Also available from
the American Academy of Pediatrics

Caring for Your Baby and Young Child
Birth to Age 5

El Cuidado De Su Hijo Pequeño
Desde Que Nace Hasta Los Cinco Años

Caring for Your School-Age Child
Ages 5 to 12

Caring for Your Teenager

Your Baby's First Year

El Primer Año De Su Bebé

Guide to Your Child's Symptoms
Birth Through Adolescence

Guide to Your Child's Sleep
Birth Through Adolescence

Guide to Your Child's Allergies and Asthma
Breathing Easy and Bringing Up Healthy, Active Children

Guide to Your Child's Nutrition
Making Peace at the Table and Building Healthy Eating Habits for Life

New Mother's Guide to Breastfeeding

Nueva Guía De Lactancia Materna

Guide to Toilet Training

Guía Para Enseñar Al Niño A Usar El Inodoro

ADHD: A Complete and Authoritative Guide

Baby & Child Health: The Essential Guide From Birth to 11 Years

For more information, visit www.aap.org/bookstore.

Heading Home With
YOUR NEWBORN
FROM BIRTH TO REALITY

By

Laura A. Jana, MD, FAAP, and Jennifer Shu, MD, FAAP

American Academy of Pediatrics
DEDICATED TO THE HEALTH OF ALL CHILDREN™

AAP Publishing Staff

Director, Department of Marketing and Publications
Maureen DeRosa, MPA

Director, Division of Product Development
Mark Grimes

Manager, Consumer Publishing
Eileen Glasstetter, MS

Director, Division of Publishing and Production Services
Sandi King, MS

Manager, Editorial Services
Kate Larson

Manager, Editorial Production
Theresa Wiener

Manager, Print Production Services
Leesa Levin-Doroba

Manager, Graphic Design
Linda Diamond

Director, Division of Marketing and Sales
Jill Ferguson

Manager, Consumer Product Marketing and Sales
Susan Thompson

Cover design by Stephen B. Starr Design, Inc.
Pencil drawings by Anthony Alex LeTourneau
Book design by Linda J. Diamond

Library of Congress Control Number: 2004111854
ISBN: 1-58110-157-0

The recommendations in this publication do not indicate an exclusive course of treatment or serve as a standard of medical care. Variations, taking into account individual circumstances, may be appropriate.

Statements and opinions expressed are those of the authors and not necessarily those of the American Academy of Pediatrics.

Products are mentioned for informational purposes only. Inclusion in this publication does not imply endorsement by the American Academy of Pediatrics.

CB 0037
9-131/0405

WHAT PEOPLE ARE SAYING

A special book that new parents will want to read cover to cover before their little one arrives. No matter what challenges new parenthood throws your way, Drs Jana and Shu are sure to leave you feeling both confident and competent. *Heading Home* is the perfect shower gift!

Barton Schmitt, MD, FAAP
Professor of Pediatrics at the Children's Hospital of Denver

In short, easy-to-read chapters, these pediatrician authors explore all the topics…which are part of every new baby's life. Their sections on car seat safety and traveling with an infant are especially informative and up to date. The authors' supportive reassurances and sensitive advice will be particularly helpful to parents whose baby does not fit the norm. Without a false note anywhere, the authors have made a gift to parents of their own confidence and experience. This book is a fresh contribution to adults just beginning the parenting journey.

Molly Frederick
Senior Associate Editor, formerly of *Contemporary Pediatrics*

Drs Laura Jana and Jennifer Shu combine their experience as moms and their expertise as pediatricians in a chatty yet essential handbook that guides the new mom through the inevitable avalanche of advice… and sorts through common worries…. Based on their experiences, the authors know only too well that caring for a newborn is not easy… but, they advise, prepare for a great adventure.

Mary Hager
Medical Correspondent, *Newsweek Magazine* (retired)

This book will lower your stress about raising your child. It is a wonderful narrative that reads as if it was a conversation among friends…. You can have a shared learning experience with the authors who are moms, docs, and daughters and really do know.

George A. Strait
Associate Vice Chancellor UC Berkeley,
Former Medical Correspondent, ABC News

In an era of one-size-fits-all parenting advice, this book truly stands out. Doctors Jana and Shu offer the kind of advice that will help new parents keep their expectations reasonable, while giving them the confidence and encouragement they need to be great parents, and to have fun at the same time.

Armin Brott
Author of *The Expectant Father: Facts, Tips, and Advice for Dads-to-Be* and *The New Father: A Dad's Guide to the First Year*

A family-friendly, easily read…guide to the unique experience of caring for a newborn that is both practical and medically sound.

Lillian Blackmon, MD
Chair, AAP Committee on Fetus and Newborn

The advice you'd get from your sister or best friend, if she had her baby only last year.

Gil Fuld, MD
AAP News Editorial Advisory Board

To everyone who humored us when we told them we were writing a book and, more importantly, to those who actually took us seriously.

—LJ and JS

ACKNOWLEDGMENTS

As we kick back and marvel at the fact that our book has at long last become a reality, we realize just how grateful we are for our family, friends, and colleagues. As cliché as it may sound, we really couldn't have done it without their love, support, understanding, and continued reassurances that what we had to say was well worth putting into print. For that they are deserving of both recognition and our sincerest thanks.

First and foremost, we are thrilled to be in this partnership with the American Academy of Pediatrics (AAP). After years of hard work and climbing our way up the steep learning curve in the world of publishing, we couldn't have found a more perfect fit. Executive Director Errol Alden, MD, and Past Executive Director Joe Sanders, MD, have offered us an incredible opportunity to work with the AAP, which we truly believe represents the gold standard in caring for children. Past President Louis Z. Cooper, MD, was instrumental in getting our book in the right hands to make it to the publishing stage. Eileen Glasstetter has been a phenomenal help with coordinating all the work that goes into making a book—especially when she's had to work with 2 type A personalities. Kate Larson's attention to detail as copy editor has been invaluable. Also indispensable have been Mark Grimes, director of the Division of Product Development, and Maureen DeRosa, MPA, director of the Department of Marketing and Publications.

We owe our gratitude to the many experts who reviewed our text for technical accuracy: Emilio Arispe, MD; Lillian Blackmon, MD; Paula Duncan, MD; Gil Fuld, MD; Robert Needlman, MD; Richard Pan, MD, MPH; Marilyn Bull, MD, for her expertise in injury prevention and control; and lactation consultants Kathleen Craig and Nanette Bellavance of Dartmouth-Hitchcock Medical Center's Birthing Pavilion for their input on breastfeeding.

We would also like to recognize the American Medical Association's 2004–2005 President John Nelson, MD, MPH, as well as Mike Lynch, vice president of media relations and advocacy communications, and Lori Bolas, former media manager of news and information, for their enthusiastic support of our book.

Other supporters we would like to acknowledge include Armin Brott; Mary Hager; Barton Schmitt, MD; George Strait; and Tom Tonniges, MD.

Personal Acknowledgments

Laura Jana, MD: I have been fortunate to have crossed paths with several people whose faith in my abilities has helped me to believe in myself. Perhaps one of the most influential to my career was Dr Benjamin Spock, who not only took me seriously years before I had a degree behind my name, but was an incredibly insightful man whose love of life and understanding of both children and parents continues to inspire me. I also want to thank pediatricians Dr Robert Needlman, who first demonstrated to me how to practice the art of pediatrics, and Dr Barton Schmitt, whose kind words of support mean far more to me than he probably realizes. Others who have played meaningful roles in helping me to figure out what my dreams really are and how to reach them include Dr Susan Wentz, Dr Marjorie Greenfield, Dr Paula Duncan, Dr Emilio Arispe, and Denise Baddour. And finally, I owe a special thanks to Dr Georges Peter, whose commitment to involving young pediatricians and women in the AAP is what brought me back in touch with Dr Jennifer Shu years after we trained together in San Francisco. I feel so fortunate to have Jennifer as one of my closest colleagues and friends, as our partnership has unquestionably changed my life.

My 3 precious children—Bethany, Alex, and Ryan—help remind me every day what is truly important in my life, and I am forever grateful for their willingness to let me test out (and fine-tune) my parenting techniques before sharing them with others. My twin sister, Ellen Levy, did far more than her fair share in making sure that this book would be published, while my brother Philip Levy's repeated votes of confidence in my abilities have been invaluable. My mother, Dr June Osborn, has always done everything in her power (and then some) to make sure that I was able to pursue my dreams, and my father has made sure his pride in my accomplishments is ever-apparent. Above all else, I want to acknowledge my best friend and husband of 10 years, Dr Ajoy Jana, who has not only given me his unwavering support, but his unconditional love. To his parents, I am eternally grateful for raising such a wonderful son and for including me in their family, because it is the life and family we have created together that define who I am and are my greatest accomplishments.

Jennifer Shu, MD: Space prevents me from personally listing all the important people with whom I have crossed paths in life. Many of you have given me the encouragement and confidence to become the person I am, and for this I am most grateful. I would like to give my utmost appreciation to my husband and son who have patiently supported a book that took more than 3 years to come to life; you are truly my best friends. Thanks to my parents, who taught me to believe that I could be anything I wanted to be. A big shout-out goes to my sisters who have been my peppiest cheerleaders. To my extended family of in-laws: Thanks for welcoming me into your lives as a daughter/sister/friend. My 10th-grade English teacher, Mr Paul Lankford, told me that I would be a star no matter where I went, and I was naïve enough to believe him—I know he has similarly influenced many other students in a tremendously positive way and I would like to recognize the impact he has had. My heartfelt thanks go to my pediatric colleagues, coworkers, and mentors who have guided me in this ongoing quest to be a better pediatrician. My friends from all the stages of my life have been incredibly supportive and tolerant of my quirks and tendency to share my excitement about this book. I would also like to extend my gratitude to all my patients, who have taught me just about everything I know about newborns. And lastly, a big woo-hoo to my coauthor Laura— we finally finished it; I'm glad we've gone through this amazing experience together and am so excited that this is only just the beginning!

TABLE OF CONTENTS

The Current State of Parenting Affairs

If you're standing in a bookstore as you read this, it will be obvious to you that we are by no means the first authors to write about the wondrous but admittedly daunting journey called parenthood. The fact of the matter is that we live in a time where parenting experts all but grow on trees, and parenting books, magazines, and Web sites are overflowing with advice. Given the sheer magnitude of information already available, you may wonder why we decided to toss our hats into this overcrowded ring and set out to write books on the subject of raising children. To be perfectly honest, we almost didn't.

A Journey of Our Own

Originally, we set out in search of what we knew parents (our patients, our friends, and ourselves) wanted—a parenting book that was informative and practical, that offered explanations right alongside recommendations and, most of all, that was firmly grounded in the realities of modern-day parenting. At the end of the day (or several years later, to be more exact) and hundreds of parenting books, patient visits, baby showers, and play groups later—not to mention several children of our own—we still hadn't found a book that reflected our own unique perspective on parenting. In fact, what we discovered was that new parents were reading "all of the baby books" and were still left with questions about the realities of caring for their newborns. It was then that we decided that there was room for at least one more parenting book on the shelf, and we set to work creating a book that would specifically focus on the first few weeks of parenthood.

Following the Rules: Parenting by the Book

Nowadays it seems you can find well-defined rules about everything from feeding and sleeping schedules to dating someone's teenage daughter. As convenient as it may seem to have someone write out for you an exact recipe for parenting success, we believe that there is not just one right way to do things. As with diapers and baby clothes, we are convinced that parenting techniques are not simply one size fits all. Our goal is to help familiarize you with the basics of baby care, and even more importantly to build your confidence as a parent right from the beginning during what many consider to be an overwhelming time—the newborn period. With a little knowledge and a positive attitude, you will find that you are very capable of anticipating and reasoning your way through even the most challenging aspects of what lies ahead. It's a great feeling to find yourself comfortable enough in your parenting abilities that you don't have to live life with a quick reference guide—ours or anyone else's—tucked in your back pocket.

Parenting With Style

We have found that it is a rare parent—new or seasoned—who isn't also on the constant lookout for good, practical parenting advice to make life a bit easier, less expensive, safer, or simply more fun. We like to think of these little pearls of wisdom as parenting revelations—the "wow, what a good idea…I never thought of that" or "you know what, that really makes sense—I wish I had thought of that sooner" kind of revelation that comes when fellow parents share their insights—or, in this case, when we share ours. After all, we firmly believe that parenting is not only a lifestyle, but that it can be done in style.

From Birth to Reality

As parents ourselves, with 4 young children between us, we have first-hand knowledge of what parenting questions tend to arise and what dilemmas have a way of presenting themselves in the course of a typical day—or night—with a newborn. Opportunely enough, we both also happen to be pediatricians. The years we have spent in pediatric training and practice have provided us with an added understanding of babies, children, and parents—not to mention what obstacles they (and you) are likely to run into along the way. We have had the opportunity to talk and listen to thousands of parents just like you—and believe us we have listened! Not only have we listened in our offices to concerns about first fevers, flat heads, and breastfeeding and helped parents sort out their babies' common (and not so common) medical ailments, but we have answered questions about everything from the family bed and first airplane trips to installing car seats and choosing infant attire.

Parent-Tested, Pediatrician-Approved

And now we're ready to share what we've learned—not just in medical school, but also from everyday life and everyday parents just like you—as we guide you through the transition from birth to the reality of being a parent. While we have complete faith in your ability to figure things out for yourself, we thought you might find it helpful to hear our thoughts *before* you have to do it all on your own! *Heading Home With Your Newborn* represents a blending of our experiences and brings you the best of both worlds—a book that presents the *reality* of parenting from a parent's perspective, but with a pediatrician's stamp of approval. Instead of being "kid-tested, mother-approved," our book is "parent-tested, pediatrician-approved" all wrapped into one convenient package.

Anticipating Change

You may have heard people say that life is never the same after having a baby. Until you have lived through the experience yourself, it may be difficult to truly imagine exactly what heading home with your newborn will mean for you and your family. One thing that you can count on, though, is that your life *will* certainly change—physically, emotionally, and financially. By this we're not just referring to the shedding of pregnancy pounds, the psychological stress of sleep deprivation, and the cost of baby bedding (not to mention college, which is forever looming in the distance), but also your general perspective on life. The phrase "Toto, we're not in Kansas anymore" springs to mind.

Great Expectations

How you deal with the inevitable changes and challenges of parenthood is likely to be colored by your initial expectations of what life with your newborn is going to be like. While we will provide the information to help prepare you for the day-to-day tasks of life with a newborn, in the end it will be up to you to create a positive mental attitude. After all, we firmly believe that an important part of preparing for life with a newborn involves getting into the right mindset.

Rude Awakenings

Fairly often we find that new parents expect too much of their newborns (and themselves). While we've dedicated entire sections of this book to the topics of breastfeeding and sleep, they make for perfect examples of unrealistic expectations. Suffice it to say that although the "textbook" pattern of feeding may be 15 minutes on each breast every 3 hours, a newborn who nurses sporadically and frequently throughout the day and night is much closer to the norm. And if you're expecting a full night's sleep right from the start as opposed to being grateful for a 4-hour stretch—we're sorry to say you're likely to be in for many rude awakenings. We could use any number of similar examples to support our belief that expecting too much inevitably sets parents up to *feel* like they've derailed when in reality they are usually still right on track.

Keeping It Real

Whether you are heading into the homestretch of your pregnancy or are already homeward bound, take a minute to ask yourself how you feel about your parenting abilities. Some people find themselves petrified while others maintain a cool confidence. As you get ready to go from birth to the sudden reality of parenthood, we suggest adopting the mantra "I think I can, I think I can, I think I can…" long before you ever formally become acquainted with *The Little Engine That Could* (much less find yourself reading this timeless children's book aloud for the hundredth time). Whether your expectations of yourself and your newborn simply need some fine-tuning or a major readjustment, we hope you'll head home confident and soon be saying, "I *knew* I could, I *knew* I could, I *knew* I could…."

High Hopes

We have the highest hopes and sincerely believe that you and your baby will settle into a manageable lifestyle. After all, millions of parents before us have had newborn babies and still choose to have second, third, fourth…children. In the short term, we encourage you to set your sights not so much on the day-to-day challenges but on the more intangible aspects of parenthood—the joy, pride, and sense of awe and accomplishment that is the essence of parenthood. These should be your great expectations. We can all but guarantee that the joy will outweigh the fatigue, and your overall sense of accomplishment will erase many of the doubts you may have.

The Price of Things to Come

Labor and delivery ....Painful

Furnishing, decorating, and stocking
the nursery...Expensive

Keeping up with your newborn's eating
and (not) sleeping schedule ....Tiring

Forgetting to brush your teeth or shower ....Unhygienic

Being a parent ....Priceless

 BRAVE NEW WORLD

While you have many years ahead to familiarize yourself with the nuances, joys, and responsibilities of raising a happy, healthy child, we want to help make the first baby steps you take up the new-parent learning curve a little less wobbly. We decided that the most logical way to begin this journey is with a look at one of the most unforgettable events of parenthood—when new parents like you pack up their things at the hospital, take a deep breath, place their precious new babies in carefully selected car seats, and boldly go where they have never been before. We call it heading home.

PART I

into the mouths of babes

INTRODUCTION

As the parent of a newborn, you'll undoubtedly be spending a good deal of time paying attention to what goes into your baby's mouth. Whether by breast or by bottle, the frequent task of feeding a newborn has the potential to raise a whole host of questions ranging from how to know if your breast milk has come in or how to prepare your baby's formula to the facts about sucking and whether it's OK to use pacifiers.

Before we really dive in, let us first point out that infancy isn't referred to as the oral stage for nothing. At the risk of sounding like an academic textbook, it's nevertheless worth acknowledging what professionals as far back as Freud himself once proposed: What goes into your baby's mouth during this stage of the game is going to be a big part of her life experience (not to mention yours). Not only will eating and growing be one of her biggest and most important responsibilities for many months to come, but her mouth will also play a valuable role in allowing her to comfort herself and discover the world around her long before she learns to use her hands and other senses to explore.

With that mouthful in mind, you may find that you look at your baby's cute little lips with new respect and awe. The rest of this chapter is dedicated to taking a hands-on look at the *reality* of feeding your newborn—not only as a nutritional necessity, but a wonderful opportunity for you to bond with your baby. Our ultimate goal is to help you settle into a comfortable routine and give you a clear idea of what you can expect as well as what to look out for.

Now to turn our attention to the substance of the matter at hand—breast milk and/or formula. For the sake of convenience, we have tried to separate breastfeeding from formula feeding—a well-defined separation in print that is not always so clear-cut in real life. That's because quite a few parents ultimately find themselves relying on some combination of breast milk and formula. Once you've finished the part that applies to you—whether it's breast, formula, or both—we encourage you to keep reading because later in this chapter we address subjects that are likely to be of interest to all of you. They include pacifiers, feeding schedules (or the lack thereof), and supplemental vitamins. And you'll be able to brush up on the basics of bottle-feeding—from supplies to technique and cleanup—in a section meant to be useful to anyone who plans to use a bottle, regardless of what you choose to put in it.

 DOLLARS AND SENSE

If the decision about whether to breastfeed or formula feed were based solely (or even partly) on finances, breastfeeding would win hands down. The added expense of breastfeeding includes the cost of a few extra calories a day for mom (somewhere around 25% more) and the cost of nursing bras, breast pumps, breast pads, or any of a multitude of other optional supplies you happen to pick up along the way. With formula feeding, on the other hand, most of the inherent costs are not optional. As you may have already discovered, formula tends to be quite costly. Recent estimates report a year's average cost of formula to be anywhere from $1,300 to $4,000, depending on the type used (more on the actual types later in Chapter 2).

breastfeeding

In our humble opinion, the most significant contribution we stand to make to your breastfeeding success is to start you off with realistic expectations. To do that, we have taken the time to address many of the common breastfeeding myths and misconceptions that tend to weigh new parents down. We have found it particularly helpful for new and expectant parents to remind themselves of 2 reassuring facts.

1. Millions of mothers before you have been able to breastfeed their babies successfully.
2. The first couple weeks of breastfeeding are by no means representative of what your entire breastfeeding experience will be like.

While a handful of fortunate new moms do ease into breastfeeding as if they were born to do so and are quickly rewarded with an overwhelming sense of accomplishment, in reality there is usually a period of self-education and on-the-breast training. Consider this time to be one of trial and error—a "get acquainted with and accustomed to the process" phase in which breastfeeding your baby may take a bit more time, thought, and effort than it will in your not-so-distant breastfeeding future. With a few safety precautions and an eye on the prize, you will likely be able to dodge many common obstacles—both perceived and real. And if you're coming to us already frustrated and all but resigned to giving up any hope of breastfeeding altogether, we hope to offer you a new lease on breastfeeding life.

A Comment on "Breast Is Best"

As you enter the world of parenthood, you will undoubtedly encounter the phrase "Breast is best." That's because it has become an almost universal slogan that graces the pages of parenting magazines, Web sites, medical textbooks, and formula advertisements alike. Given that breast milk is impossible to duplicate and the health benefits it offers invaluable, we wholeheartedly support the American Academy of Pediatrics (AAP) recommendation to feed your baby breast milk as long as possible—ideally 1 year or even longer. With that as a backdrop, what we have to say about your decision to breastfeed may therefore come as a bit of a surprise—especially from 2 pediatrician moms who are fully aware and in support of the idea that there are great benefits to breastfeeding. We feel the need to mention that we have come across instances in which breastfeeding has not always worked out for the best. Now lest the preceding statement be regarded as a letdown to breastfeeding advocates everywhere, let us explain.

The standard consideration in favor of breast milk is very straightforward. Breast milk is currently unrivaled as the ideal food for infants. The infection-fighting antibodies it contains just can't be bottled in even the most expensive of commercial formulas, and it has been shown to reduce a newborn's chance of developing everything from ear infections, allergies, vomiting, and diarrhea to pneumonia, meningitis, and potentially even sudden infant death syndrome. There are also health benefits to nursing mothers. Just about the only caveat we feel compelled to mention is that for some caring and devoted new mothers, when it comes to putting recommendations into practice, sometimes breastfeeding just doesn't work out right. Whether it's a matter of modesty, attitude, medically related issues, or the disappointment of unsuccessful attempts, breastfeeding is a potential source of frustration for some new moms. Worse yet, difficulties with breastfeeding can be the cause of some serious feelings of parental inadequacy—leaving devoted mothers questioning their overall ability as parents. Too many of these new parents are led to believe—either by convincing themselves or by being told by others—that to be a good mother, breastfeeding is an absolute requirement.

We will now say to you what we suggest to every new or expectant mother that comes to us with questions or concerns about the early days of breastfeeding: First decide for yourself whether you are looking for breastfeeding help or secretly hoping someone will tell you that it's OK *not* to breastfeed. If you've already made the *informed* (and by informed we mean not only having all the facts, but also discussing your choice with a qualified health professional) decision that breastfeeding is not for you, then you have our full support in flipping directly to the formula-feeding discussion of our book without experiencing unrelenting pangs of guilt. If, on the other hand, you've never given much thought to breastfeeding, you find yourself questioning your ability to do it successfully, or you have run into a few bumps on the road to what will almost surely be breastfeeding success, we hope you will read on. We want to take a stab at boosting your confidence and make sure your breastfeeding experiences are not only successful, but also enjoyable.

 BREASTFEEDING AROUND THE WORLD

Compared to 30 some years ago when essentially no new moms in the United States attempted to breastfeed, the fact that 57% of women tried their hand (or breast) at it in 1994 represents a significant change. While the popularity and number of women breastfeeding in the United States has continued to grow over the past 10 years, we are still nowhere near competing with other "enlightened" parts of the world when it comes to breastfeeding accomplishments. In Sweden, for example, 98% of new mothers start out breastfeeding their newborns. Then again, such success isn't so surprising coming from a country that grants new moms nearly 2 years of maternity leave (with a full year of it paid!).

How Far We've Come and How We Got Here

Anyone looking at breastfeeding popularity in the United States over the past several decades is sure to notice what we like to call a roller coaster phenomenon—up in the '70s, down in the '80s, and back up again starting in the '90s. And of course, what was considered to be "best," not to mention socially acceptable, has varied considerably not only over time, but also based on many other factors such as what area of the country parents live in, their age, and their background. While we've certainly come a long way from the days when breastfeeding moms were the exception to the rule and ostracized for their choice, we have not come so far that there aren't still outdated, hard to believe, and even downright comical laws that prohibit public displays of breastfeeding.

BREASTFEEDING WITHIN YOUR LEGAL RIGHTS

Believe it or not, there are laws in most states that protect a woman's right to breastfeed. Some make it perfectly clear that it's legal for mothers to breastfeed in public, while others are more outdated and make it difficult for nursing moms to do so. Some of the more creative pro-breastfeeding laws we've come across exempt nursing mothers from jury duty or remove sales tax from lactation supplies. If we've piqued your interest and you somehow manage to find yourself some spare time, you can check out the La Leche League's Web site at www.lalecheleague.org to brush up on breastfeeding rights and regulations in your own state.

Getting Started

What's "Natural" Doesn't Always Come Naturally

Yes, the act of breastfeeding is "natural," but the truth of the matter is that it doesn't always come naturally. All too often, new parents expect to be handed a newborn who gracefully latches on, nurses no more than 15 minutes on each breast every 3 hours, and delights in a plentiful supply of breast milk within a few short days. While we can only wish this scenario on all of you, clinging to this idealistic picture of breastfeeding bliss is all but guaranteed to set most of you up for perceived failure. If, however, you prepare yourself for the distinct possibility that your newborn may lack interest or sucking stamina, that each feeding may be different, and your nipples may be a little worse for wear early on, well then you only stand to be pleasantly surprised. The most likely scenario: Breastfeeding may be natural, but expect it to be a learning process for you and your baby. Some babies are quick learners, while others take their own sweet time.

Advice Abounds

As you try to educate yourself or start your on-the-job training, you're almost certain to find that anyone who has ever breastfed (or been remotely involved in breastfeeding) considers themselves a full-fledged expert. Some of the advice you get will undoubtedly prove to be very helpful, but be aware that you'll probably get your fair share of unsolicited suggestions and contradictory, confusing, or just plain wrong advice—even when it comes from moms who have nursed a virtual litter of children, are highly intelligent, and have the best of intentions. Just keep in mind that at the end of the day, there are only a few universally accepted facts about breastfeeding. The rest of what you do and how you do it will be a matter of establishing your own personal breastfeeding style.

Sending Out an SOS (in Search of Support)

Breastfeeding really does have its rewards, but it also can be a very demanding and tiring 24-hour-a-day job. If you find yourself experiencing feelings of frustration, isolation, and even feelings of entrapment—especially given that 21st-century moms are less likely to have their own mothers or other family members nearby to turn to for advice—one of the worst things you can do is try to cope alone. Of course it's not any better to find yourself in the company of a well-meaning grandmother who is just waiting for the opportunity to tell you how easy bottlefeeding would be in contrast. Please take a moment and tell yourself that you are absolutely not alone and don't need to be figuring out the tricks of the trade the hard way! We strongly suggest that if what you really need is a supportive shoulder to lean on, put down this book and find one (or several). It may seem like yet one more thing you don't have time for, but finding that you don't have to learn to breastfeed alone can make all the difference in the world.

- La Leche League International has local chapters throughout the world. You can either check your phone book or go to their Web site (www.lalecheleague.org) to find area leaders and meeting places and times.

- Get help from your hospital. Labor and delivery staff, nurses on the mother-baby unit, and hospital lactation specialists are a great place to start exploring what types of support are available in your community before, during, and after you deliver.
- Turn to your pediatrician for advice and/or assistance. As pediatricians, we routinely observe newborns breastfeeding in our offices and are very accustomed to providing practical advice and troubleshooting tips.
- Don't be afraid to enlist your spouse, partner, friends, family members, or neighbors—anyone you think might be able to lend a hand and/or offer emotional support. Even though no one else can breastfeed for you, we've never met a new mother who couldn't use a little help with cleaning, cooking, laundry, or watching the baby for a bit so she can get a break every now and then.
- In the wired world we now live in, virtual breastfeeding support groups, discussion forums, and chat rooms abound; you can find them by doing a search or through different parenting Web sites. As with any Internet activity, you should of course be careful about any private information you might divulge and look for credible sources of information.

 ### A BREAST A DAY KEEPS THE DOCTOR AWAY

Based on many studies done in the United States and elsewhere around the world, we know that breastfeeding is not only nutritionally sound and decreases the risk of sudden infant death syndrome (SIDS), but can translate into fewer colds, allergies, infections, hospitalizations, and visits to the doctor's office. That's because protective proteins called antibodies, along with other infection-fighting cells found in breast milk, are continually transferred from you to your baby for as long as you breastfeed. This added level of defense against bacteria and viruses is particularly beneficial during the first several months of your baby's life when his immune system isn't yet functioning at full speed.

My Baby, My Breasts, and I

Becoming a new breastfeeding mother really does involve a fundamental shift in one's view of the world—a shift that is lifelong in the sense of awe you get from nurturing a child of your own, but more immediately in a practical, concrete way. That is, you are suddenly thrust from a world primarily focused on "me, myself, and I" (or perhaps "me, my spouse, and I") to one that inevitably is structured around "my baby, my breasts, and I." As you set out to master the fine art of breastfeeding, you are likely to look on your breasts in a whole new way, and most likely give them far more consideration than ever before (regardless of how significant they were to you in your pre-breastfeeding past). In fact, we are of the strong belief that if your baby's health provider doesn't ask you how you, your baby, *and* your breasts are doing in your early days of breastfeeding, he or she has, for lack of a more tactful description, completely missed the boat.

First Attempts

Assuming that all goes well with the birth of your baby and both of you are doing well in the minutes and hours immediately following delivery, then the best time to attempt your first breastfeeding is as soon as possible. While this may seem obvious, it's easy to find yourself feeling like you have no say or control in what takes place during your hospital stay, much less in your own delivery room. If you wait for someone to tell you what to do and when, then whether you are encouraged to breastfeed right away will depend on your hospital's attitudes toward breastfeeding.

Helping Hands at the Hospital

Your goal for breastfeeding in the delivery room (and throughout your stay at the hospital) should be to make sure you and your baby work out the concept of latching on correctly. At some hospitals it is standard for labor and delivery nurses to not only bring mothers their newborns within minutes of delivery, but to offer plenty of breastfeeding instruction and encouragement. At other hospitals, however, it is still routine for newborns to be taken off to the nursery to be cleaned up and even given a bottle while their mothers get some rest. If you want to get off to a good start, don't be afraid to take things into your own hands and give breastfeeding a try while you're still in the delivery room. Many babies tend to be temporarily wide awake right after delivery. After all, they've just been through a pretty eye-opening experience right along with you. If and when you get the chance, take advantage of your baby's temporary state of alertness (which we liken to a honeymoon period). Within a matter of hours you may well find you have a very sleepy baby on your chest.

   ROOMING IN

Depending on the hospital where you deliver, your baby will either be allowed to room in with you for most of your hospital stay, or will be kept in a centralized nursery and brought into your room on occasion. If you're planning to breast-feed, we strongly recommend exploring your options and, if available, choosing a so-called baby-friendly hospital that actively promotes breastfeeding and will accommodate your desire to stay close to your baby and nurse frequently.

Getting Comfortable

Given that just about all new moms are prone to focusing their attention on their breasts (and their babies) when they first sit or lie down to nurse, we also want to remind you to take a moment and make yourself comfortable. Supporting yourself with extra pillows, making sure you have on convenient and comfortable clothing, and having anything you might want or need within arm's reach (a glass of water, a book, the phone, or the TV remote control) *before* getting down to business can definitely make the experience more enjoyable. When it comes to the actual position you try, the choice is really up to you. In case you aren't aware of them, we will briefly describe several of the most popular options.

- **Cradle hold.** This is the position most new breastfeeders start with, and the one that many new moms prefer. The most common exceptions are new moms who have just had cesarean sections and find, for obvious reasons, that they want to avoid having their newborns pressing on their bellies. While sitting up (preferably with lots of comfy pillows and good back support in place), you simply lay your baby across your lap side-ways so that she is facing you with her head in line with your breast. In the typical cradle hold, you will use your right arm to support your baby's head and body while she nurses on your right breast (her head resting in the crook of your right arm with your hand supporting her bottom), and then your left arm for support while she is nursing on your left breast. To help ease the strain on your back, shoulders, and neck, try putting a regular or specially designed breastfeeding pillow or two across your lap to help raise your baby up to the level of your breast. And while you may be content with cradling your baby in your arm(s) as she nurses, trust us when we tell you that a few well-positioned pillows placed under your arms can work wonders and spare you some unnecessary aches and pains. As you get into the finer points of positioning, you also can try what is referred to by breastfeeding experts as the cross-cradle hold. With your baby lying across your lap ready to nurse on your left breast, you can use your right arm instead of your left, as in the typical cradle hold, to support your baby's head and body. For either type of cradle hold, whichever arm you are not using to support your baby's head and body is free to help position your baby's mouth onto your nipple.

- **Football hold.** To position yourself for breastfeeding using the so-called football hold, some parenting books suggest you picture a football player holding a football under his arm as he runs downfield. We're willing to bet that conjuring up this mental image just won't be enough to help many of you avoid some unnecessary roughness or fumbling. As you sit down and try to replicate the position with your baby, here's an explanation we hope you will find more practical. Unlike the cradle hold, where your baby lies across your lap, the football hold requires that you lay your baby to one side of you or the other. If you're going to start nursing on your right breast, position your baby so that her face is level with your breast while her body rests against your right side. You can then use your right arm to support her body. Well-placed pillows under your baby—this time placed along your side instead of across your lap as in the cradle hold—can really take a lot of strain off your supporting arm, shoulder, and neck. Quite honestly, we're not sure how many moms actually prefer this hold. We ourselves never had much success scoring touchdowns with it, but for your purposes all that really matters is that it works well for some moms and not so well for others, so feel free to try it out for yourself.

- **Side-by-side or lying down.** In this position, you and your baby lie down facing each other, with your baby's mouth in line with your breast. You'll probably find yourself using your lower arm to support your own head, leaving your upper arm to help adjust your baby (and/or breast) as needed. While most women seem to prefer nursing from their lower breast (ie, when lying on the right side, they offer their right breast), there are no hard-and-fast rules. If you find yourself recovering from a cesarean section, or even if you're just plain exhausted and don't feel like sitting up, you may decide this is a great way to nurse with less effort—especially once you get the hang of it.

Breathing Room

Regardless of what breastfeeding hold works best for you, a couple of simple "rules" apply to all positions. Once you've brought your baby to your breast, make a point of allowing him to move his head as needed instead of holding it firmly against your breast. Yes, his head needs support, but you can relax your hold (and yourself) a bit once your baby has latched on and is nursing, allowing him to adjust himself whenever necessary. You can also help make sure he has adequate room to breathe at all times by making sure at least one nostril is visible and not completely covered by your breast.

WHAT'S FOR DINNER?

Your breasts are likely to start producing colostrum even before your baby is born—as early as the second trimester. Colostrum provides most newborns with everything they need for the first several days of life. By the end of the first week, if not sooner, your body should begin to make a larger volume of milk that is less yellow and more watery—known as "transitional" milk. This milk is definitely more likely to satisfy your baby's hunger and help him settle into somewhat of a more predictable pattern of feeding. How you choose to approach the waiting period until its arrival is up to you, but we suggest you put a positive slant on things and view your colostrum-producing breasts as half full, rather than half empty.

Catching On to Latching On

Anyone who's ever breastfed can tell you that there's a big difference between getting babies to latch on and getting them to latch on *correctly*. For nursing mothers everywhere this can mean the difference between smooth sailing and choppy waters, as defined by sore, cracked, or even blistered nipples. For babies it can mean the difference between actually getting some milk in return for their efforts and the equivalent of sucking on the closed end of a straw. To nurse effectively, babies need to use their tongues to essentially lap or massage milk out of the breast. This requires that the tongue be positioned under the breast in such a way that the baby can draw the nipple *and* the darker colored area around it (the areola) into her mouth as she sucks. If your baby starts out nursing by simply pursing her lips around your nipple and sucking away, you'll very quickly realize 2 important facts: The harder she sucks the less likely she is to get anything, and the more likely your nipples are to suffer the consequences.

Lending a Helping Hand

With any luck you will find that there is at least one nurse or other health professional present in the delivery room or available on the mother-baby floor of your hospital who is skilled at assisting new mothers with getting newborns to latch on correctly. Even if there's not, you can play an active role and facilitate.

- **Expressing interest.** Gently expressing a few drops of breast milk onto and around your nipple can help your baby hone in on his intended target.
- **Rooting for success.** If your baby still doesn't seem interested in opening his mouth, try lightly stroking his cheek just to the side of his mouth to stimulate what's known as the rooting reflex—a reflex that should cause him to open his mouth in search of your nipple.
- **Open wide.** If he doesn't open his mouth wide enough, you can gently help him open it further by pushing down on his chin.
- **If at first you don't succeed.** By all means, if he doesn't get it right the first time, don't be fooled into thinking that any latching on is better than none. If it seems that your baby's mouth didn't open wide enough to assume the necessary position on your breast, he seems to have only gotten your nipple in his mouth, or it continues to hurt when he sucks, then don't hesitate to take him off and encourage him to try again.

GOING FOR THE GUSTO

Newborns have been shown to have an amazing and inborn drive to nurse. In one study, newborns actually demonstrated their impressive ability to inch their way up from their mothers' bellies all the way to their breasts in search of food within mere *minutes* of being born. Given that this is a book about practicality, however, we don't suggest you sit around waiting for your own newborn to propel herself up to your breasts before offering her the opportunity to breastfeed.

Getting It Right

We are well aware of the fact that telling you to take your baby off your breast and getting him to try again until he gets it right is sometimes easier said than done. For lack of a better analogy, many infants are like leeches when it comes to latching on. Once they're on, they're on tight and holding on for dear life. Getting them to let go by attempting to pull them off is therefore a misguided and potentially painful prospect, but there is a relatively easy solution (that does not involve the use of the salt or matches commonly recommended for leech removal). Before removing your baby from your breast, gently slide one finger into his mouth to break the seal of his lips around your nipple. Once the seal is broken, you'll find it much quicker, easier, and less painful to take him off and have him start over again. You can also use this technique whenever you need to interrupt or end a feeding. While it's true that most babies don't like being taken off the breast in the middle or even the start of a feeding, this can actually work in your favor. If your baby subsequently cries in disapproval, he's all but guaranteed to open his mouth wider, increasing the likelihood that he'll latch on correctly on his next attempt.

Breastfeeding Irritations

During the first days and weeks of breastfeeding, it's entirely normal for mothers to experience a certain degree of irritation as their nipples grow accustomed to repeated sucking and stimulation. How then, you might wonder, are you supposed to know the difference between the discomfort associated with starting out anew and the pain and irritation that result when a baby doesn't latch on correctly? Beyond paying close attention to how your baby latches on, try also to figure out whether the irritation tends to subside as your baby gets into a rhythm of sucking. Mild irritation or discomfort that occurs only at the start of each feeding is generally associated with the newness of nursing. As you and your nipples toughen up over the days and weeks to follow, you're likely to find that this type of irritation quickly fades away (thank goodness!). Nipple pain that persists or gets worse as your baby nurses, on the other hand, is more likely to be a sign that she is not latched on correctly, and is often accompanied by cracked or blistered nipples—the thought of which is enough to make anyone (especially breastfeeding moms) cringe.

Nurturing Your Nipples

In the spirit of being honest and preparing you for what may lie ahead, the bad news is that cracked or even blistered nipples can appear after even just one nursing session gone wrong. The good news, however, is that nipples do heal. With the proper care, patience, and a little extra attention, they can get better within a matter of days. Given that this never seems fast enough to those of us who've experienced such nipple insults firsthand, here are some temporizing measures you can try if you happen to find yourself with sore, dry, cracked, or blistered nipples.

- **Hang in there.** This is not what breastfeeding is all about. As the saying goes, "This too shall pass."
- **Latch assessment.** First and foremost, readdress how your baby is latching on. Sometimes, rather than having your baby latch straight onto your nipple like a target, you may find more success by using what's called an "assymetric" latch, where your baby's mouth centers more on the lower part of your areola.
- **The lesser of 2 evils.** If one breast feels any less sore than the other, then by all means go with the lesser of 2 evils and offer that one to your baby first because babies tend to suck harder when they first start nursing.
- **Smooth things out.** Consider the use of specially designed nontoxic creams such as lanolin (available in most stores that sell baby products) after breastfeeding or even use a little dab of your own breast milk on your breasts, then expose them to open air.

- **Bare yourself if need be.** If the pain doesn't start to resolve despite your best efforts or if you have any questions, you should seek professional help sooner rather than later—as in within a day or so at most—to get things back on the right track. This should be from someone accustomed to offering breastfeeding advice and ideally someone that you are comfortable baring your nipples to, if need be.
- **Options are out there.** It's well worth remembering that there are many more options, techniques, and tricks of the trade available to nursing mothers who find themselves sore, frustrated, and with seemingly un-cooperative breasts. They include, but are not limited to, pumping, breast shields, and supplemental nursing systems.

WHAT'S BEHIND BURNING NIPPLES

If you happen to experience nipple irritation, better described as a tingling, burning sensation, then a yeast infection may be to blame. Yes, yeast like moist areas and don't discriminate between your baby's mouth (see "Thrush Attack" on page 234), rear end (see "Diaper Rashes" on page 128), and your nipples. Letting your nipples air-dry before stuffing them back in your bra or under moist breast pads can help lessen your chances, but once yeast have taken up residence on your nipple(s), you'll want to discuss appropriate yeast-fighting measures with your doctor. Sometimes all it takes is a little appropriately applied yeast medication—on your nipples and in your baby's mouth—to clear things up and get your nipples on the fast track to full recovery.

Cramping

While you may have heard plenty of tales of sore breasts and nipples from others who have ventured to breastfeed before you, they may have forgotten to forewarn you about the associated cramping (of the uterus) that some new mothers experience during the early days of breastfeeding. By this point in the chapter you may be asking yourself if the fun ever stops, but trust us when we say that breastfeeding isn't all about enduring pain. It's just that when you sit down to breastfeed, your uterus is likely to cramp (described by some as resembling a contraction) in response because the signal that is known to cause contractions is the same one responsible for triggering your body to make milk. So while the cramping itself isn't exactly pleasant, you can look at it in a different light and consider it a good sign that your baby is latching on correctly and sending your body all the right signals. In fact, this dual response also plays a significant role in helping your body recover more quickly from pregnancy and childbirth—decreasing the likelihood of uterine bleeding and shortening the amount of time it takes your uterus to shrink back down to its normal size.

Going With the Flow

A Simple Matter of Supply and Demand

Once the latching on part of breastfeeding is squared away, many parents find themselves worrying about whether their babies are getting enough to eat. If you want to know the truth, in many ways the answer is no. Now let us clarify. Yes, your baby will be getting enough to live on until your full volume of milk comes in, but what he is getting is a relatively small volume of a milky, yellowish-white substance called *colostrum*. While colostrum is rich in protein, it is lacking in fats, sugar, and overall calories, as well as sheer volume. The fact that a new mother's body comes equipped with colostrum makes perfect sense in the grand scheme of things. Nature has made it so that newborns get just enough nutrients to get them through the first few days, but at the same time leaves them hungry soon after each feeding. This causes them to want to nurse more frequently, thus helping to ensure that their mothers' milk production will increase in response. During your first few days of breastfeeding—and for as long as you continue to nurse your baby—the more he nurses, the more your body will sense his increased demand and respond by stepping up the milk production, thus increasing your supply of breast milk accordingly.

 SIZE MATTERS

You may be relieved to know that milk production is not proportional to breast size. While everyone's bustline tends to expand during pregnancy in preparation for breastfeeding, rest assured that when it comes to breastfeeding success, mothers who barely fill their A-cups can rival their D-cup colleagues.

The Turning Point: How Will I Know When My Milk Comes In?

You may think that knowing when your milk has "come in" is another one of those "you can't relate until you experience it yourself" scenarios, but chances are good that when your breasts have gotten the message and respond by making larger volumes of milk, it probably won't be an occurrence that goes unnoticed. We can think of no clearer way to describe it than how my (Laura's) husband put it the day my milk came in. He matter-of-factly said, "Wow! You definitely did not have those when I married you." One's milk coming in is more often than not accompanied by a not so subtle change in breast size.

Some new mothers find that the change from producing colostrum to transitional milk takes place over a couple of hours. For others, the course of change is spread out over a day or two. In either case, most moms experience a noticeable increase in breast size accompanied by a feeling of fullness. That said, new moms can sometimes be deceived into thinking that they're producing enough milk before their breasts actually get the hang of it. If you don't experience a reassuringly noticeable change, or if there is even any question in your mind as to whether your milk has started to flow and your newborn is getting enough—especially during these early days and weeks—take your questions or concerns to your baby's doctor without delay.

Progressive Production

The changeover from colostrum to transitional and then mature milk is an important one. It gives you and your baby's doctor reassurance that all is going well. Because the actual transition is not always so clear-cut, as some women notice very little change in their breasts as their milk supply increases, it is useful to be aware of several other clues that can help you figure out that everything is moving ahead as planned. They include

- Your breast milk is white instead of yellow in color and appears thinner or clearer.
- Your baby makes more obvious gulping and swallowing noises when nursing.
- Your baby begins to pee and poop much more frequently (see "What Goes In Must Come Out" on page 59).

- Your baby no longer is losing weight or just holding steady, but instead has begun to gain weight relatively noticeably both on and off the scale (see "Weighing In" on page 30).

GETTING THE GOOD TIMES TO ROLL

New mothers who breastfeed typically experience a clear increase in milk production, commonly referred to as having their milk come in, anywhere from 2 to 5 days after the birth of their babies. How well you keep up with your fluid intake, your baby's ability to latch on correctly, how often you are able to nurse in the first few days, and many other factors can all play a role in the timing of this much anticipated turning point. If your milk supply hasn't come in by day 4 or 5 (or you're unsure as to whether it has), or if your baby is sleeping more and nursing less, then you should definitely call your baby's doctor for help, guidance, an evaluation, or reassurance.

The Let-Down Tingle

While the sensation that typically accompanies let-down isn't exactly the same for everyone, and for that matter isn't present at all for some breast-feeding moms, most women do experience what is often described as a tingling, a prickling, or even an electrical-like feeling in their breasts. Such sensations at the start of a feeding are helpful but not necessary in signifying that your milk has started to flow. As an aside, you may find (if you haven't already) that there are plenty of other potential triggers of milk let-down besides just a latched-on baby at your breast—including but not limited to the sound of a crying baby (yours or someone else's), a breast pump, nipple stimulation, sexual arousal, a warm shower or, on occasion, nothing at all.

Alleviating the Discomfort of Engorgement

For some of you, "fullness from breast milk" will be a purely euphemistic way of describing engorgement, a word familiar to many new breastfeeding moms and defined as being filled to the often painful point of capacity or congestion. Yes, your body may well have some work to do in the first days and weeks of breastfeeding before your breasts learn to control how much milk they make and spare you the discomfort of over-distension. Until your milk production matches your baby's needs—your breasts making as much as she needs, when she needs it, without going overboard—you may find yourself in some uncomfortable positions. Fortunately, there are things you can do about engorgement.

The 2 mainstays of managing engorgement are to wear a supportive bra (as sort of a "push-back" measure to decrease milk production) and to express a little milk whenever necessary to relieve the pain. When it comes to the latter, be sure to think about the concept of supply and demand we mentioned earlier before expressing a lot of milk; you'll find that there's a fine line between expressing enough breast milk to relieve the pain and expressing so much that you give your body the unintended message to produce even more. Using a warm compress, expressing milk, and feeding your baby more frequently may help relieve your symptoms.

  MASTITIS

If you are a breastfeeding mom, it's going to be well worth your time to be on the lookout for mastitis. In mastitis, bacteria infect the breast ducts that store milk, resulting in painful, red, swollen breasts. Be forewarned that mastitis has a way of sneaking up on nursing mothers. That's because the more obvious signs of breast infection may not be obvious until a day or two after you start to feel achy, sick, and/or feverish. As long as you're familiar with mastitis, you stand a fighting chance of noticing it early on, getting the necessary medical advice, and getting treated with antibiotics sooner rather than later.

It's Not Worth Crying Over Spilt Milk

Having also experienced leaky breasts firsthand, we readily admit that they all too often come with the territory as your body adapts to breastfeeding. While they may represent a mild nuisance for some, they can be a source of considerable frustration and great embarrassment to others. It's not clear why some women's bodies seem to have better control of their milk flow than others—experiencing only minimal leakage limited to the few days after milk comes in instead of a more pervasive problem that can last for weeks (or even months) into the course of breastfeeding. If nothing else, we can offer you some words of advice and encouragement that we hope will help you take this potential fact of breastfeeding life in stride.

- **The power of perspective.** You may hear an occasional account of someone whose breasts never quite contained themselves and proceeded to leak the entire time she breastfed. Statistically speaking, your own chances of "recovery" are actually quite good. Any leakage you may experience at the outset will most likely subside or even resolve completely over time. And just because you leak a lot with your first baby doesn't mean that you are destined to leak a lot with every subsequent child. OK, so it may not be that much of a consolation this time around, but at least there's light at the end of the next tunnel!

- **Breast pads.** Breast pads are a very useful invention. Feel free to try out the thin cotton disposable ones if you have only minimal leakage, but head straight for the washable reusable (and generally more absorbent) type if the disposable ones don't do the trick. And for those of you whose breasts just haven't gotten the hang of holding on to the milk until your baby requests it, you wouldn't be the first to decide to stuff a burp cloth, hand towel, or even a clean cloth diaper in your bra to keep things under control while sleeping or lounging around in the privacy of your own home.

- **Provide back-pressure.** Back-pressure helps. If you start to leak (or are blessed with some advanced warning of impending leakage in the form of a let-down tingle), put pressure on your breasts to slow or stop the flow. When in public, you can subtly fold your arms across your chest and squeeze firmly. This gives new meaning to assuming an arms-crossed power pose.

- **Contain yourself.** Taking extra measures to contain yourself, so to speak, such as wearing a supportive bra during the time when you are nursing, is not only said to decrease your odds of being left with saggy breasts after your breastfeeding days are over, but doing so can also help to decrease the likelihood of engorgement and leakage. While it may not be a common topic of public discussion, believe us when we tell you that plenty of new moms (particularly those who are prone to leakage and/or engorgement) take up the habit of wearing a bra 24/7 for as long as it takes for the flow to ebb.

If the Bra Fits...

As a general rule—even before pregnancy and breastfeeding are factored in—we firmly believe that splurging on comfortable bras and underwear is well worth whatever it costs you. You've probably already discovered that pregnancy is often responsible for increasing one's bust size, as is breast-feeding. By how much varies, but it's relatively safe to say that the bras that once fit you in your pre-pregnancy days are not going to be of much use for a while. With that in mind and the task of bra shopping at hand, we suggest you

- **Consider comfort and convenience.** Above all else, look for bras that offer comfort *and* convenience. After all, you'll be breastfeeding as many as 12 times a day, and this is a garment that you may well find yourself wearing 24 hours a day! You'll have enough going on with your breasts that the last thing you'll need is to add another potential source of discomfort or irritation.

- **Expect expansion.** Expect that you'll keep expanding until your milk supply comes in. While you may want to invest in some new, bigger bras during pregnancy, don't assume that's the last bra shopping you'll need to do.

- **Evaluate for ease of use.** Nursing bras nowadays come with all sorts of modern-day conveniences—not the least of which are flaps that can be opened on each cup to allow easy and more discreet access. Be sure to try on a couple to see not only if they are comfortable and fit well, but also if the flaps are easy to fasten and unfasten.

- **Go with what works.** Regular bras are also an option. Some women find that wearing a regular bra and simply pulling the shoulder strap (and therefore the cup) down or partially opening a front-fastening bra is as easy as wearing a true nursing bra, not to mention less expensive and in some cases more comfortable.

How Much Is Enough? How Much Is Too Much?

Unlike their formula-feeding counterparts who are able to rely on the ounce-by-ounce markings displayed on the sides of their babies' bottles, breastfeeding parents typically have questions and concerns about exactly how much breast milk their newborns are getting, and whether it is enough.

To address this understandable but often unnecessary concern, it's helpful to first distinguish between the several days *before* your milk comes in and the period *after* this turning point. As we've already discussed, the 2- to 5-day period preceding your milk coming in is inherently going to be a different breastfeeding experience—for you and your baby—than what you should expect as soon as the tide has come in, so to speak. By breastfeeding as often as you can during the first few days, without letting yourself become *too* irritated or sore, you can help ensure that your baby doesn't become dehydrated before your body reaches full milk production. Practically speaking, we recommend that you nurse more frequently during the day (at least every 2–3 hours, but more often if your baby is ready, willing, and able), while letting up a little at night (set your alarm for every 4–5 hours at the most if your baby will sleep that long). If your baby is jaundiced (see "Seeing Yellow: Jaundice" on page 261) or you suspect he may be getting dehydrated, you'll definitely want to have him checked out, as well as discuss specific feeding recommendations and expectations with your baby's doctor.

Settling Into a Routine

Once your milk supply comes in, be prepared to enter into a new phase of nursing that more closely resembles the mental image many new parents have about breastfeeding—one that includes frequent feedings accompanied by lots of wet diapers and soft if not outright liquidy poop (more on that subject in "What Goes In Must Come Out" on page 59). What you should not expect, however, is that you and your baby will fall into a regular routine defined by a set feeding schedule. Even after the first week or two, you may still find that there are days when your baby wants to nurse every hour or two—a pattern that often signals a growth spurt (see "Growth Spurts" on page 53). At other times she may sleep her way through 4 or more hours and still show no signs of waking up to eat. These considerations are what make the strictly defined patterns of feeding so often touted in some parenting books unrealistic. That said, a somewhat predictable feeding schedule would not be misguided unless you try to get your baby to adhere to it without exception from day 1. Overall, it is reasonable to expect to feed your baby at least every 2 to 3 hours as a baseline, with the goal of one longer stretch of 4 or more hours (preferably at night) within a few weeks.

Remember that this is a work in progress over the next several weeks or possibly months.

Breastfeeding on the Go

While a handful of new moms seem to be as comfortable baring all on a bench in the middle of a mall, in the center seat on an airplane, or at the home of a friend as she is in the privacy of her own home, there's nothing wrong or prudish about you if you aren't ready to tackle breastfeeding in public—now or ever. It's all about your own comfort level. There's certainly a sense of liberation that comes with learning some of the tricks of the trade that will ultimately allow you to breastfeed discreetly in public places (some of which we will be sharing with you elsewhere in this book), but unless you're ready, don't worry about mastering it now. For many mothers, this is but one of the many differences between the first and subsequent children.

  EXTREME BREASTFEEDING

As a point of interest and caution, there are occasionally those women who give breastfeeding on the go new meaning—such as the woman who made national news in 2003 for breastfeeding her 7-month-old while driving more than 60 mph on the Ohio turnpike. Even if there is apparently no shortage of loopholes in the law when it comes to extreme breastfeeding, we certainly hope that those of you who are already comfortable with the whole "baring your breast for the sake of breastfeeding" routine don't decide to engage in such risky acts in the name of good nutrition.

Breastfeeding by Numbers

The following are some handy definitions and rules of thumb to use when establishing your own approach to a breastfeeding routine:

- **Feeding intervals.** If you haven't started breastfeeding yet, it's probably hard to imagine how this can be a source of confusion. The issue at hand has to do with the starting point—whether to use the *start* of a feeding or the time at which your baby actually *finishes* the meal to determine when it's time to feed again. The pokier your newborn is at nursing—with some babies taking upwards of an hour to actually complete a feeding—the more this subject will apply to you. The standard convention is to use the time from the start of the first feeding to the start of the next. And yes, this may well mean starting a second feeding within an hour or two of finishing the previous one. What this means in real life: If you are attempting to make sure your baby eats at least every 2 to 3 hours and he starts nursing at 10:00 am, has to be woken up several times along the way, "requests" a diaper change at 10:30 am, and requires your active encouragement to latch back on to the second breast before finishing at around 11:00 am, you may still be looking at sitting down for another feeding no later than noon or 1:00 pm. While there are certainly new moms who have confided in us that this schedule can feel like a life sentence, you can take great comfort in knowing that it is likely to last no more than the first few weeks of your breastfeeding experience.

- **Breastfeeding frequency.** The most commonly recommended schedule for newborn breastfeeding is every 2 to 3 hours, which translates into a minimum of 8 to 12 feedings during any given 24-hour period. The reason it's so important for you to focus on fitting in this many feedings a day is to make sure that your baby is getting enough to eat to avoid dehydration and gain weight. Newborns who are still waiting for their mothers' milk supply to come in or those who are slow to catch on, latch on, or nurse even after milk is made abundantly available to them may end up having less energy and becoming increasingly more interested in sleeping. When newborns start to go longer periods between feedings—especially when they have yet to establish themselves as good eaters and regain their birth weight—they run the risk of getting even less to eat, becoming even more fatigued, and a vicious cycle can ensue. It is this cycle that you should be aware of, and which you are working so tirelessly to avoid with all of your round-the-clock feedings.

 SKIPPING MEALS

Conventional wisdom tells us it's not a nutritionally great idea for us to skip meals. When a newborn decides to do so 2 or more "meals" in a row for any reason—whether out of disinterest, lethargy, or difficulty feeding—you need to take heed and consult your baby's doctor without hesitation to find out why.

- **Weighing in.** You will find that just about everyone tends to focus on how much babies weigh in the days and weeks after they are born. That's because it gives us a measurable, objective way of determining if babies are getting enough to eat. Newborns are expected to lose as much as 10% of their birth weight in the week or two after birth (mostly in the form of water weight). A useful rough rule of thumb is that they should gain it back by 2 weeks of age. With that in mind, if you find that your baby goes in for his 2-week checkup and comes out weighing well over his birth weight, then you can take it as a reassurance that breastfeeding is going well. On the other hand, if you have concerns that your newborn isn't gaining weight or is continuing to lose weight, don't wait for the routine 2-week check to consult with your pediatrician. It is absolutely no reflection on you or your success at your first attempts at parenthood if you end up on the phone with your doctor's office several times in the first week or two of your parenting journey. That is, after all, what they're there for!

One Breast or Two

The often-debated question of whether it is better to breastfeed a baby on one or both breasts at each feeding does not, in fact, have a single right answer. Some experts in the field recommend one—allowing babies to drain the breast fully and therefore get to the "dessert equivalent" of breast milk known as hind milk, which has been shown to be richer in fat. Others recommend the double-breasted approach—noting that 15 minutes of nursing on each side typically drains most of a breast's total milk volume and offers the more practical benefit of preventing women from becoming "lopsided" after each feeding. Some women choose to drain the first breast fully to be sure their baby gets the hind milk and then nurse as long as possible on the second. From a practical standpoint, we've found that it is reasonable to go either way.

- If your baby is a poky eater who can hardly be woken up to tackle the second breast after nursing from the first—especially if she happens to have a hard time latching on, is finicky, or rebels whenever you attempt to take her off the first and switch her to the second—well then the "one breast per feeding" approach may better suit your needs. Just remember to keep track of which side your baby last nursed on and then alternate breasts at each feeding. This routine may require you to actually write down which breast your baby fed from last, because many a new mother has found that her memory isn't quite what it used to be before being in a chronic state of sleep deprivation. Or simply put an extra breast pad on the side you need to nurse on first as an easy reminder for the next time.

- If, however, you find that your baby is content to switch from one side to the other during the course of a feeding, or if you find that your "neglected" breast becomes uncomfortably engorged when you alternate—then you may decide to settle into the 2-breast routine. Depending on how your baby acts at any given time of day, you may just want to follow her lead and try to keep each side as even as possible. As we mentioned earlier, this is more of a consideration when it comes to engorgement, leaking, and milk production in the first couple weeks of breastfeeding than it is down the road.

When all is said and done, your body will learn to accommodate whatever pattern you and your baby settle into, and you will have more flexibility in deviating from your standard routine.

Falling Into Bad Habits?

Even though you may be a relative newcomer to the world of parenthood, you've nonetheless probably already been warned not to let your baby use your breasts as a pacifier or a snack bar, not to let him fall asleep while nursing lest he become dependent on doing so for months if not years to come, and to try to get him onto a set feeding schedule as soon as you can. Well, here's news that will make your life easier: These warnings and recommendations don't apply to you during the first several weeks of your baby's life. Spoiling is not and should not be a concern at this stage. In fact, resisting the urge to follow the scheduled approach to feeding, especially early on, and instead offering your baby the opportunity to nurse frequently now can actually help establish breastfeeding in such a way as to ensure future success. Once you and your baby have gotten comfortable and settled into the whole breastfeeding routine, you can more appropriately consider your options when it comes to feeding schedules and nursing as a pacifier substitute if you so choose. And let us just add, for those of you who may have already read other parenting books, that trying to keep a *newborn* from falling asleep while nursing is, in our experience, nothing short of an exercise in futility. All of these things will come in time, but you don't need to worry about them for several weeks.

The Confusion About Nipple Confusion

A good deal of attention seems to be paid to the notion that babies who are in the process of learning to breastfeed can sometimes be led astray by the introduction of any sort of artificial sucking device—whether it's in the form of a nipple on a bottle or a pacifier. Again, even the experts seem to be divided when it comes to supplementing with a bottle or offering pacifiers to breastfed babies. We have found that it is entirely feasible to do either or both without sabotaging your chances for breast-feeding success if you understand a few simple concepts and follow a few basic rules.

As we said before, your baby's mouth is and will continue to be the center of her universe. Quite simply, babies naturally want to suck—and some more than others. In the first days and weeks of life, this urge to suck certainly can work to everyone's advantage in speeding up a nursing mother's milk production, but once the milk is in and breastfeeding is well established, some new mothers find themselves in the challenging and sometimes uncomfortable position of having a baby who *constantly* wants to suck (or so it seems). That's because for some babies, sucking is not just about getting fed. This additional interest is referred to as nonnutritive sucking and is the reason why pacifiers (or fingers) can and often do come in handy in consoling a fussy baby. While there's nothing inherently wrong with letting your young infant nurse long after your breasts are drained and in between feedings (unless it is causing you undue pain), it is perfectly acceptable to use a pacifier instead (see also "Practical Pacifier Principles" on page 56). It may help to limit the pacifier use to when your baby really wants it, and not offer it to her all the time. Be sure to talk to your baby's doctor if you have more questions about the use of pacifiers.

Nipple Confusion Defined

The problem that some experts have with artificial nipples is that they have the potential to confuse a baby who is being breastfed. During the time when a baby is learning to breastfeed, sucking on the nipple of a bottle to get milk is thought to be considerably easier than the effort required to effectively lap milk out of a breast. The concern, therefore, is that babies not yet fully accomplished at breastfeeding may opt for the "easy way out," or become confused about the necessary way to suck when returning from bottle to breast. Although pacifiers aren't responsible for supplying an alternate source of milk, they too require a baby to suck differently than he would on his mother's breast. That said, we have found that most breastfed babies do just fine with the introduction of a bottle and/or pacifier if their parents wait long enough to introduce it. How long is long enough? The practical answer is: long enough to let your baby get the gist of breastfeeding first, but not so long that he will accept no substitute. There's definitely a fine line between long enough and too long. While the exact timing is debated, if your baby is latching on, nursing, peeing, pooping, and gaining weight well, then we have found somewhere in the vicinity of 2 to 6 weeks to be a perfectly reasonable time to introduce an artificial nipple onto the sucking scene.

Supplementing Scenarios

The decision to give a breastfed baby additional breast milk or formula from a bottle—better known as supplementing—may be strictly a matter of choice and convenience for some mothers, but born out of nutritional necessity for others. In reality, something as simple as needing to get a single stretch of sleep longer than 3 hours in the course of several tiring weeks motivates some exhausted new and experienced moms to supplement. Other motivating circumstances typically include babies who have latching and/or feeding problems and are getting dehydrated and/or jaundiced, and mothers who are struggling to increase their milk supply or have physical/medical limitations or work responsibilities that impact their ability to breastfeed. In any of the previous scenarios, supplementing is an acceptable option. Tempting though it may be, we do want to make sure that those of you who are struggling to breastfeed and beginning to question your abilities don't find yourself reaching for a bottle for lack of perceived alternatives. Instead, we urge you to enlist the help of your pediatrician or a local lactation consultant and explore all of your breastfeeding options first.

 ## PUMP IT UP

With only occasional exception, it's technically never too soon to start pumping your milk and building up a stockpile for present or future use. Pumping can help stimulate a new mom's milk supply to come in, increase her milk production, or relieve engorgement once the supply has been established. That said, adding pumping into the already rigorous newborn feeding schedule can be quite challenging and a whole lot of extra work. Unless you are used to pumping or need to pump out of necessity, we suggest waiting until you are comfortable with nursing and your milk supply is well established. When you are ready to get started, consider how much and how often you plan to pump because you'll want to get the type of pump that best suits your pumping needs. If you plan to pump infrequently, you may get by with a manual pump (or even manual expression). For anything more frequent, we highly recommend an electric version. Let us also mention that there are some women (Jennifer included) who have little luck with pumping (much less manual expression) and are perfectly content to supplement their nursing with a bottle of formula when deemed necessary and/or convenient.

Into the Mouths of Moms

In addition to potentially finding yourself thirstier and with an increased appetite once you enter the milk production business, you may also find yourself the recipient of a whole lot of advice about exactly what you should and shouldn't be eating and drinking—all given in the best interest of your milk. We've found that most moms who are new to breastfeeding, however, benefit a great deal from a little practical perspective on this subject.

- **The scoop on eating for 2.** Some breastfeeding moms figure they can eat just about anything they want. Others become overly focused on quickly regaining their figures and set out to diet. As a breastfeeding mother, you are certainly entitled to take advantage of eating for 2. However, just as in pregnancy, breastfeeding should not serve as an open invitation to let your cravings run wild. Rather than doubling how much you eat and overindulging in desserts and empty calories with little nutritional value, it is perhaps more prudent to increase your daily caloric intake by 25% (in some cases up to 50%) and try to eat a relatively well-rounded diet while nursing.

- **The good, the bad, and the spicy.** Given that much of what a nursing mother eats or drinks has the potential to ultimately end up in her breast milk, you might be convinced that you are in for many months of a bland diet. You may be relieved to know then that most breastfed babies happily tolerate a lot more variety than you'd think—even if your favorite foods include garlic, onions, cabbage, broccoli, or the like. Unless you have a strong family history of certain food allergies or can pinpoint a particular food that seems to upset your baby, there's no need to take the spice out of your life—or your food.

- **Staying well hydrated.** While there is no truth to the old wives' tale that you need to drink milk to make milk, drinking plenty of liquids and staying well hydrated can definitely help keep things flowing. Some moms actually experience strong pangs of thirst associated with milk let-down each time they breastfeed—conveniently ensuring that they remember to take time to drink. Even if you don't, use your nursing times as reminders to make sure you take time to drink and stay well hydrated.

Medications

Regardless of whether you are going to be taking herbal remedies or prescription, over-the-counter, or homeopathic medicine(s), it's safest to assume that any medication you take may affect your breast milk and harm your baby (or decrease your milk supply), so always check with your doctor first. In reality, some medications don't find their way into the breast milk at all and some do but are perfectly safe and have little or no effect on nursing babies.

INDULGENCES AND VICES

Caffeine. If you didn't already quit caffeine cold turkey when you were pregnant—or you did but now can't wait to welcome caffeine back into your life—you may be relieved to know that breastfeeding and enjoying a little caffeine every now and then aren't mutually exclusive. In fact, La Leche League International reports that up to 3 cups of caffeine-containing beverages per day pose no inherent harm to nursing mothers or babies. That said, if you notice your baby is irritable or fussy, you might want to try decreasing or gradually eliminating your caffeine intake.

Cigarettes. If you were able to quit smoking during your pregnancy, then congratulations—now is most definitely not a good time to restart. And if you didn't attempt or manage to quit before—now is as good a time as any (if not better) to succeed, for your baby's health and your own. While you undoubtedly know that smoking cigarettes isn't good for you to begin with, it may still come as a surprise to some of you that doing so while breastfeeding allows chemicals to pass into breast milk and cause dangerous side effects. Secondhand smoke increases your baby's risk of infections, asthma, and sudden infant death syndrome. If you do choose to smoke, the American Academy of Pediatrics (AAP) recommends doing so right after you finish nursing your baby, limiting yourself to a few cigarettes per day, and never smoking around your baby or even in your house or car.

Alcohol. Breastfeeding legend suggests that drinking alcohol increases a nursing mother's milk supply. According to the AAP *New Mother's Guide to Breastfeeding* book, "Contrary to popular myth, drinking beer does not increase your milk supply." What we do know for sure is that alcohol, if consumed in large amounts by breastfeeding mothers (and more importantly, during pregnancy), can harm babies. If you choose to have an occasional drink of alcohol, it is best to do so right after you finish breastfeeding, knowing that it will show up in your breast milk soon thereafter (within 30–90 minutes) and will likely be cleared within 2 hours. You can either wait the 2 hours it typically takes for alcohol levels in breast milk to drop before starting the next feeding, or decide to take the more purist approach and "pump and dump" the next feeding's worth of breast milk.

CHAPTER 2

formula for success

We admit it. In many ways, feeding your baby formula may seem much easier than breastfeeding, especially in the beginning weeks. After all, you don't have to worry about having enough of a supply, it's rather painless (if you don't count the sleep deprivation that comes with round-the-clock

 ## A VERY BRIEF HISTORY OF
FORMULA AS WE KNOW IT

In addition to being a prominent mainstay of modern-day parenthood, formula is very big business. Despite the many options that make their way to the grocery store shelves, there are only a handful of major manufacturers in the United States, all of whom must meet the same well-defined standards established by the US Food and Drug Administration. As you might imagine, a quick look back tells us that this was not always the case.

Mid-1800s: Most attempts to create a substitute for human milk before this time were met with disastrous results. Almost everyone stuck to breastfeeding.

1867: In the mid-19th century, researchers began to analyze breast milk in an attempt to create a reasonable substitute, and the first in today's formula lineage was introduced. A liquid containing wheat and malt flour was mixed with cow's milk, cooked with bicarbonate of potash, and billed as the "perfect infant food." We're not exactly sure what potash is or if this primitive formula was met with open mouths, but by the late 1800s, the foundation of modern-day formula had been laid and the marketing of artificial infant formula had begun.

1951: The first non-powder infant formula hit the shelves and rapidly became the most popular product available on the infant formula market.

1950s: The developed world fully embraced artificial infant formula, and it soon became the feeding method of choice.

feeding), and it's easy to monitor your baby's intake. Granted, formula can be costly, you have to wash your supplies, and on occasion a baby will be finicky about which nipple and formula she is willing to accept, but at some point during their child's first year, most of today's parents end up using formula. With that in mind, we intend to give you a practical approach to formula, buying and cleaning bottles and nipples, and troubleshooting for newborns who don't seem to play by the rules.

Sifting Through the Formula Facts

In this day and age, all it takes is a casual glance down the formula aisle at the grocery store or baby super center to become overwhelmed by the number of formula options available to you and your baby—a little "ultra lipid powder" here, some "lactose-free concentrate" there.... We therefore thought it might be useful to simplify the world of formula a bit and give you a quick overview. It's easiest to start by categorizing formula into the 3 most commonly used types: those that are *cow's milk-based;* those that are *soy-based;* and those that are *specialized, hypoallergenic,* or *elemental*— meaning that their components are broken down to be more easily digestible. While you may have heard a lot of talk about babies needing to be switched from one formula to the next, most babies are started on cow's milk-based (or soy-based) formulas and do just fine. In fact, most babies spend their entire formula-consuming careers drinking the same formula they were given on day 1. The fact that most babies do well with cow's milk- and soy-based formulas is financially fortunate because while these 2 types of formula tend to be comparable in price (with soy typically costing only pennies more per ounce), the elemental formulas are significantly more expensive (as in nearly twice as much). Thankfully, this third category of formulas is generally reserved for babies who have reactions to cow's milk- or soy-based products (see "Tales of the Truly Intolerant" on page 39) and better tolerate the broken down and more easily digested proteins found in hypoallergenic or elemental formulas.

Formula Intolerance

Some babies have a clear preference for one type or even brand of formula over another. Some prefer the smoothness of ready-to-feed formula to the consistency of prepared powder formula. Others demonstrate a penchant for cow's milk-based formula over soy-based (or vice versa). In some instances, preferences are subtle. For some babies, however, the word "preference" is an understatement. In search of a formula cure for a lot of extra fussiness, gas, spitting up, or any number of other ways that babies reject certain types and voice their opinion, parents are prone to a fair bit of formula trial and error. The good news is that most newborns do quite well with whatever form, brand, or type of formula they are given. While many even tolerate being switched back and forth between different brands without any problems, we should caution you that this is generally not recommended by health professionals. If, however, you find yourself with a finicky eater on your hands, we suggest that you talk to your baby's doctor to discuss a reasonable approach to formula switching and determine if your baby happens to be one of the handful of infants who are truly intolerant.

 TALES OF THE TRULY INTOLERANT

As many as 10% of all babies are truly intolerant of milk- or soy-based formulas—a condition known as *milk soy protein intolerance* (MSPI) where the intestinal tract is irritated by the proteins found in both of these types of infant formulas. Babies with MSPI typically aren't happy. They fuss and tend to react soon after eating. They often spit up a lot, become gassy (sometimes to the point of pain), or have problems with pooping (either constipation or diarrhea). If you suspect that your baby may have a formula intolerance, be sure to discuss your suspicion with your pediatrician. By running a quick test on your baby's poop (looking for traces of blood and other incriminating substances), he or she can help to determine if your newborn's intestinal tract is reacting to the formula. If your baby is truly intolerant, your baby's doctor can recommend an alternative formula for you to try and discuss with you the game plan for future feeding.

The Importance of Being Iron-Fortified

It is very important that your baby gets enough iron during the many months before he starts eating iron-rich foods. With that in mind, take a closer look around and you may be surprised to see that some formulas are sold as low-iron preparations. The reason we considered this important to mention is because there seems to be a common misconception among parents that the iron in regular formula causes constipation or stomach pain in babies and that low-iron formulas are therefore a reasonable solution. While this assumption is understandable, especially coming from any parents who have ever suffered the uncomfortable side effects of having taken iron supplements themselves for any length of time, it does not hold true for infants. That's because the impressively high levels of iron listed on the formula label don't, in fact, reflect how much iron your baby is able to process and actually use. While sparing you the biochemistry of iron absorption, we want to reassure you that your baby will only end up making use of a fraction of the iron you put in his mouth, and most babies tolerate regular formula without any complaints. If your baby seems to be developing a rash, excess spitting up, pain, or problems pooping, we (as you might suspect) suggest a quick consult with your pediatrician before considering changing formulas.

 CHEWING THE FATTY ACIDS (DHA AND ARA)

In recent years, 2 fatty acids known as DHA (docosahexaenoic acid) and ARA (arachidonic acid) have been added to some infant formulas. In their naturally occurring forms, these fatty acids are thought to be crucial for a baby's development—especially of the eyes and brain. How much difference they actually make when they are added to formula has yet to be proven. According to the government agency that oversees the production of infant formula (the US Food and Drug Administration), "the scientific evidence is mixed." But the addition of the fatty acids is known to be safe, and you'll surely spot them on your next stroll down the formula aisle—either by reading the ingredient labels or looking for prominently displayed words such as "lipids," "Lipil," "Advance," or just plain "DHA and ARA."

Formula Form and Function: Powders, Concentrates, and Ready-to-Feed

Infant formulas generally come as ready-to-feed liquid, concentrated liquid, and powder. Which type is going to work best for you is likely to depend on how much formula you plan to use, where you plan to use it (ready-to-feed is definitely very convenient when you're out and about), and how much you want to spend.

Just as pregnancy taught most of you to think in weeks instead of months, bottle-feeding your baby will require you to think in ounces and adopt it as your standard unit of measurement. To prepare you accordingly, we'll first clarify the basic measures you'll need for formula success.

1 ounce = 30 cc (cubic centimeters) = 30 mL (milliliters)

8 ounces = 1 cup

32 ounces = 1 quart

Now that you have some frame of reference, we'll move on to the actual substance of formula preparation.

2 scoops + 4 ounces water = 4 ounces of mixed formula

- **Powder.** The simple concept here is that you add water and shake a lot. In what we can only assume was an enlightened attempt to eliminate room for mixing errors, all powdered formula is mixed according to the same recipe: *one scoop of powder to every 2 ounces of water.* Powdered formula comes in cans containing enough powder to make anywhere from 100 ounces to more than 200 ounces of prepared formula. It is certainly your most economical choice, and quite frankly works perfectly well for most babies. You can decide whether to mix it up as you go or prepare a full day's worth (or two) at a time and refrigerate it.

2 ounces concentrated formula + 2 ounces water = 4 ounces of mixed formula

- **Liquid concentrate.** This is the "just add water as directed and shake" formula option. Mixing and measuring is again quite straightforward, because all brands of concentrate call for equal amounts of water and concentrate. If you intend to end up with a total of 4 ounces of prepared formula, you'll need to mix 2 ounces of concentrate with 2 ounces of water. Of course many people choose to mix an entire can of concentrate (13 ounces) with an equal amount of water. The resulting 26 ounces of now-ready-to-feed formula can be covered and put in the refrigerator to be used over the next 48 hours. While some parents find concentrate to be easier, neater, and/or more convenient than powder, it is a convenience for which you will pay more.

- **Ready-to-feed.** This is your no-mixing, no-measuring, no-mess option. Sold in either 8-ounce cans (4 or 6 cans to a pack) or 1-quart (32-ounce) containers/cans, the use of ready-to-feed formula is hopefully self-explanatory—what you see is what you give. While the fairly small "Ready-to-Feed" caption isn't always prominently displayed on the label, you'd be hard pressed to miss the distinguishing price tag (see "Comparing Ounces to Ounces" on page 43). While buying ready-to-feed formula inevitably costs the most, it leaves almost no room for error (assuming that you don't mistake it for concentrate and dilute it with water). Unopened cans can be conveniently stored at room temperature. Once opened, unused portions can be covered and then refrigerated for up to 48 hours.

Pour 4 ounces of ready-to-feed into a 4-ounce bottle.

COMPARING OUNCES TO OUNCES (FOR WHAT IT'S WORTH)

Based on a recent check of prices at the local grocery store, we thought it would be helpful to give you a general idea of how the different types of formula stack up ounce for ounce at the checkout counter. To do so, we compared one particular type and brand of formula, and did not factor in sale prices (which can unquestionably save you a lot of money). Also keep in mind that the ounces we are comparing—and that you can easily compare for yourself—are the ounces of *prepared* formula once it is ready to feed to your baby.

Type	Size	Price Per Prepared Ounce
Ready-to-feed	Four 8-ounce cans	25 cents
Ready-to-feed	1 quart	18 cents
Concentrate	13-ounce can	15 cents
Powder	Small can	11.5 cents
Powder	Large can	12 cents

To compare ounces to ounces for yourself, first look at the formula container and figure out how many ounces you'll be able to make from it once it is properly prepared. Then simply divide the price by the number of prepared ounces and you're guaranteed to be a better-informed formula-buying consumer in no time!

Formula Buying Tips

Buying formula is a significant expense of parenthood. If you are so inclined, we've put together a little list of ways you might save a bit along the way.

- **Do the math.** We realize that it's not always easy, fun, or feasible, but it can be quite worthwhile to take the time and figure out how much you're paying per ounce (as we demonstrated previously). You may be surprised by what you find by comparing prices between brands as well as by comparing types and sizes. Once you've looked at the label and figured out how many total prepared ounces you'll be getting in any given can or container, divide the cost by that number.

- **Stock up.** To do this, you'll first want to make sure that your baby is perfectly content with the formula he's getting. Then take advantage of any sales and coupons you may spot along the way. While we're not really sure just how important formula expiration dates really are, you'll want remember to check the expiration date printed on the cans before stocking up if you're going to take them seriously. While many will have expiration dates well in excess of a year, you won't want to get stuck with a bunch of cans whose time will be up before you can use them.

- **Save receipts.** Early on it's more difficult to know for sure that the formula you buy now is going to be the formula you buy forever after (ie, through the end of the first year). While you're still settling in over the next several weeks, we suggest tucking your receipts away somewhere for safekeeping and easy retrieval.

Mixing It Up

Be sure to read the instructions carefully when preparing formula. Any incorrectly prepared formula, whether it's too concentrated or too dilute, has the potential to cause problems. While ready-to-feed formula is just that—you can pour the room-temperature contents directly into a bottle, screw on the nipple, and have your baby feed away—the others require accurate preparation. As for the water you use, you may want to use boiled or purified (bottled or filtered) water, at least in the first month or two. For most normal healthy babies, regular tap water is acceptable. Check with your pediatrician or water department before using well water, or if you have any concerns about the purity of your tap supply. If you have any questions about mixing your formula, don't hesitate to contact your baby's doctor for recommendations. Although rare, mixing mistakes can, in fact, cause very serious problems for infants in a period of only days.

PRACTICAL POSSIBILITIES FOR POWDERED FORMULA

Short of using the more expensive but ready-to-feed formula, we've found that the best way to have plenty of easily prepared formula on hand is to put premeasured amounts of powdered formula into several of your baby's bottles, complete with nipples and lids. As an important insight, be sure your bottles are *completely* dry before putting powdered formula in them. A few drops of water left inside a bottle can make the powder stick to the sides in a manner reminiscent of cement and consequently make future bottle cleaning a significantly more challenging proposition. Once the premeasured powder is sealed in a few dry bottles, they're ready for use whenever it's time to feed your baby. The added benefit: No heating time is required. Instead of having to heat up previously prepared and chilled formula, you can simply add an appropriate amount of warm or room-temperature water to a bottle at each feeding time.

CHAPTER 3

bottles and nipples

Whether you plan on bottle-feeding your newborn with formula or pumped breast milk, you will obviously need to properly equip yourself with a supply of bottles and nipples. Nowadays, you can choose from lightweight plastic bottles, glass bottles, collapsible (disposable) plastic bottle bags, angled bottles, colored bottles, contoured bottles, and countless shapes, sizes, and consistencies of nipples. Although we're certain that many of you would like to have all your bottles in a row in anticipation of your baby's arrival and most babies really could not care less, there's just no good way to know ahead of time if your baby will agree with your initial choices. That's because when it comes to nipples, and even the bottles you choose, be forewarned that one size does not always suit all. If your baby happens to be less than tolerant of the type/brand you've so carefully selected, you may be faced with a trial period as you test out the different shapes, sizes, colors, and brands of bottles and nipples in an attempt to find a good match. We therefore recommend starting off with the basics and waiting to buy in bulk until you find a keeper. If you are set on stocking up on a particular type of bottle in advance, simply hang on to your receipts. Once a sample bottle and nipple has been met with your baby's approval, you'll be all set.

The Model Bottle

We've found that in reality, most babies go along with their parents' taste in bottles and there really isn't such a thing as a single "model bottle"—one that outshines all the rest. Nevertheless, we have found the following considerations to serve bottle-buying parents well:

- In general, a transparent (ie, not colored) 4-ounce bottle is the most practical choice for newborns.

- Larger (6- or 8-ounce) bottles are fine if you don't mind using them half-full until your baby is bigger.
- Angled bottles and those with a "frame" and disposable nurser bags are said to help decrease the amount of air your baby swallows (although regular bottles held at the proper angle will also).
- Disposable bags have the added benefit of, well, being disposable; you only have to wash the nipples after each feeding.

CHAPTER 4

going with the flow

One of the main considerations in choosing a nipple is finding one that
allows the right amount of milk flow for your baby. Because different babies
can handle different flows at different ages and levels of development, you'll
soon discover (if you haven't already) that nipples come in many different
sizes. They are typically marketed based on a baby's age, with the preemie
and 0- to 3-month nipples allowing for slower flows than those nipples
designed for use by 6- or 9-month-olds. Voracious eaters, however, may do
perfectly well with a faster-flow nipple even as newborns, while others may
take months before being able to drink from the age-appropriate nipple
without having large volumes of milk streaming down the sides of their
mouths. As for the openings—not only will you find yourself with a choice
of 1-hole, 2-hole, and 3-hole nipples, but also nipples that are cross-cut and
who knows what else. For practical purposes, all you really need to pay
attention to is how fast the milk flows—too fast, too slow, or just right.

While neither of us had to spend much time in search of a suitable nipple for our babies, it is worth mentioning that nipples also come in many
shapes and sizes, from regular to orthodontic and beyond. If your baby is
finicky, then you'll want to pay more attention to the vast array of nipples
and choose whichever shape your baby decides to accept. We will add that
most experts we've asked don't believe that the orthodontic shape adds
much, if any, benefit.

Heating Things Up

While there is no inherent medical, nutritional, or even comfort-related
need to warm your newborn's bottles, if you're like a good many parents
these days, you'll be spending the next several months heating formula

(or expressed breast milk) for your baby. The recommended way to do this is to put a bottle of breast milk or formula into a bottle warmer or saucepan of warm water until the milk is warm. That said, you would not be the first parent to be tempted by the microwave. Before you succumb to temptation, let us point out that microwaves are known to heat unevenly, creating potentially dangerous hot spots, not to mention destroying the protective antibodies found in breast milk. For these reasons, almost all experts recommend avoiding the use of the microwave altogether. If you make the decision to still use the microwave, we strongly suggest you do so only with formula, only for several seconds at a time, and that you take extra precautions to mix the formula well before giving it to your baby. Regardless of how you choose to heat things up, always be sure to test a few drops of the well-mixed liquid on your inner wrist before feeding your baby.

WHAT WILL THEY THINK OF NEXT

Many of the bottle-warming and bottle-cooling products now fall into parenthood's "what will they think of next?" category. These include bottle warmers you can plug into your car's lighter as well as the all-in-one bottle-cooler-heater-alarm clock that you can plug in next to your bed at night. There are mini-coolers, compact refrigerators, and insulated baby "lunch" bags that come equipped with ice packs. We think you will see a pattern here. It's always refreshing to know that people are looking out for ways to make life easier for parents these days! To be perfectly honest, if it's ease of use you're looking for, we suggest a trial run of unwarmed formula or breast milk before you convince yourself that you and your baby can't live without the latest in milk-warming technology.

Finally—The Feeding Part

Once you've found a good bottle-nipple combination and have formula or breast milk on hand, you are ready to bottle-feed your baby. One of the most helpful things to remember when bottle-feeding is to angle the bottle. By holding the bottle fairly upright in your baby's mouth instead of horizontal, you will avoid feeding your baby air and make sure she is getting only the milk. To do so,

- Lean her back at a slight recline while supporting the back of her head and neck.
- If she isn't already open-mouthed in eager anticipation, you may find it helpful to stroke the side of her mouth or cheek with the nipple to get her to open her mouth (see "Rooting for Success" on page 17).
- Then insert the nipple into her mouth and hold the bottle with the end tilted up enough that the milk completely fills the nipple as your baby drinks.
- As the bottle empties, you may find you need to hold the bottle almost upright.

Bottle-feeding by Numbers

You've probably read enough by now to know that we have no way of telling you exactly how many ounces your newborn will take. As you get a feel for feeding your baby (and the associated peeing and pooping that should accompany it), here are a few numbers for you to use as general guidelines.

- **First feedings.** Newborns typically take anywhere from 1/2 to 1-1/2 ounces at each of the first few feedings.
- **Daily totals.** After the first several days, most newborns drink between 12 and 24 ounces during the course of each 24-hour day.
- **Feeding frequency.** On average, formula-fed babies drink every 3 to 4 hours, while those given bottles of breast milk still tend to eat every 2 to 3 hours. Regardless of feeding frequency, any newborn who refuses feedings 2 or more times in a row should be brought to the immediate attention of his doctor.
- **Weighing in.** The true test of whether your baby is drinking enough is if he is gaining weight as expected. This holds true for breastfed and formula-fed infants (see "Weighing In" on page 30).

DOUBLE SIPPING

We recommend filling each bottle with only as much as you think
your baby will take—with a little extra for good measure in case she happens
to be particularly hungry. That way you can minimize the amount you end
up having to discard at the end of each feeding. The party line is that it's
OK to hang on to leftover formula or breast milk for a little while in hopes that
your baby decides to finish it off—especially if you've got a grazer on your
hands or your baby decides to drink less than you expected. However, you
should plan on keeping leftovers around no longer than about an hour
before throwing them away, because bacteria from your baby's
mouth are known to multiply fairly rapidly in milk.

Cleaning Up

Sample nipples obtained from the hospital or doctor's office conveniently
come in sterilized packages for the earliest feedings and are meant to be disposed of after a single use. After that, the standard recommendation is that
all feeding supplies and pacifiers should be washed and, whenever possible,
sterilized prior to first use.

- You can easily sterilize your supplies by placing them in boiling water
  for about 5 minutes. Commercial sterilizers are also available for
  this purpose.
- In general, many parents are content to hand wash bottles and nipples
  in hot, sudsy water and rinse right after feedings to keep the remaining
  contents of the bottle from sticking/drying to the sides, nooks,
  and crannies.
- Bottle and nipple brushes are inexpensive and invaluable for cleaning
  even the hard-to-reach places.
- You can either re-sterilize your bottles and nipples between uses or
  wash them in a very hot dishwasher.
- There are plenty of dishwasher-safe plastic baskets on the market specially designed to serve the sole purpose of holding all of the small items
  involved in bottle-feeding—the nipples, lids, and other baby accessories
  that will likely take up a sizable chunk of your dishwasher's upper rack.

Schedules and Routines

Setting a Schedule or Going With the Flow

Getting babies to follow some semblance of a feeding schedule is a subject of great interest to many parents of newborns—ranking right up there with longing for predictable sleep schedules (see "Sleeping Like a Baby" on page 87). You should know that it is also a topic that inspires great debate. You'll find many differing opinions depending on whom you ask, what you read, or where you look. While we certainly don't presume to have the one and only answer to the eternal question of whether one should feed on demand or follow a set schedule, we can certainly give you the background you'll need to choose a practical and safe approach to the whole issue of when and how much to feed your baby.

Schedules Gone Awry

As you're probably already aware, we are not advocates of strict feeding schedules—at least not in the true sense of the phrase. That's because more often than not babies aren't either. While there are some general feeding rules of thumb, babies aren't exactly aware of them and often choose not to play by the rules. Following are several of the more common and normal variations in newborn feeding habits that are all too often perceived as schedules gone awry.

Day-to-Day Variability

We feel compelled to point out that nobody (with rare/eccentric exception) eats the same thing, in the same amount, at the same time, every day, day in and day out. Babies are no exception, so prepare yourself for a reasonable amount of variation in the amount your baby drinks on any given day and focus your attention instead on making sure that your newborn is waking up to feed, getting enough to drink, and growing as expected.

Growth Spurts

Until we had our own children, growth spurts were merely a concept we learned about as pediatricians. They sounded logical enough—involving intermittent brief periods of rapid growth accompanied by increased hunger—but they didn't seem to us to have that much bearing on reality.

And then reality set in (as it does for most new parents). Your first introduction to a growth spurt will probably come when your baby is 2 or 3
weeks old. Everything will seem to be going just fine, you'll have just started
to feel like you have control of things (and of your milk supply if you are
breastfeeding), and then out of nowhere your baby will let you know otherwise. Almost overnight he's likely to be less easily satisfied, more frequently
fussy, and seemingly hungry all the time. While formula-feeding parents can
certainly be thrown for a loop by growth spurts, adding an extra ounce or
two to their babies' bottles and/or feeding more frequently can quickly settle
everyone back into a comfortable new routine. For breastfeeding moms,
accommodating growth spurts can take a little more time and flexibility.
During the several days it may take for your breasts to compensate for your
baby's increased needs and demands, don't start to question your breastfeeding abilities. Instead of letting growth spurts shake your confidence,
remind yourself that it is only natural for newborns to be fussy and to seem
like they're temporarily not getting enough milk. Based on the concept of
supply and demand as it applies to breastfeeding, this is the only way your
baby will be able to tell you to increase the amount of milk you are producing to meet his growing needs.

Cluster Feeding

Cluster feeding is just as it sounds—when a baby decides to defy those
who dare to suggest feeding every 3 hours or more and instead decides to
eat several times in a relatively short period. This pattern is sometimes
also known as grazing—especially when a baby is a frequent feeder with
seemingly little stamina and seems to be taking the snack-bar approach
to breastfeeding in general. In your newborn's first days and weeks we
strongly recommend you follow your baby's lead—whether that means
feedings that are evenly spaced or clustered together, long sessions or short.
Even after your baby's feeding patterns become relatively predictable, it's
worth mentioning that a good many babies still choose to cluster feed—
most commonly in the evening before bedtime. Without scientific data
to support it, let us just say that some parents swear by cluster feeding
as a way to top off the tank, subsequently buying everyone involved a
longer stretch of nighttime sleep before hunger strikes again.

Routine Considerations

The Merits of an All-Liquid Diet

For the next several months, your baby will get all the nutrition he needs from breast milk and/or formula. While we are well aware of the fact that babies of generations past were given rice cereal as young as a few weeks of age, giving any form of solid food to babies before 4 to 6 months is no longer recommended (except under certain circumstances such as reflux). Doing so is thought to increase a baby's risk of developing allergies, constipation, and even choking. Even if you find yourself pressured by well-meaning grandparents or friends who swear by it, we suggest you suppress the urge to give your baby any type of solid food until 4 to 6 months of age, or until you discuss it with your pediatrician and you get the go-ahead.

Where Does Water Fit In?

In response to a question many parents ask: Yes, water is a liquid, but no, your newborn baby does not need any. It's fine to give her a sip or two on occasion, for example if she has the hiccups and they're bothering you (because babies don't tend to care), but giving a young infant more than that runs the risk of filling her up and leaving her less room for the more nutritious breast milk or formula she needs to grow. In addition, too much water can even make your baby very ill.

No Milk (for Now)

Until your baby reaches 1 year of age, you should continue to reach for the breast milk or formula instead of regular cow's milk. This recommendation is based on the fact that cow's milk is less easily digested, contains higher concentrations of proteins and minerals, offers inadequate amounts of vitamins and iron, and has the potential to place unrealistic demands on your baby's kidneys and intestinal tract.

    VITAMINS FOR NEWBORNS

With only a few exceptions, most healthy full-term newborns get all the vitamins they need from breast milk and/or formula. The American Academy of Pediatrics does, however, recommend that exclusively breastfed newborns receive vitamin D drops (200 IU per day) starting at the age of 2 months because breast milk does not contain enough of this vitamin. Babies getting at least 16 ounces of formula per day, on the other hand, should not require any extra vitamin D.

Sucking Sense and Sensibility

It's a rare parent who doesn't find the classic "baby sucking thumb in utero" ultrasound picture worthy of framing—or at least showing off to friends or around the office. But the ability to suck is more than just cute. It's important for other reasons as well. While babies are sometimes caught on ultrasound sucking their thumbs as early as 18 weeks or less, the sucking and swallowing efforts necessary to drink from breast or bottle don't become coordinated until closer to 34 weeks. Not only do babies perfect their sucking skills once they are born in the name of good growth and nutrition, but most of them rely on sucking to soothe themselves—some relying on it more heavily than others. The fact that babies don't have enough control over their fingers and hands to reliably get them to their mouths and suck on them for many weeks after they are born naturally leads many parents (and us) into a discussion of pacifiers.

Practical Pacifier Principles

Pacifiers have proven themselves to be yet one more source of parenting controversy. Breastfeeding purists say stick to your guns and keep them out of your newborn's mouth (see "The Confusion About Nipple Confusion" and "Nipple Confusion Defined" on pages 32 and 33)—even when your baby is not yet able to use his own fingers as an alternative. (We would note that if and when your baby is able to find his own fingers, it's OK to let him continue using them as natural pacifiers.) Others forewarn that pacifiers are simply a bad habit waiting to happen. Well fear not, as long as you understand a few practical pacifier principles and pitfalls. Whether you choose to breastfeed or bottle-feed, or a combination of both, here are some tips for if and when you decide to give your baby a pacifier.

- **Soothing through sucking.** Pacifiers can be invaluable in soothing babies as well as satisfying those who want to suck all the time. You need not worry about your baby developing a lifelong dependency on them. Just be very careful not to offer your newborn a pacifier at times when he really should be fed instead—especially in the first couple of weeks—because pacifiers can pacify hungry babies as well as those who are looking for comfort.

- **Picking out the perfect pacifier.** These days, picking the perfect pacifier may seem like a considerable task, given all of the various brands and styles on the market. To the best of our knowledge, there's no correlation between price or marketing strategy and effectiveness, so we simply recommend trying one out and seeing if your baby likes it.

- **If at first you don't succeed.** When you first offer your baby a pacifier, don't be surprised if he seems uninterested, outright angry, or spits it out even when you know he's not hungry and just wants comfort. For breastfed babies, sucking on a pacifier inherently requires a different technique, and one that may take a few tries. For breastfed and bottle-fed babies alike, a nipple that does not provide milk may not be quickly welcomed. As you offer your baby a pacifier, try lightly stroking just to the side of his mouth and then gently holding the pacifier in his mouth for a moment as he starts sucking to keep it from popping right back out.

- **A practical pacifier substitute.** The cheap, easy, and ever-present pacifier substitute: your pinky finger. If you find yourself in the position of wanting to soothe your baby by giving him something to suck on other than your breast, you can always use your (clean) little finger. Simply turn your hand palm-side up and let your baby suck on your pinky finger, allowing it to rest gently in the roof of his mouth. As a word of caution for anyone with longer fingernails than ours—you may want to rethink how much you value your long nails, or at least the one on your little finger. You may find that it's a small sacrifice to make to clip it shorter for the sake of having a contented baby. Some babies will learn to find their own fingers to suck on earlier than others, so do your best to make sure those fingers are clean and have clipped nails too.

- **Passing on pacifiers.** If your baby just isn't that much of a "sucker," he may not need to be soothed by sucking on a pacifier at all. Just be thankful that there's one less thing to keep track of and wean him from in the future.

what goes in must come out

INTRODUCTION

This section is devoted to a subject that, if nothing else, will help you realize just how far you're about to come—from your days as an expectant parent to master of body fluids and functions. A very basic understanding of how your baby's body works—combined with some reflection on a few of your own life experiences—should be more than enough to tell you that a good deal of what goes into your baby's mouth will eventually come out in one form or another. Granted your baby will be putting a significant portion of whatever is going into her mouth toward her growth and development, but all the indigestible, unnecessary, or undesirable stuff—be it solid, liquid, or gas—is all but guaranteed to make its way out on a very regular basis. First and foremost, pee and poop will soon be in abundant supply—at least after you've made it past the first few days when your baby's system will still be gearing up for "bigger and better" things. Don't be surprised if these and other previously less than tasteful subjects indiscriminately make their way into your casual (and not-so-casual) conversations. In fact, we consider the contemplation and shared discussion of such topics to be a defining feature of parenthood.

Looking Into What Comes Out

In this section, we will take a close look at the inner workings of newborns and what's behind all of the peeing and pooping, not to mention the gas, hiccups, burps, spit-up, and vomit that comes along with having a baby. Your personal day-to-day experiences will certainly leave some of you scratching your heads in wonder, confusion, or amazement. Don't worry if it doesn't all sink in right away. Trust us when we say that it soon will (refer to "Stain Removal" on page 151).

Peeing and Pooping

If we were attempting to write a medical textbook, we would now be turning our focus to the topics of urine, stool, and bowel movements. The fact of the matter is that 1) this is not in any way meant to resemble a medical textbook and 2) once you've been buried in a sea of diapers over the first days, weeks, and years of parenthood, there's just nothing academic about it. Given that most parents we've talked to over the years simply refer to it as good old pee and poop, we will too. With our choice of words thus briefly explained, let's get to the real substance at hand. To give you some context, the reason why pediatricians seem to care so much about whether a baby is peeing and pooping normally is because it is one of the easiest and most reassuring ways we have to determine if a baby is getting enough to eat, all systems are in good working order, and he is generally healthy.

As you settle into your own daily feeding "routine" (a term we use loosely, as explained in "Into the Mouths of Babes" on page 1) and attempt to gauge if your own baby is getting enough to eat, drink, and be merry, you'll find that pee and poop play a leading role. First, to figure out whether your baby's plumbing is working normally, you'll need a good understanding of just what is meant by the word "normal."

CHAPTER 5

to pee or not to pee

How Wet Is Wet Enough?

The answer to this question depends on how you're feeding your baby (breast or bottle) and how old your baby is, because the first few days can be far fewer than the by-the-book 8- to 10-plus wet diapers a day. For formula-fed newborns who are taking well to the bottle, it's perfectly reasonable to expect a good 5 or more wet diapers a day within the first day or two. Breastfed newborns, however, can be a little trickier to assess during the first several days before their mothers' milk supply comes in (see "Breastfeeding" on page 5). While breastfed babies get their necessary calories from the early milk (colostrum), this first form of breast milk comes in a much smaller volume. It therefore stands to reason that breast-fed newborns pee less frequently—sometimes only 2 or 3 times a day— and in much smaller amounts until their mothers' full-volume milk supply comes in (anywhere from 2–5 days after delivery). Once you reach this breastfeeding milestone of milk production, *then* you can expect your baby to catch up to her formula-fed colleagues and have at least 5 (if not 8 or 10) wet diapers in any 24-hour period. When everyone's drinking and peeing are up to full capacity, *then* the standard 8 to 10 wet diapers a day applies. If at any time you are concerned that your baby is not peeing as much as she should, this is as good a reason as any to enlist the help and expertise of your pediatrician.

IN SEARCH OF A LITTLE PEE IN A BIG DIAPER

Detecting small amounts of pee in a newborn's super-absorbent disposable diaper can at times be likened to finding a needle in a haystack. If you're having difficulty determining whether your newborn's diaper is wet, try putting a cotton ball or folded tissue inside of it—toward the front of the diaper near the penis for baby boys and lower in the crotch area for baby girls. Then be patient. Any subsequent pee will now be much easier to detect and the challenge of detecting it most likely short-lived. It shouldn't be more than a few short days before you find yourself faced instead with the problem of overly soaked diapers and laughing at the thought of cotton balls and tissue.

For additional information on difficult to identify diaper contents, see "The Art and Science of Diapering" on page 115.

CHAPTER 6

poop happens

When it comes to newborn poop, it helps to be aware that there is a normal and expected poop progression that takes place over the first week or so. Most doctors expect newborns to demonstrate their pooping ability before sending them home from the hospital. And most newborns happily oblige—doing so without much difficulty or delay. The very first newborn poops you'll see, usually in the first 24 hours or so, are typically thick, tarry, and black. This lovely, gooey mess is simply the poop your baby made before being born and is referred to as meconium.

The Scoop on Poop

As breast milk or formula begins to make its way through your baby's system over the next few days, you can expect your baby's poop to become more of a pasty brown color (the so-called transitional stool) and then ultimately become the standard mustardy yellow and seedy poop typical of breastfed babies, or the more pasty/formed and variably colored poop of formula-fed babies. For all babies, but especially for those who are breastfed, the establishment of frequent poop that has gone through this predictable color change is a good indication that they are getting enough to eat. For the breastfed baby, it also suggests that the eagerly anticipated full-volume milk supply has arrived.

 PRECOCIOUS POOPING

In some instances, babies actually poop before they are born—allowing meconium to mix into the amniotic fluid. While this is a reassuring sign that all's well in the poop department, such babies may require closer observation in the period immediately after being born to make sure that the meconium hasn't made its way into the lungs.

The Many Colors of Poop

Long after adjusting to parenthood and your role as principal poop watcher and wiper, you may still find yourself fretting over changes in the color of your baby's poop. In reality, once your baby has pooped enough to get rid of the tarry meconium, all the varying shades of yellow, brown, and even green are considered perfectly acceptable. While mustardy yellow is the color of choice for most breastfed babies, and yellow-tan with hints of green for those who are formula-fed, being presented with a changing palette of colors is not uncommon, particularly later on down the road when your baby is introduced to such things as solid foods and snotty nose colds (which adds swallowed mucus to the mix).

Black, White, and Shades of Red

There are a few colors of baby poop that, should you see them, always warrant discussion with your baby's doctor. They are

- **Red.** Seeing red can mean blood, especially in the newborn period when your baby isn't eating or drinking anything red-colored that could be mistaken for blood when it comes out the other end. Blood should not signal you to panic immediately, but you should bring it to the attention of your pediatrician, who will be able to help you sort out the cause. It is possible for babies to swallow some blood during delivery that presents itself shortly thereafter—either in the baby's spit-up or poop—but, nevertheless, any amount of bloody poop should be evaluated because it can also be a sign of a problem.
- **Black.** Black-colored poop sometimes represents old blood because blood is known to turn from red to black over time in the intestinal tract. Remember that this black color alert does not apply to your baby's first few meconium bowel movements, which you can fully expect to be black and tarry looking.
- **White.** White poop is quite rare, but needs to be brought to the attention of a doctor ASAP because it can be caused by an underlying liver problem. The earlier it is addressed, the better—either for peace of mind or medical management.

The Eating-Pooping Connection

You'll find that for many young babies, a little thing called the gastro-colic reflex (*gastro* referring to the stomach and *colic* referring to the colon—the end of the road in the intestinal tract) is responsible for making eating and pooping occur nearly simultaneously. In fact, many newborns have such a strong gastro-colic reflex that they poop just about *every* time they eat—sometimes even in *anticipation* of being fed before any milk has graced their lips. If you stop and think about it, you may find that you're already quite familiar with this particular reflex because it is not unique to infancy. While generally less exaggerated and hopefully less immediate, a good many adults never fully outgrow this gastro-colic reflex. Unlike newborns, however, most adults are able to control the urge long enough to finish their meals before needing to excuse themselves to the bathroom to take care of business.

 FULL SPEED BEHIND

Once your baby has gotten the hang of eating—especially if you have chosen to breastfeed and your milk is fully in—don't be surprised to find yourself faced with poop that can be described as nothing less than explosive. Remember the problems Southern Californians had in the 1990s with paintball shooting sprees? If not, let us summarize: Wayward teenagers drove around with paintball guns terrorizing neighborhoods by firing off blobs of paint at high speeds, targeting whomever and whatever happened to cross their paths. Well that's the best analogy we've come up with yet to convey the potential forcefulness (and subsequent mess) that can result when a breastfed baby's intestinal tract is fully up to speed. Having now been forewarned, we suggest you review our diapering chapter to make sure you're comfortable with your diapering technique. And remember to keep your baby's back end securely contained whenever possible—or be prepared to take cover and suffer the consequences!

Consistency: A Word About Diarrhea and Constipation

Many parents are concerned (usually unnecessarily) that their new babies have diarrhea. And with the definition of diarrhea typically involving the words "frequent" and "watery," it's certainly not hard to understand why. In fact, most young babies simply have well-functioning intestinal reflexes and everything that goes in one end comes flying out the other. That said, if you are concerned or simply want a reality check that what you're seeing in your baby's diaper is normal, then go right ahead and grab a poopy diaper (if you have one available to submit as evidence), stick it in a plastic bag, and head on over to check things out with your pediatrician.

 ## TRULY INTOLERANT POOP

On occasion—somewhere on the order of 5 to 10 out of every 100 babies to be exact—a baby's intestinal tract doesn't react well to formula and/or breast milk. Known as *milk soy protein intolerance* (or MSPI for short) by those who are confronted with it, this type of intolerance is worth being aware of. Fortunately, MSPI doesn't present itself as a mildly fussy, spitty, or gassy baby, or one who simply has "loose" bowel movements (because, as we mentioned, that would include a whole lot of perfectly healthy, "tolerant" babies). More commonly, babies with MSPI make their intolerance known by acting quite uncomfortable, fussy, or colicky; vomiting; and/or having diarrhea—especially after or while being fed. Every now and then, blood turns up in their poop. As a parent, it is admittedly not always easy to pick apart MSPI from your more run-of-the-mill crying, fussy, spitty baby who poops a lot. And you shouldn't feel as though you have to. If you have questions about whether the formula or breast milk you are feeding your baby is not being well received by his intestinal tract, pack up your baby (and a recent poop sample, if you can) and head on into your pediatrician's office.

Pooping by Numbers

Once babies have proven themselves capable of clearing out their meconium and have moved on to dishing out the "real thing," you can be relatively assured that their plumbing is in good working order and turn your attention to the so-called normal pooping patterns of infancy. What's considered normal at this stage of the game (and for months to come) ranges anywhere from one poop every several days to several poops every day. Some are like the sprinters of the pooping world—fast and furious—while others are more like distance runners—slow and steady. In general, breastfed babies poop more than formula-fed ones, and younger babies poop more than older ones. Newborn babies and young infants also tend to have several tiny poops in succession, so as a point of practicality we recommend waiting a few minutes until your newborn is convincingly finished rather than jumping into diaper-changing action after the first signs of activity. From your pediatrician's perspective, the actual number of poops is likely to be less important than the fact that everything is generally moving along.

 ENOUGH IS ENOUGH

Enough is enough when it comes to newborn poop, but any more than that may well be too much. In the spirit of helping you distinguish between the healthy but fast and furious pooper and those newborns at risk, physician experts in the field of newborn care suggest the following rule of thumb: Any time a newborn's poop becomes progressively more watery or outpaces feeding frequency, it's time to seek medical advice.

When the Pooping Gets Tough

On the flip side of loose or watery poop, many parents have questions about constipation as soon as their babies begin to grunt, strain, or get red in the face while trying to poop, or the first time they go several days without a poopy diaper. Fortunately, true constipation—as defined by hard, difficult to pass, or infrequent poop—isn't a big issue for most young infants. Believe it or not, going as many as 5 to 7 days between poops is not inherently going to be a problem for babies who have already proven themselves fully capable of pooping during their first couple of weeks and are now eating and growing well. As long as your baby's poop is fairly soft and comes out easily when it does appear, you can breathe with relative ease despite the exaggerated degree of discomfort your baby seems to display. Even if your baby occasionally seems to have difficulty getting the poop out, remind yourself that pooping while lying flat on one's back isn't exactly natural. Given that your baby won't have many options for a while, you can try to facilitate by pushing your baby's knees up toward her chest while she's lying on her back to give her some resistance against which to strain. If, however, your baby consistently seems to have problems pooping—she does so infrequently or with apparent pain, or you notice blood or poop that just doesn't seem right to you—be sure to check in with your baby's doctor about what (if anything) you should do to remedy the situation.

(see also "Formula for Success" on page 37).

Persistent Problematic Pooping (Hirschsprung Disease)

When all of a baby's parts are in working order, poop makes its way southward and comes to rest in the last part of the digestive tract—called the large intestine or colon. It accumulates there while awaiting its release from the anus. Every now and then, the nerve cells that control the anus (and sometimes those in the lower part of the colon) don't develop properly. As a result, the muscles responsible for letting the poop out can't relax. This condition is known as Hirschsprung disease. Only about 1 out of every 7,000 babies have it. In extreme instances, the anus is unable to open at all—in which case pooping is noticeably absent from birth. Some babies with this condition, however, lack only some of the nerve cells and are still able to relax enough to let some poop out, but not as easily or as often as expected. This form of Hirschsprung can seem to be constipation, as characterized by infrequent or difficult poops, and may not signal a problem until the parents or pediatrician begin to notice a chronic pattern over time. While we've only taken the time to give you the quick and dirty explanation, it should be enough to give you some sense of what to keep in the back of your mind if you find yourself concerned about your newborn's pooping practices.

CHAPTER 7

other unmentionables and inconveniences

In addition to peeing and pooping, parents of newborns seem to encounter a disproportionate number of other "unmentionables and inconveniences"—namely gas, burping, spitting up, and vomiting. The following 2 chapters will help you sort through what's considered normal, what's considered a nuisance, and what should not be ignored.

Full of Hot Air

With all the gulping some babies do during feedings and crying, it's no surprise that they swallow quite a bit of air. Once air makes its way in, there are only 2 logical ways for it to escape—up and out as a burp or down and out as gas. Air that is destined to be passed as gas must travel through many feet of intestines—a process that invariably takes longer and is often believed to cause more fussing and discomfort than if that same air manages to come back out in the form of a burp. While we can't honestly say that this theory has been proven, it doesn't usually take a lot of convincing to believe that gassy babies tend to be uncomfortable babies. For this reason alone, it's worth taking some simple steps to minimize the amount of air your baby swallows.

- **Feed early and often.** Whenever possible, feed your baby *before* she is screaming her demands at you. The more she cries before a feeding, the more likely she is to fill up with air.
- **Rise to the challenge.** When feeding your baby, keep her body at somewhat of an upright angle—at least so that her head is resting in a position higher than her stomach. Try to do this even if you have

already figured out how to nurse lying down. This theoretically allows the liquid to sink to the bottom of a baby's stomach while the air stays on top—thus making it easier (and less messy) to burp out. Any air bubbles trapped below the milk will be burped up with liquid (spit-up) or have to pass through the intestinal tract.

- **Bottoms up.** When bottle-feeding your baby, hold the bottle at an angle so that there is always milk filling the entire nipple. This helps keep babies from sucking air.

- **Let things settle.** During and/or after each feeding, keep your baby upright for a few minutes to let things settle and then try to burp her.

Burping

Babies and parents alike seem to get significant relief from getting out whatever gas happens to make its way in—and the sooner the better. The next best thing to helping your baby avoid sucking in a lot of air in the first place is to get any resulting air bubbles to come out in one big satisfying burp (or two) shortly afterward. That said, some babies really seem not to be bothered by the presence of stomach gas—in which case you don't need to exert too much effort in the following burping endeavors.

The Technique

Given the amount of attention paid in parenting books, in magazines, and on Web sites to the topic of burping babies, you might be led to believe that nothing short of a class on the subject could properly prepare you. Well, in hopes of bursting your bubble, let us stress that burping is not rocket science by any stretch of the imagination. Burping is actually a relatively natural process that you simply stand to help along. If anything, most parents just benefit from a little guidance on if, when, and how vigorously to do it. We've seen many a parent frantically trying to elicit a burp every few minutes during and after each feeding. The fact of the matter is that some babies just don't swallow as much air or need to burp as much as others, and if your baby is going to burp, he will probably do so within a few minutes of having his back patted. Ideally, you simply want to decrease your baby's chances of discomfort by coaxing out whatever air has found its way into your baby's stomach. That said, here are some basic burping techniques.

- **Positioning.** The classic burping technique (and often the most popular) involves holding up your baby facing you against your chest with his head resting just over your shoulder. You can also sit your baby upright on your lap, supporting his trunk by putting one hand across his chest and under his armpits while patting his back with the other. Or you can lay your baby on his belly across your lap or on the floor to help compress his stomach and press the air out.
- **Patting.** Pat or rub your baby's back for a couple of minutes after he drinks. Your patting should be less forceful than an all-out clapping motion, but harder than a soft touch. Many parents either burp a little too delicately or—on occasion—with a little too much enthusiasm.
- **Planning.** If your baby hasn't burped within a couple minutes, you can stop and if necessary plan to try again later if he seems uncomfortable. Quite honestly, many babies are able to muster a burp all on their own. If you find your baby is very spitty, swallows a lot of air, or is uncomfortable during feedings, you can certainly try stopping and burping him in the middle of each feeding. Just be forewarned that in our combined experience, babies hate to be interrupted while eating without good cause.
- **Patience.** Accept the fact that some babies do not need to burp (or be burped) with every feeding—especially when they don't swallow much air, aren't prone to spitting up, or just plain don't tend to burp much. It's definitely not worth losing sleep over if you're unable to elicit a burp.

Pumping Gas

Despite your best efforts, some air will inevitably make its way past the stomach and into your baby's intestines. If you find that your baby seems uncomfortable as a direct result of gas, try laying her on her back and "bicycling" her legs to help work the air bubbles out. You can also try gently putting her face down along your arm, her legs straddling either side with your hand palm up under her belly, chest, and chin. If you're now wondering how to go about coordinating this whole one-arm thing—which hand, and facing which direction?—then you can opt to do what we do and rest your baby belly down on top of a flat surface. Lifting up slightly on her belly, use your fingertips to lightly massage or squeeze her tummy area for a few minutes. These motions seem to help break up gas bubbles—or at least help make gassy babies and their parents more comfortable with their predicament. Although it is not always the case, some babies reportedly respond well to over-the-counter anti-gas drops containing simethicone—the key ingredient found in Mylicon, Gerber Gas Drops, Phazyme, and certain colic drops. You'll notice we say "reportedly respond" because to tell the truth, it has been our experience that the effort and expense of anti-gas drops doesn't usually pay off. If, however, you feel your baby may benefit, don't let us stand in the way. There's usually no harm in trying them as long as you consult with your pediatrician first—just as we hope you would before using any medication. Be sure to hang on to your receipt because should you find them to be ineffective, we've recently been informed that some companies will reimburse your money.

Hiccups

The good news about hiccups is that they're not dangerous and they are almost always more bothersome to parents than they are to babies. At best, your baby won't get any at all, or only have an occasional cute little run-in with them. At worst, they'll make their presence known at all hours of the day and night and effectively disrupt what may already be a delicate balance in your baby's stomach—giving your baby yet one more excuse to wake up and/or spit up. The fact of the matter is that newborns have a lot of very active reflexes, and hiccupping can be one of them—sometimes even popping up before birth. Hiccups are thought to occur when a baby's diaphragm is "tickled" for any reason—by sudden swallowing or irregular breathing—or for no apparent reason at all, and it is our understanding that any form of breath-holding (which, for a newborn, is pretty much limited to sucking or crying) effectively helps to stop them. If you're convinced that your baby is uncomfortable you can try offering a pacifier or, if you just can't resist trying it out, you can experiment by giving a little "sip" of breast milk, formula, or water to see if it stops the process. If you ask us, however, breath-holding doesn't seem to work so well—often even for adults—and you might be just as well off ignoring the hiccups, knowing that they're harmless and likely to be short-lived.

CHAPTER 8

spitting up and vomiting

We have found that many baby books describe spitting up as a harmless nuisance that goes away over time, while at the same time cautioning parents that vomiting—sometimes described as projectile—is to be taken seriously. They then proceed to offer up such definitions of spitting up and vomiting as follows:

- **A typical definition of spitting up:** The easy flow of stomach contents through the mouth that may or may not accompany a burp.
- **A typical definition of vomiting:** The forceful flow of stomach contents through the mouth.

Now for a little reality check: Does anyone else besides us happen to think the definitions seem somewhat similar? Well that's because in real life, spitting up and vomiting can be somewhat difficult to distinguish—especially for those who have never had to give it much thought before. If you've already discovered you've got a spitter on your hands, you may be wondering just how forceful is "forceful" and just how projectile do stomach contents have to be and over what distance do they have to travel before qualifying for the upgraded status of vomiting. Don't beat yourself up if you discover you were born without the innate ability to distinguish between the two. The distinction between happy spitters and those with bigger issues has been known to elude doctors at times too. We will do our best to prepare you for the run-of-the-mill spit-up challenge, while at the same time familiarize you with warning signs that can signify something more serious. Take the following descriptions for what they're worth, do what you can to distinguish between easy and forceful flow, and then go with your own gut instinct as to whether you need to involve your pediatrician.

Esophagus

Lower esophageal sphincter

Pylorus

Stomach

Spitting Up

If you are fortunate, you will be blessed with a baby who, from birth, has the ability to politely keep whatever he drinks to himself and realizes that spitting up does not count as sharing. The information that follows will not be as relevant to you as it will be to those new parents who quickly become conditioned to expect that some part of every feeding will inevitably come back up and out. If you happen to already be sitting with a spit rag over your shoulder(s) and protective coverings over most of your furniture, then you'll undoubtedly be able to relate to this part of the chapter—the part we like to think of as the "what you've worked so hard to put in always seems come out, even when you don't want it to despite all your best efforts to keep it in" section.

For most babies, spitting up is simply the result of a not yet fully developed muscle that is supposed to serve as a gatekeeper at the top of the stomach—in general allowing food (drink, in this case) into the stomach and then *keeping* it there. For those of you who are dying to know the name of the muscle most likely to blame for your spit-up woes, it is called the *lower esophageal sphincter* or LES for short. For a clearer picture, take a minute to visualize your baby's stomach as an upright water balloon with a narrow opening at the top—in the case of a spitty baby, a water balloon left a little too loosely secured. It's not hard to imagine how any amount of applied pressure—a poke or squeeze on the side—or a change in position could cause its contents to overflow, especially at times when the balloon is relatively full. For some newborns, a simple gas bubble or a press on the belly is often quite enough to overpower a novice sphincter muscle and allow a baby to spit up. Most of the time, spitting up doesn't bother babies. For the parents of these so-called happy spitters, a loose sphincter simply means being more diligent about burping, stockpiling a larger supply of burp cloths or spit rags, and investing in a bottle (or 3) of stain remover.

THE SHAPE OF THINGS TO COME (UP)

No matter how curdled or "spoiled" your baby's spit-up appears, you can reassure yourself that it doesn't really matter. The curdled appearance just reveals that your baby's stomach had already started processing it before it managed to escape and nothing more.

Remedies for Spitty Babies

Burping and spitting up often go hand in hand for newborns. The air in a baby's stomach decides to come up, and the stomach contents often opt to tag along for the ride—a tendency that serves to explain why you'll find a fair bit of overlap between burp prevention and spit-up avoidance techniques. If you find that your newborn tends to spit up quite a bit, there are several things you can try to remedy the situation.

- Position your baby's head higher than the rest of her body when she's eating.
- Step up your burping efforts. You can either just put a little more effort into eliciting a good burp after each feeding, or even try burping more frequently during the feeding—after every 5 minutes of breastfeeding or every ounce or so from a bottle. Only you and your baby can decide whether the interruption in feeding is worth the results.
- Hold or position your baby relatively upright for a good 20 to 30 minutes after meals.

- While some parents find that simply switching brands of formula (see "Formula Intolerance" on page 38) or eliminating certain foods in a breastfeeding mother's diet can help decrease the amount of spitting up, it's always worth checking with your doctor before considering such changes (see "Into the Mouths of Moms" on page 34). While on occasion a change might help, for many newborns and their parents it's an unnecessary inconvenience.

 THE PATH OF LEAST RESISTANCE

Many parents get alarmed when liquid comes spewing out of their baby's nose, but let us reassure you that this is an anatomically normal (albeit potentially surprising and/or unpleasant) occurrence. In case you haven't already discovered it for yourself, we all have a direct connection between the backs of our throats and our noses. Stomach contents expelled by spitting up or vomiting usually follow the path of least resistance, so depending on the circumstances—your baby's positioning and the force of the eruption to name a couple—the exit route may be his mouth and/or his nose.

Assessing Your Losses

Only rarely do babies spit up enough that it becomes more than a matter of inconvenience and affects their overall nutrition and weight gain. That's not to say that the amount an otherwise healthy baby spits up doesn't seem impressive from a parent's-eye view. When looking at the spit-up stains on your baby's clothes (or your own), it is very easy to overestimate the amount of lunch actually being tossed. If you don't want to just take our word for it and are determined to get a better idea of the true volume, you can try pouring some milk or water in measured increments onto a clean towel or cloth diaper. You'll see that the liquid will spread out quite a bit on the dry fabric. Compare the size of a spot made by 1 teaspoon, 1 tablespoon, or 1 ounce of fluid to the spot made by your baby's spit-up or vomit and you may be reassured that all has not been lost. The bottom line: A spitty baby who continues to eat well and gain weight well does not generally need much, if any, intervention. On the other hand, any newborn who isn't eating well, isn't gaining weight as expected, or is increasingly spitting up larger amounts more frequently and/or more forcefully needs to be seen by a doctor.

GERD

GERD is simply the acronym for gastroesophageal reflux disease. In simpler terms, you can think of it as the baby equivalent of heartburn—the result of stomach contents making their way back up into the esophagus, sometimes causing discomfort and on rare occasion resulting in possible complications. It is often the diagnosis given to babies who spit up enough to warrant a discussion, evaluation, and potentially even medical treatment by their doctors. This is not something a book can (or should) diagnose for you—only make you aware of its existence. If in doubt, get it checked out.

Vomiting

More often than not, new parents worry about vomiting when what is coming out of their babies' mouths more closely fits the admittedly vague definition of spitting up. Although less common, newborns can and do vomit for a variety of reasons. Your baby may occasionally vomit if, for example, she has a particularly sensitive gag reflex and/or you have a particularly forceful milk let-down when breastfeeding, or if she's a little overly eager and happens to overfeed. Some babies who seem to have more persistent vomiting may be intolerant of whatever it is they are being given to drink, have an underlying infection, or have a problem in their digestive tract that doesn't allow things to flow through as directed—all instances that should be discussed with and evaluated by a doctor. That said, if you suspect true vomiting, you should be on the lookout for fever or any other signs of being sick. You can also keep an eye out for blood in the poop, diarrhea, and excessive fussiness and gassiness—all of which may indicate intolerance to formula or breast milk and will be helpful symptoms to report to your pediatrician. Because vomiting can cause dehydration and electrolyte imbalances much more quickly in newborns than in older children and adults, don't wait until your baby seems truly lethargic or dehydrated (less pee, dry mouth, doughy skin, sunken eyes and fontanelle, and weight loss) to contact your pediatrician—just do it right away.

THE TRUE MEANING OF PROJECTILE

Projectile is a word that is often used in the context of spitting up and vomiting. Some parents graphically describe their baby's vomiting as "shooting across the room." While moderately forceful spitting up or vomiting can cause liquid to "jump" or "gush" out a few inches from your baby's mouth, truly projectile eruptions—more force, longer distances, etc—especially when they occur on a regular basis, may indicate more serious problems.
For more information, read on.

How Much Is Too Much? When to Consider Pyloric Stenosis

At the point when vomiting seems to be getting progressively worse and becoming more and more out of hand, you and/or your pediatrician may suspect a condition called pyloric stenosis. The pyloric sphincter is simply the muscle at the far end of the stomach that serves as gatekeeper— allowing food to pass into the intestinal tract (see diagram on page 76). In contrast to its often too lax counterpart at the top of the stomach, this sphincter muscle can sometimes become a bit too thick and strong for its own best interest (or anyone else's) and consequently does too good of a job regulating what can get out of the stomach into the intestinal tract. Stenosis simply refers to any type of narrowing; in the case of pyloric stenosis, the opening at the bottom of the stomach becomes progressively narrower than it should be. The more difficult it becomes for stomach contents to go down and out through this narrow region, the more they head up and out instead.

Occurring in about 3 of every 1,000 babies and being much more common in first-born boys and those with a family history, pyloric stenosis causes babies to start spitting up in the first few weeks—usually around days 21 to 28. Unlike the frequent happy spitters or even the intermittently impressive vomiters, babies with pyloric stenosis vomit with increasing force and frequency—most often building up to the full-fledged projectile vomiting by 6 to 8 weeks. If your baby's vomiting is persistent and progressing, it's worth contacting your physician sooner rather than later. If your baby does, in fact, happen to be diagnosed with pyloric stenosis, there is a sure-fire remedy to stop the vomiting; babies with pyloric stenosis require an operation to widen the pylorus muscle's opening at the bottom of the stomach. Babies usually recover quickly and begin feeding normally within a couple of days following surgery.

DOUBLE TROUBLE

If an infant vomits most or all of a feeding for 2 or more feedings in a row, it should be taken as a potential warning sign of something potentially more serious, and prompt medical evaluation is needed.

Gagging and Sputtering

Some babies tend to have more sensitive gag reflexes than others, which on the one hand is a very good thing because it is the gag reflex that is responsible for keeping food (or in your newborn's case, breast milk or formula) from "going down the wrong way" and getting into the lungs. On the other hand, a gagging or sputtering baby can admittedly be very scary for parents. If your baby starts gagging or having trouble breathing while feeding, you can promptly sit him upright, pat his back, turn his head to the side or slightly face down to let any milk or saliva run out of his mouth, and let him catch his breath. In almost all cases, babies quickly recover from such episodes on their own. If your baby has frequent gagging episodes, or especially if he ever stops breathing even briefly or turns blue for a moment during a gagging or coughing spell, be sure to seek medical advice.

FOR SAFETY'S SAKE

For safety and peace of mind, we recommend that you and any of your baby's potential caregivers find the time to take a CPR course in case any emergencies arise regarding your baby. You can start by contacting your pediatrician, local Red Cross, or local hospital for class information.

activities of daily living

INTRODUCTION

Included in the following chapters are many of the newborn topics we consider to be the bread and butter of parenting. In them, you will find answers to the most commonly asked questions new parents typically have about each of the activities you are likely to be partaking in day in and day out once all the baby showers have passed, the waiting and wondering is over, and you've finally checked out of the hospital and headed for home. Sandwiched between the ins and outs discussed in the preceding sections and looking ahead toward heading out and about (to be addressed in the section to follow), we now focus our efforts and your attention on those important aspects of everyday life with a newborn that will initially dominate your thoughts and occupy much of your time, but soon will become second nature: the topics of newborn sleep, crying, diapering, bathing, and clothing.

CHAPTER 9

sleeping like a baby

It is for good reason that sleep (and a new parent's relative lack thereof) always seems to top the list of popular parenting topics. There's no doubt about it, heading home with a newborn is quite an eye-opening experience, literally and figuratively speaking. Even years of being on call as pediatric residents didn't prepare us for the interrupted sleep schedule that typically characterizes life with a newborn. It's safe to say that few things will change more dramatically than your sleep habits—at least for the foreseeable future—when you suddenly switch roles from expectant parent to new parent. Even beyond the basic questions of when, where, and how much to expect your baby (and you) to get, you may also find yourself wondering what to do about your newborn's blatant disregard for the "rules" of sleep—including but not limited to the sanctity of nighttime sleep, the importance of "beauty" sleep, and just plain letting everyone in the household get enough. As you head into the first few weeks of what is all but guaranteed to be relative sleep deprivation, we suggest that you remind yourself of one thing: This too shall pass.

What a Difference a Day (or Two) Can Make

During the first day or two after you have your baby, you might find yourself impressed with and thankful for how much your baby is sleeping. Many a mother of a newborn gets her best rest in the hospital, only to come to the conclusion she is destined to be one of the lucky few whose baby is destined to sleep through the night from day 1. Although we really don't enjoy bursting anyone's bubble, we feel obliged to give you a heads-up on what changes are likely to be right around the corner: These first couple of days are most likely just a honeymoon phase in the grand scheme of newborn sleep patterns. Many newborns spend their first few days on the outside catching up on sleep after the exhausting effort it took to get them there. It's almost as if they are briefly too tired to realize they are now out in the real world where there is so much to see and so much fun to be had. But once they wake up to the fact that they have at their disposal new scenery; parents to "play" with; and a lot of eating, peeing, and pooping to do—and they are no longer being lulled to sleep in the cozy confines of a uterus complete with soothing background noise—well then all bets are off and the games typically begin. As you first set out to learn the rules of this "can you survive your newborn's sleep habits?" game, you'll find that there are, in fact, very few rules. And even for the few rules there are, your baby may not be much for following them. With time (a few weeks), patience, and a bit of endurance mixed in, you and your baby will catch on and adjust.

Back to Sleep

Chances are good you were raised as a "belly baby"—spending all of your non-waking hours (as well as many of those when you were awake) lying comfortably on your belly. Yes, we acknowledge the fact that parents in generations before us did the best they knew how and all of you reading this book obviously managed to make it to the point where you are trying out parenthood for yourself. Since those days when we were so tenderly laid belly down to rest, new information has come to light about the potential role sleep position plays in sudden infant death syndrome (SIDS)—an occurrence that is admittedly rare but nonetheless terrifying to think about. Based on an ever-increasing amount of evidence linking belly sleeping to an increased risk of SIDS, the American Academy of Pediatrics (AAP) launched its major Back to Sleep Campaign in 1992. After a full decade of education aimed squarely at getting parents and caregivers to place infants to sleep on their backs instead of their tummies, SIDS prevention efforts have been impressively successful—in how babies are put to sleep *and* more importantly in significantly decreasing the number of babies who die from SIDS. If you're interested in the actual numbers, we are happy to oblige: As of 1998, more than 75% of babies were estimated to be put to sleep on their backs, in contrast to 25% in 1992. Over this same period, there was a dramatic decline in the number of SIDS deaths—by some estimates as much as 40%.

THE REALITY OF SIDS

Sudden infant death syndrome (SIDS), sometimes called crib death, is the sudden, unexplained death of an otherwise healthy baby. It is certainly not a topic we, as parents or pediatricians, enjoy bringing up with excited new parents, but it is one that is definitely worth being informed about. While SIDS is always a tragedy for the roughly 2,500 babies and families it affects each year in the United States, the odds of it happening to your child are very low and it is well within your power to lower them even further. Although SIDS rarely occurs during the first month of life (the risk is greatest from 1–4 months), there are simple things you can do to protect your newborn right from the start. Back sleeping and breastfeeding have been shown to lower the risk of SIDS, as has allowing infants to go to sleep using a pacifier. Things that increase the risk of SIDS: belly sleeping, putting a baby to sleep with another child or adult who might roll onto him, exposure to cigarette smoke, prematurity, overheating, and loose or soft bedding.

Putting Back-Sleeping Concerns to Rest

We're willing to bet that this isn't the first time you've been introduced to the benefits of raising a back-sleeping baby. Most new parents today are well informed when it comes to SIDS and why back sleeping is so strongly recommended. We'd be missing the boat, however, if we didn't acknowledge the fact that you may find yourself with some practical concerns when faced with putting principle into practice. For the most part, the following concerns cause parents to worry unnecessarily:

- **Spitting up and vomiting.** The most common back-sleeping concern we hear time and time again is the fear that babies will spit up and choke while asleep. Fortunately, several reassuring studies as well as the test of time have demonstrated that healthy babies put to sleep on their backs are not only able to turn their heads and/or protect their airways if and when they spit up, but are no more likely to have breathing or digestive-related problems than their belly-sleeping counterparts of days past.
- **Flat heads.** It is true that the shape of your newborn's head is not yet set in stone, and that there has been a general increase in the number of

babies "walking" around with flat heads since back sleeping came into vogue. The fact of the matter is that it's really not that much of a problem for most back-sleeping babies. In large part, that's because you have a good deal of control over the situation. All you need to do is try to make sure your baby gets laid to rest alternating the way she faces her head (turned to either side or looking straight up) each time she's on her back—while she is asleep and also while she is awake. By offering your newborn plenty of tummy time and time spent in positions other than flat on her back while she is awake, you can also help decrease the likelihood of a flat or misshapen head. For more on newborn heads, see "The Shape of Things to Come" on page 224.

- **Taking sides.** Perhaps the most tempting and readily available products marketed to those parents who just aren't convinced of the safety of back sleeping (despite all the information we have included previously) are infant side sleepers. These wedge-like cushions come in various shapes, sizes, and colors and allow parents to position babies on their sides while preventing them from rolling over as they sleep. It is true that the initial SIDS prevention recommendations included back and side sleeping as reasonable alternatives to belly sleeping, but the "new and improved" back-sleeping campaign does not leave room for interpretation. The recommendation was shifted to and continues to encourage only back sleeping. Perhaps side sleeping was eliminated from the "side or back" recommendation because there was a good possibility that side-sleeping babies would end up on their bellies before night's end (a concern that is admittedly addressed by side-sleeping wedges), but the AAP recommendation still stands: "Devices designed to maintain sleep position…are not recommended since none of these have been sufficiently tested for their safety or effectiveness."

- **Delayed milestones.** Some of you will undoubtedly hear or read that back sleeping has been associated with delayed motor development. In addressing the question of delayed milestones—or more specifically, a delay in the time when back-sleeping babies first begin to roll over— it all seems to even out in the end. Even if your baby doesn't take to rolling quite as early as her belly-sleeping counterparts of generations past and present, to our knowledge no college application has ever asked applicants how early they mastered the ability to roll over (or, for future reference, sit, crawl, walk, or toilet train). When it comes to strengthening the muscles your baby needs to roll and, at the same time, decreasing your baby's chances of ending up with a flat head, just be aware that both can be easily accomplished by allowing your baby plenty of time on her belly when she's awake.

- **Improving the air we breathe?** Not too long ago, there was an exposé done on one of the prime-time television shows about infant mattresses that reportedly prevented babies from re-breathing air during sleep. Despite inflated claims that this type of improved air flow around a baby's face effectively decreased the risk of SIDS, the investigative report subsequently uncovered evidence supporting the AAP stand: Re-breathing devices are not proven to be effective. What are they good for? Preying on a parent's greatest fear. When it comes to deciding whether to purchase a SIDS-preventing mattress, we suggest you stick to the basic and proven approach and instead buy a good, firm one that fits snugly in your crib (see "Crib Safety Considerations" on page 102).

Good Night, Sleep Tight

We'll be the first to admit that going belly up doesn't always seem to agree with all babies. While not true of all babies, we've found that quite a few are prone to startling themselves awake from peaceful slumber. That's because all babies are at the whim of their own reflexes—which, by definition, they cannot control—and are born with one particularly inconvenient reflex (the startle, or Moro, reflex) that causes them to jerk suddenly, flail their arms and legs, and even cry out in response to being startled—hence the name (see "Reflexes" on page 248). And yes, even when you've gone to great lengths to create a startle-free environment for your sleeping baby, he may just take matters into his own hands (and feet), startle himself awake, and then proceed to flail around like a bug stuck on his back until someone comes to his rescue. But don't give up on uninterrupted sleep just yet, because there is something quick and easy you can do: a handy little technique we call the "burrito wrap."

The Burrito Wrap

In other words, we suggest you wrap your baby up as snug as a bug in a baby blanket before putting him down to sleep. Hands down, the most talented people we've ever seen at this sleep-saving technique are the nurses in the newborn nursery. These baby-bundling experts take uncomfortably free and exposed newborns and almost effortlessly have them bundled in blissful, no flailing allowed slumber in the blink of an eye. If you have an opportunity, we highly recommend watching these professionals in action. For those of you who are already home and either missed out on the hospital demonstration or could use a little refresher course, we've laid out the details for you as best we can without actually being there to demonstrate in person.

1. Lay a baby blanket out like a diamond in front of you.
2. Fold the top corner of the blanket down a bit so that the folded corner almost reaches the middle of the blanket.

3. Place your infant on his back, centered on the blanket with his arms at his sides and his head just above the folded edge and his shoulders just below it.

4. Take one of the side corners of the blanket and fold it over your baby's shoulder and across his body, making sure to tuck the corner underneath him on the opposite side.

5. Then take the bottom corner of the blanket (below your baby's feet) and fold it up over your baby. If the blanket is large enough that the bottom corner reaches up to (or over) your baby's face, you can simply fold it back down until his face is no longer covered or bring it over one or the other shoulder and tuck it under him.

6. Finally, take the only remaining corner and pull it over your baby's other shoulder and across his body. Again, tuck this corner snugly under your baby's opposite side.

Once you have the general idea, remember that variations are perfectly acceptable. Feel free to play around with what works best for you and your baby. While the exact details and the order in which you do them may not matter too much in the end, we will point out that there is a good reason why we recommend folding the bottom of the blanket up *before* flipping the last corner across (ie, step 5 always before step 6) and always tucking corners under your baby: Doing so helps to keep your handiwork from coming undone quite as easily.

Hands-free Bundling

Some of our esteemed parenting colleagues suggest doing whatever it takes (with regard to bundling, that is) to ensure that your baby's arms and legs stay snugly secured in the blanket. Other equally convincing and respectable experts recommend *never* restricting your baby's arms—focusing your bundling attention on just your baby's legs while allowing her arms free rein. We personally have tried bundling both ways with good results. If you find that your baby seems unhappy having her arms "pinned down" by her sides instead of up next to her head, then just go ahead and burrito wrap her without placing her arms inside.

A NEWBORN'S PERSPECTIVE ON THE COMFORTS OF HOME

In addition to being at the mercy of their own reflexes, babies also tend to take a while to adapt to their new and often less appealing living (and sleeping) quarters. Keeping in mind that your newborn has just spent almost a year inside a continuously warm, dark, snug, and soothing environment, it becomes easier to understand how the sudden transition to lying sprawled out flat on one's back can seem like nothing short of a rude awakening—one that your newborn may take some time adjusting to.

Sleeping by the Book

"Sleeping like a baby" can mean different things to different people—usually depending on whether they've ever had or taken care of one before. For just about all newborns it fairly predictably means having the ability to sleep at any time and in any place, while at the same time being completely unwilling to entertain any "suggestions" as to how, when, or where to put such talent into practice. You may come across those who have ventured down the path of parenthood before you who simply shake their heads sympathetically and wish you luck in getting your newborn to wake up when you want/need him to, and even better luck getting him to go to sleep when you want. Because we're obviously committed to helping you set appropriate expectations for yourself and your baby, we're going to approach the whole subject of sleep by first helping you get into the right frame of mind. We decided to start out by providing you with some basic sleep-related milestones.

- **Daily sleep.** The average newborn spends at least 16 hours a day sleeping, but there can be big differences from one newborn to the next. The total amount of sleep babies need in any given 24-hour day gradually decreases over time, but still totals just over 14 hours at 6 months of age and just under 14 hours at 1 year.

- **Naps.** Sure, many newborns nap in 1- to 2-hour spurts, but before you go planning your schedule around any preconceived idea of nap time, let us add that the length of most newborns' naps are also very variable and tend to be scattered throughout the day (and night) in a completely random and therefore unpredictable manner. The 3-nap-a-day schedule with which you may be familiar should be considered a sleep pattern you should aspire to down the road, because most newborns don't settle into this type of nap routine for at least a month or two. Even then, it can take a few additional weeks or months before you can count on a morning, early afternoon, and early evening nap.

- **Night versus day.** During the first few days and weeks of parenthood, you are likely to find that there's not going to be a whole lot that distinguishes your days from your nights. More often than not, they just seem to blend together into one big sleep-deprived blur. That's because it will be almost completely up to your newborn when he chooses to be awake and when he chooses to sleep, and most newborns spend equal amounts of time sleeping during the day and night—a tendency that can be quite challenging for those of us accustomed to more of an awake-by-day, asleep-by-night approach. By the end of their first month, most newborns do manage to figure out how to consolidate their sleep into longer stretches and start to get at least one extended stretch of sleep each 24-hour day. So with any luck, you'll be blessed with a baby who decides to choose nighttime as the right time to do so. And for the real light at the end of the tunnel: By 3 months of age, many babies get approximately two thirds of their total daily sleep during the night.

Reversing Day-Night Reversal

Some babies, however, settle into the newborn sleep routine dreaded by many expectant parents—the so-called day-night reversal. As the description implies, newborns are known on occasion to mix up their days and nights. These temporarily backward-sleeping babies often begin to increase the amount of sleep they get each time they go to sleep according to plan, but simply do so more during the day while demanding to be fed, changed, *and* entertained throughout the night. As painfully exhausting as this upside-down approach to sleep may be for those of us accustomed to getting most if not all of our sleep at night, the assurance that this too shall pass once again comes to mind. We can all but guarantee you that hope is not far away. In most instances, the fact that your newborn is learning to replace lots of short little catnaps with longer stretches of sleep—whether they happen to fall during the day or at night—bodes well for a more "civilized" sleep routine in your not too distant future.

Lights On, Lights Off

If your baby seems determined to "play" during the night and sleep during the day there's really no quick fix, but there are some easy things you can do early on to set the stage for more acceptable sleep habits in the future. During your first few weeks at home with your baby, try to establish an atmosphere that clearly differentiates night from day. A good night's rest may not result overnight, but this approach can help get you there sooner.

- **Allow for active sleep.** During the day, have your baby sleep in more active areas of the house—in rooms with the lights on, or perhaps even in the car seat or stroller when you determine that you are ready to make your way out of the house.
- **Consistent contrast.** Don't spend much time worrying about background noises such as talking, telephones, or music during daylight hours. In contrast, try to make your nighttime interactions calm and quiet.

- **Maintain focus.** Whenever possible, take a more focused approach to your nighttime interactions—limiting them to feeding, burping, changing, and gentle soothing when necessary.
- **Soft-spoken approach.** Get in the habit of taking the aforementioned measures in a dark room using a soft voice whenever you want to signal to your newborn that it would be a fine time to sleep.

Learning to Sleep, Drink, and Be Merry

Before lying down, closing your eyes, and simply considering yourself lucky that you have a baby who has precociously caught on to sleeping long stretches at a time, you'll want to first consider whether prolonged periods of sleep could get her into trouble. That's because some babies— especially those who are born small, who have not yet mastered breast-feeding, or who are just a bit too sleepy for their own good—can be drowsy enough that they don't remember to wake up and eat. Just how long should you let your newborn sleep at any one time and how often should you feed her? The answer will depend on a variety of factors, not the least of which will be based on your pediatrician's assessment and subsequent recommendation.

Let Sleeping Newborns Lie?

Some pediatricians buy into the idea that full-term, healthy babies do not need to be woken up to eat during the night as long as they are eating and gaining weight well. Others feel very strongly that all young infants—at least for the first several weeks—should not be allowed to sleep for more than 4 or 5 hours at a time (at most) without being woken up to eat. Our opinion on the matter: Wait at least until you are sure your newborn has fully mastered breastfeeding or bottle-feeding, proven himself capable of keeping up by taking a regular interest in eating, and regained his birth weight according to plan within the first 2 weeks after being born before kicking back and enjoying the luxury of 4 or more hours of uninterrupted sleep. Whatever you do, be sure you discuss any sleep habits that seem too good to be true (and may, in fact, be falsely reassuring) with your baby's health care provider before reveling in the thought of a good night's sleep.

Waking Up Is (Sometimes) Hard to Do

Now is as good a time as any to discuss briefly the age-old adage "never wake a sleeping baby." Many expectant parents take this advice to heart and prepare themselves and their homes accordingly. In anticipation, they begin by locating the ringer on/off switches on their phones and making signs to tape over their doorbells that read, "Please knock quietly—baby sleeping." After bringing home a newborn of your own, however, you're far more likely to discover that most young infants (older babies are a different story) can sleep through just about anything—vacuums, doorbells, and the ringing of telephones included. Instead of figuring out ways to ensure peaceful slumber, many new parents find themselves (with ringers off and doorbells covered) wondering if, in fact, their babies would awaken to the sound of a freight train going by or the house being hit by a tornado. You'll find that as your baby gets older she will probably become a lighter sleeper, but for the time being you can feel free to relax a little on the noise control, unless of course you need it so you can sleep.

How to Wake a Sleeping Baby

As we mentioned at the outset, newborns have an impressive ability to ignore the world around them when they see fit to sleep. If you find yourself in the position of needing to wake up your baby, here are some simple techniques that sometimes (notice we said "sometimes") work.

- **The kinder, gentler approach.** You might as well start out with the kinder, gentler approach to baby waking and see what kind of response you get. This can include such basic measures as talking, singing, and gentle stimulation. Pick your baby up, talk to him, move his arms and legs around, even tickle the bottom of his feet or rub his cheek—whatever works to arouse him.
- **Dressing down.** Whether it's the physical stimulation or the increased exposure to cool air that does it, many newborns absolutely hate to be undressed. Your newborn may find it well worth the time and effort it takes to awaken and voice his opinion.
- **Double-duty diapering.** Even if your baby doesn't technically require one, going through the motions (even reusing the same diaper) may help if undressing alone doesn't do the trick. This works especially well

for those babies who have a tendency to fall asleep before finishing their meals. We think of it as dual-purpose diapering because not only do diaper changes tend to wake up sleeping babies, but this also tends to be a time when newborns are more likely to actually need to be changed (see "The Eating-Pooping Connection" on page 67).

- **Cleanliness is next to wakefulness.** Giving sleepy babies a bath certainly takes things a step beyond undressing and changing diapers, but has been known to work when all else fails. While we certainly don't approve of cruel and unusual punishment in any way, shape, or form, there may be times when some of you simply have no other choice than to resort to a bath to get your baby to wake up. This more "drastic" measure is most appropriately used sparingly, such as in the event that a newborn is long overdue to eat, and can be modified to accommodate your baby's umbilical cord as needed (see "Baby Bath Basics" on page 131).

The approaches we have described to you are obviously based on the assumption that your newborn is healthy. While it is true that newborns are known to be challenging to wake up at times, you should also be aware that babies who are not arousable or responsive despite their parents' best efforts need medical attention. Do not wait to discuss any questions or concerns you might have about your baby's sleepiness with your baby's doctor: Seek medical help immediately if your newborn seems increasingly sleepy, unresponsive, or hard to arouse.

Now I Lay Me Down to Sleep

Many new-baby books matter-of-factly lay out the merits of teaching babies to fall asleep on their own (without parental assistance). You know: no rocking, no nursing, and no driving circles around the neighborhood in search of sleep. If you have taken heed, you may be wondering to yourself exactly how you are supposed to go about getting your newborn to fall asleep without guaranteed screams of protest. In case you hadn't noticed, let us point out that most of the "don't rely on sleep aids to get your baby to sleep" advice is usually meant for babies as they approach 4 months of age. Instead, we suggest you avoid wasting your time worrying about whether you are doing yourself and your newborn a great disservice by occasionally allowing her to fall asleep cradled in your arms, snuggled

up on your chest, or in the back of your car secured in her car seat instead
of her crib and just do it ("it" being whatever you need to do, within
reason, to get you both some rest).

> ### TO SLEEP, PERCHANCE TO DREAM
>
> Even though they have shorter sleep cycles than adults, overall the average
> newborn spends far more time in what is known as active (REM) sleep. Not only
> is this the stage of sleep where dreaming takes place, but also where there is
> likely to be a lot more sucking, kicking, grunting, and moving going on.
> This is also a good time to catch a few first smiles.

Suitable Sleep Sites

At first, we figured we ought to allot a good bit of time to addressing the
various sleep-site options available to you—starting predictably with the
crib and then running through everything from bassinets, cradles, co-
sleepers, and playpens to car seats and dresser drawers. Then it occurred to
us that most parents we talk to seem to handle this part of new parenthood
pretty well on their own, and either don't care too much or already have
their hearts set on one or the other (or several) of the options. Given that
there are plenty of informative baby product books like *Baby Bargains* and
Girlfriends' Guide to Baby Gear around, we decided not to take up too much
of your time on the subject. Instead, we are going to lay out for you what we
consider to be the practical considerations and safety tips most useful in
deciding where to lay your baby down to rest.

The Great Debate: Sleeping Solo or Filling the Family Bed

Probably since the beginning of time, babies and parents around the world
have slept together in what has come to be commonly referred to as "the
family bed." In recent years, particularly in industrialized nations including
the United States, the trend has been to have children sleep separately starting from infancy. Whatever you choose, be sure you let common sense
prevail; if you or your baby aren't safe, content, or able to rest well in your
sleeping arrangement of choice, it's probably time for a change. As you
explore your options, we have one additional insight into your sleeping
future to offer you: Your selection of sleep arrangements now will not

inherently translate into a long-term commitment, but it can certainly turn into one. If you have no intention of bed-sharing in the future, then you'd be well-advised to give serious thought as to just how long you plan on letting your newborn become comfortably accustomed to the idea of a family bed at the outset—whether it's just a few weeks, many months, or any number of years.

- **The family bed.** Whether due to space limitations, cultural norms, or a strong belief that cosleeping is an integral part of parenting, parents have slept with their babies for thousands of years. In many parts of the world and in a good 60% of US households, many babies still do sleep in bed with their parents at least on occasion, despite recent trends toward solo sleeping. Followers of attachment parenting seem to feel quite strongly that parents and babies benefit most from bonding whenever possible, including during sleep. Proponents also feel that cosleeping makes breastfeeding easier—making new mothers more responsive to their babies' cues of hunger long before they wail to be fed and requiring less effort to feed them.
- **Sleeping solo.** In the United States, there has been a definite shift toward putting babies to sleep independently, whether in a crib, cradle, or bassinet. Our country's movement toward independent sleep may well be, in part, attributable to recent concerns that cosleeping may increase the risk of SIDS (see "The Reality of SIDS" on page 89). Other practical reasons why parents opt for solo sleeping: They find it to be safer, sounder (for the baby and her parents), and less intrusive on their "adult" time.

Cosleeping Safety Considerations

Many new parents are tempted to take their newborn into bed with them—often times out of fatigue and convenience, as well as for cultural and philosophical reasons. Whether cosleeping is safe, however, has been the subject of much debate. Recent studies suggest that cosleeping may significantly increase the risk of infant suffocation, so you'll find that many experts now strongly advise against it and instead suggest the very practical and safer alternative of sharing the same room, but not the same bed. If you do choose to sleep with your baby in your bed, even if only infrequently, here are some simple but extremely important safety considerations.

- Cosleeping and the use of tobacco, alcohol, or drugs (including over-the-counter or prescription medicines) don't mix. These substances may cause excessive drowsiness—making you potentially less aware of your baby.

- In our book, the heavy blankets, comforters, pillows, and other accessories that are typically found on adult beds and that could potentially suffocate or smother your baby have no place being in the same location where your newborn sleeps. While we're on the subject of simple yet potentially life-saving measures, we also strongly recommend removing any and all such items that may have already taken up residence in your baby's crib.

- Make sure you protect your baby from falls or from the possibility of being trapped between the mattress and the wall, headboard, or other furniture.

The Convenience of Cosleepers

For those of you who find the convenience of having your baby nearby at night appealing but aren't as wedded to the idea of having him in bed with you, then a cosleeper may be just the right answer for you. If you ask us, these specially designed baby beds are ingenious. They are somewhat like playpens, generally rest at the same height as a standard adult bed, have a drop-down (or absent) side rail on the side that fits next to the bed, and can therefore be placed right alongside it for easy access. Some even have the added benefit of doubling as a portable crib, play yard, or changing table.

Crib Safety Considerations

Whether you decide to set up a crib for your baby as soon as your pregnancy test turns positive or months after your newborn's much anticipated arrival, there are a few general safety principles that you'll want to follow to ensure your baby's safety. Some may not seem particularly relevant during your baby's first few months, but given that cribs tend to be big-ticket items and the one you invest in is going to be put to the test for years to come as your baby learns to roll, sit, stand, and climb in it, it's well worth considering present and future safety concerns.

- **Crib slats.** The slats should be no more than 2-3/8 inches apart. All new cribs must meet this standard, but older cribs may not.

- **Posts and cutouts.** Steer clear of bedposts taller than 1/16th of an inch and/or cutouts in the headboard (or any other parts of the crib) where a baby's or toddler's body parts could get stuck.
- **Crib toys.** They may seem harmless, entertaining, cute, and cuddly, but it's considered wise to keep all stuffed animals (and most toys) out of your newborn's crib because they can pose a small but nevertheless real safety risk. The exceptions are the types of toys that strap securely to the side of the crib. Some babies like mirrors or toys with parts they can play with (such as spinners, rattles, and music), but your newborn probably won't be terribly interested in them for at least a few weeks.
- **Mobiles.** Mobiles are special hanging toys designed to entertain your baby and can be attached to the crib, ceiling, or wall. Some are even adorned with lights or play music. They are fun but definitely optional. If you do choose to use mobiles, make sure they do not hang low enough to entangle your baby, especially once she begins to roll. In fact, once your baby is able to sit up, it will definitely be time for her mobile to come down.
- **Crib placement.** Unless you don't mind a bit of redecorating and rearranging when your baby starts to get around, we suggest you place your crib well away from any windows and no less than an arm's reach away from any nearby dressers or table-tops. Knowing that it won't be long before anything and everything within reach will be fair game, we also recommend limiting your over-the-crib wall decorations to painted walls, wallpaper, or soft wall hangings. Picture frames and mirrors over cribs are often an accident waiting to happen. Be forewarned that even paper borders placed within reach of the crib, while safe, don't often stand up well to prying fingers.
- **Firm-fitting mattress/fitted sheet.** While they seem to be mostly standardized, cribs and mattresses can and do come in more than one size, so be sure to double-check measurements and read labels to make sure you end up with a mattress that fits snugly into your chosen crib. Any extra space between the mattress and crib frame has the potential to trap a baby's arm, leg, or head. Also make sure your fitted sheets are tight enough that they don't slip off easily, thus posing a serious safety hazard. See the following sections for more on bedding for your baby's crib.

Crib Convenience Factors

Because all cribs made now must meet the same safety standards, all the other options are just icing on the cake. Railings are almost always adjustable—meaning you can raise and lower one or both side railings. Some railings are covered by a special plastic to prevent teething babies from gnawing on the paint or wood. Many cribs have adjustable heights so you can lower the mattress as your baby gets taller and he won't be able to climb out. You will likely want to keep it at the highest level while your newborn is relatively immobile and you are coming and going frequently because it will allow you to save a good deal of strain on your back. Remember that by the time your baby is able to sit or stand up, you'll want to lower the level of the crib mattress accordingly.

Baby Bedding, Bumpers, and Blankets

If you come to find that the excitement you feel about having a new baby is wrapped up in the buying of a fancy baby bedding set complete with bumper and quilted blanket, then don't let us stop you. After all, we couldn't resist the parental urge to splurge either—at least not the first time around. For those of you who are interested in taking a more minimalist approach, now is the time for us to point out that as cute as it may be to walk into the nursery and see the lamp match the wallpaper border match the blanket match the diaper holder…you get the picture, you really don't need any of it. For safety's sake, those big crib quilts should be kept out of your baby's sleeping environment, and you should remove the bumper padding as soon as your baby starts moving around (to make sure she doesn't stand a chance of getting tangled in it). The receiving blanket(s) and/or pajamas you use to wrap your baby in should be enough for warmth. If you're really set on using a baby blanket, we suggest using a small, thin, lightweight one instead of anything thick or fluffy.

Feet to Foot

For those of you who choose to cover your sleeping babies with blankets, the AAP recommends using the "feet to foot" method as an easy and effective way to keep them from getting tangled up. Simply place your baby's feet at the foot of the mattress, cover him with a blanket, and tuck the ends of the blanket into the sides and foot of the crib.

Monitoring the Situation

Modern parents now have the option of using baby monitors to listen to, and in some cases even watch, their babies from afar. Many parents find that monitors buy them peace of mind—allowing them to roam freely around the house while still keeping close tabs on their babies. If you choose to use a monitor, you may want to keep the following considerations in mind:

- **Range.** Baby monitors are only as good as their technological limitations, so we suggest you take a look at what kind of "listening" range they each offer.
- **It works both ways.** In more densely populated neighborhoods, apartments, or townhouses you may pick up interference from other baby monitors. Not only do you run the risk of eavesdropping on neighboring households, but your monitor-owning neighbors stand an equally good chance of hearing what's going on in the monitored room(s) in your house as well.
- **Disrupting the peace.** Some of you may find that leaving the monitor on at night significantly disturbs whatever limited sleep you stand to get—causing you to be wide awake in response to your slumbering baby's every twitch or snort.
- **Channel surfing.** In this age of modern electronics there's more than enough to interfere with your monitor, including cordless phones, cell phones, and other monitors. Try to find a monitor with good reception and more than one channel to decrease the likelihood of interference. We also suggest holding onto your receipt in case you run into any unforeseen technological conflicts that become apparent only once you put the monitor to use at home.
- **Bells and whistles.** Give some thought to which bells and whistles you really want and which simply serve to raise the price. Some of the available added features include a portable receiver with a belt clip, 2-way walkie-talkie radio capability, a receiver that vibrates or flashes lights so you can leave the sound turned off, and the possibility of purchasing multiple portable receivers that can accompany a single base station.

- **Nothing beats the real thing.** Never let your baby monitor substitute for taking sensible safety measures. There is no evidence that using a monitor will decrease the chance of SIDS.

Parental Sleep Priorities

We couldn't end a chapter on newborn sleep without addressing what you can do to get yourself some much needed rest too. Typically offered by those who've been in the trenches before you, the often repeated advice to sleep whenever your baby is sleeping actually makes very good sense—regardless of whether you considered yourself the type of person to take naps in your pre-parenting days. After all, if you don't take any and every opportunity that comes your way, we're pretty sure you'll come up quite short when trying to squeeze in your own REM cycles. We encourage you to put sleep high on your own priority list and either delegate or let other activities take a back seat for the first few weeks or months. As a point of practicality, let us also mention that trying to accomplish routine but complex tasks such as balancing your checkbook, preparing elaborate meals, entertaining, or operating heavy machinery in a sleep-deprived state is best avoided whenever possible (more on this in "Taking Care of Yourself" on page 155). And in all seriousness, don't try to drive when you're extremely exhausted. Finally, take people up on their offers to help out around the house so you can get some much-needed rest. They wouldn't offer if they didn't mean it, right?

CHAPTER 10

crying

A Welcome Cry

All newborns are supposed to cry—and most of them do a very good job of it. In fact, most newborns tackle this important rite of babyhood immediately on being delivered. A newborn's first cries serve a very important purpose—helping to fill his lungs with air and thereby shift over from being dependent on the oxygen carried to him in his mother's blood to breathing it in on his own. Even without an explanation of fetal and newborn circulation, you probably don't need us to tell you that delivery room cries are worthy of eager anticipation; generally represent the arrival of a happy, healthy baby; and are almost universally met with tears of joy and relief. What cries may come in the days that follow can vary considerably from baby to baby—but more likely than not you'll find yourself with a relatively sleepy baby (see "Sleeping Like a Baby" on page 87) who only cries to be fed (see "Into the Mouths of Babes" on page 1).

Why Cry?

Once newborns have slept off the excitement of delivery and opened their eyes to the brave new world that lies before them, you can bet that they all inevitably and intermittently start crying. That said, one of the first and most helpful lessons to teach yourself is that babies don't always cry for the same reasons as adults. After all, most of us cry when we are either a) hurt or b) upset. We assume it is for this reason that many parents become distressed at the sound of their baby's cry and feel like absolute failures if they can't stop their baby's presumed cries for help, much less stop them immediately. Babies, on the other hand, have the uncanny ability to burst into tears (minus the tears, of course, which don't tend to show up for the first month or so—see "Loud and Tearless" below) if they're startled, hungry, cold or hot, tired, wet, bored, annoyed, have gas...you get the picture. The way we look at it, babies are justified in crying a lot if for no other reason than that they really don't have many other ways of communicating their feelings. If you remind yourself that crying isn't always synonymous with pain or being upset, you'll be much less likely to find yourself on the verge of tears in the months to come.

 LOUD AND TEARLESS

Most babies typically don't shed a tear in the first month—not for a lack of trying but because their tear glands aren't yet fully developed. While you may not exactly treasure your baby's cries (at least after the first one in the delivery room) you may actually find yourself a little misty when your newborn reaches this teardrop milestone and her cries are accompanied for the first time by true tears.

Tales of a Telltale Cry

Most books will tell you that your parenting instincts will quickly take over and you'll be able to identify the reason for each of your baby's unique cries. We definitely don't want to minimize the importance of taking crying seriously and we wholeheartedly agree that you should try to understand the underlying meaning of each of your baby's cries, but in our experience this is often easier said than done. When you're not quite sure why your baby is crying, look first for the "obvious" causes—hungry, poopy, wet, tired—as well as reassure yourself that it's not because of the potentially serious causes—fever and illness, poking pins, or wayward hairs or strings wrapped around fingers or toes (2 universally listed causes we felt obliged to include although they are, in reality, pretty rare). But for those of you who in the end still can't pinpoint why your newborn is/was crying and feel hopelessly incompetent as a result, we hope we can convince you to be less critical of yourself by telling you that we did not always find cry identification to be a simple task with our own newborns either. We did what we could, and we gave it our all (sometimes our "all" was a bit limited due to sheer sleep deprivation). If our children could remember their infancies and were allowed to publicly discuss our own parental "inadequacies" we're sure they would tell us they were fed when they were wet, put to bed when they were hungry, and over-stimulated when they were tired. Sure, there will be times when your baby's needs are obvious, but it's worth keeping in mind that there will also be times when you're just not sure about anything except, perhaps, wanting to pull your hair out.

 ## CALCULATED CRYING

In your first weeks and months, remind yourself that it is absolutely normal for babies to cry. A typical newborn will increase the amount he cries during any given day from about 2 hours at 2 weeks of age to a peak of up to 4 hours a day by 3 months. Light at the end of the tunnel: The amount of crying babies do then begins to gradually decrease, and the cause is usually much easier to figure out as time goes on.

Is It Colic?

Pick up any baby book and you're sure to find mention of what many parents refer to as the dreaded "C word." Even though the rule of thumb for colic is that it doesn't usually settle in until 3 weeks or so, we've included it front and center in our crying section because without any frame of reference, quite a few parents start worrying about it even before their babies are born, and then worry that every cry or fussy spell is only one step shy of all-out colic (or might signify the start of it). Quite simply, colic is defined as persistent crying in an otherwise healthy infant. For practical purposes, we like to think of colic as a spectrum ranging from babies who have crying episodes that last just a few minutes to those that cry for hours at a time. Only time will tell if your newborn will prove to be a "colicky" baby—one who has regular crying spells that present themselves usually in the evening and for no apparent reason. The good news is that most babies with colic (and even those without) outgrow excessive crying by 3 to 6 months of age.

Controlling Colic

While no one knows the true cause of colic, and many parents and experts continue to attribute the crying to stomach pain and/or something in a baby's diet, the most practical and logical analysis of colic (*and* what to do about it) was recently laid out for all parents to benefit from in a well-written, practical parenting book by a fellow pediatrician named Harvey Karp. In *The Happiest Baby on the Block,* Dr Karp takes a close look at previous colic theories and then introduces parents to the 5 Ss (swaddling, side/stomach positioning while awake, shushing, swaying, and sucking) that he—and we—find very effective in calming crying colicky babies during the first few months of life.

DOES SOOTHING = SPOILING?

You certainly don't need to hold back on responding to your newborn's cries for fear of spoiling her. In fact, for the next several months you can take spoiling off of your list of parenting concerns altogether. Each time you try to respond promptly to your newborn's cries, you simply send your baby a message that you're there to tend to her needs.

Soothing the Savage Beast

So how will you know exactly what these needs are? Well even though we've already told you it's not always simple, you are likely to find that after a few days you notice that every time your baby starts to fall asleep he has a characteristic cry. Or maybe he'll have a certain wail that stops as soon as he is fed. Once you start picking up on these cues and responding accordingly, your baby will take comfort in knowing that he's able to communicate with you, at least some of the time. If you can't identify the cry, consider the last time your baby ate, slept, or had his diaper changed. If it has been a few hours, it may be time again to tend to each of these needs. Here are some other techniques to try if your baby just won't stop crying.

- **Professional help.** Most books save the worst-case scenarios for the end of the list. Not us. We want you to know right off the bat that if at any point you feel that your baby is simply inconsolable or crying for longer than you're comfortable with, or if he seems sick or has an unusually high-pitched cry, then by all means put down the book(s) and enlist the expertise of your pediatrician without delay—that's what they're there for!

- **Soothe yourself.** OK, we're now going to assume that you've evaluated your situation and don't think it warrants a doctor's intervention. The next step is to take a deep breath and try to relax. Babies can pick up on stress around them and may start to cry if they get negative vibes. Sometimes the best first step you can take is to calm yourself down first, even if that means putting your crying baby down in a safe place and giving yourself a quick break.
- **Snug and secure.** Try swaddling your baby snugly (as described in "Good Night, Sleep Tight" on page 91). The way we reason it, newborns have all spent 9 months (give or take) accustomed to feeling snug and secure in the very close quarters of the uterus. By simulating this cozy feeling of confinement, the swaddling technique often helps with crying as well as with sleeping.
- **Keeping things moving.** Every newborn who's spent any amount of time in utero is simply not going to be born accustomed to sitting still. As a result, you may find that yours takes a while to buy into the notion that the absence of movement and activity can be pleasant and peaceful. In the meantime, you can try the time-tested methods of movement such as carrying, rocking, strolling, or driving to appease your crying or restless newborn. The ever-popular vibrating infant seats and baby swings also serve the purpose of keeping your baby comfortably moving as well. Just keep in mind that you'll want to always secure your baby according to instructions, keep an eye on him while you're using them, and buy accessories designed to accommodate newborns (additional recline, harnesses that adequately secure newborns, low settings on automatic swings, etc).
- **Simple sound effects.** Your baby may also crave the soothing muffled noises similar to amniotic fluid waves or the swishes and pulses of mom's heart and blood vessels. You may find, as many before you undoubtedly have, that the sound of a vacuum cleaner, washing machine, shower running, or human heartbeat (hold him against your chest or play a tape of heart sounds) works wonders. For some of these efforts, you will also have the added bonus of a cleaner house, clothes, or body! Whether you're musical or not, try singing or playing some music. Research has actually shown that some newborns are particularly

soothed by a song or songs that were played or sung to them even
before they were born!

- **Opposites attract.** Feel your baby's hands and feet. If they are cold,
put on another layer of clothing or wrap him in a blanket. If he's
warm or sweaty, remove a layer (and consider checking his temperature as discussed in "Fever: Trial by Fire" on page 251). See if he's
interested in a change of scenery—if it's bright, turn off the lights.
If it's dark, turn some on. If it's very noisy, turn down the volume.
If it's unusually quiet, try out some of the simple sound effects
mentioned previously. Too still? Move around. Bottom line: no
actual science involved here—more a matter of finding and fine-
tuning your own simple calming solutions.

- **Hand off.** If others are around, enlist their help until you're ready to
try again yourself.

- **Give it time.** If all else fails, just hold your baby and patiently wait for
him to settle down. Crying in and of itself won't hurt your baby, so if
you're not in a mindset to handle it, it's OK to let your baby cry for a
while. If you're at your wit's end and need a break, don't feel guilty
about putting him in a safe place (such as a crib or buckled into a
car seat) while you compose yourself.

 WHEN THE CRYING WON'T STOP

Now that we've tried to give you a better feel for why newborns cry, we want
to leave you with a general rule about newborns and crying. Even though
inconsolable crying does not always mean that there is a serious underlying
cause to blame, it always warrants a call to the doctor.

When You Feel Like Crying

While entire books are written on the subject of "baby blues" and postpartum depression, we didn't want to finish off this chapter without telling you
that if you don't feel like crying in the first few days or weeks after becoming a parent, then congratulations—you're definitely in the minority. A
whopping 70% to 80% of new moms reportedly get some form of the baby
blues. For most of you, we suggest you don't spend too much time trying to

explain your tears or wondering whether it is the hormonal roller coaster, sleep deprivation, or sheer newness of parenthood to blame. Mild depressive feelings, while common, fortunately tend to go away after a few weeks. For 1 out of 10 new mothers, however, the blues progress to full-blown postpartum depression that can last anywhere from weeks to months and usually requires counseling and treatment. If ever you find yourself overwhelmed, frustrated, anxious, persistently teary, or depressed and unable to explain or shake the feeling, please don't suffer in silence or shame. Talk to your doctor right away. Although you may well feel like it, you are not alone.

CHAPTER 11

the art and science of diapering

The Facts About Diapers

It's probably not news to you that becoming a parent will inevitably involve changing a lot of diapers—as many as 8 to 12 a day once you get into the swing of things—but who knew there was a whole art and science to the task? The fact of the matter is that most parents average 6 diaper changes a day and go through nearly 3,000 diapers during their baby's first year alone. With toilet training not often achieved until around the age of 2 or 3 years or later in the United States (although it may occur much earlier in other cultures), diapering is an unavoidable part of parenthood. Need we say more? Obviously we think so, because not everyone (ie, almost no one) is born with an innate mastery of this necessary parenting skill.

 DIAPER(LESS) TRIVIA

Did you know that in certain Asian and African cultures babies are not put in diapers? When a baby awakens or the parent notices certain cues, the parent places the baby over a bush or other designated area to pee or poop. Although you may want to adapt this technique when it comes time to potty train, based on social norms in America, we don't recommend you try this with your newborn at home!

The Debate: Cloth Versus Disposable

As newcomers to the world of parenting, some of you may not have heard of the ongoing cloth versus disposable diaper debate, especially because the use of disposable diapers has become so accepted as a modern-day convenience that many parents wouldn't dream of using a substitute. In contrast to 1955 when essentially all American babies wore cloth diapers, an estimated 90% of the turn of the 21st century babies are sporting the latest in disposable fashions. While a simple Internet search on the subject will quickly make it clear to you how strongly some people feel about the cloth versus disposable debate, we have no intention of taking sides. Instead, we figured we'd offer you some facts and practical advice related to the use of each type—with the rest of our information weighted toward disposable use only because it is clearly more applicable to most parents these days.

- **Disposable.** Disposable diapers are very absorbent, which can be good and bad. Using them may mean that your baby's skin has less contact with pee and poop, and may offer the added convenience of less frequent changing. However, it may also be more difficult to monitor exactly how much your baby is peeing—a task that is especially important during the newborn period as well as if your baby gets sick. Some cloth diaper advocates argue that babies in disposable diapers have a much higher incidence of diaper rash (presumably due to longer contact with diaper contents resulting from less frequent changing), not to mention the fact that "disposable" diapers are not biodegradable and an estimated 18 billion a year are thrown in overcrowded landfills. Interestingly, a few communities have begun recycling or composting used disposable diapers. We can only hope this becomes mainstream in the near future.

- **Cloth.** Cloth diapers are usually made of soft cotton and are supposedly more comfortable than disposable diapers (we say supposedly because neither of us has any personal recollection and we aren't exactly sure how one would otherwise prove such a claim!). Proponents also claim that babies who wear cloth diapers are 5 times less likely to develop diaper rashes than their disposable diaper-clad counterparts. But unlike disposable diapers, cloth diapers are not as absorbent, need to be changed more frequently, and usually need to be worn with an overlying stay-dry cover. These covers typically come in the form of plastic, cotton, or terry cloth. And because cloth diapers (and their covers) require a lot of washing by either the parents or a diaper service and therefore use of a great deal of water and detergent, some people in the disposable diaper camp argue that cloth diapers also have a negative impact on the environment.

CLOTH DIAPER COVERS FOR DISPOSABLE DIAPER USERS

While diaper covers are routinely used over cloth diapers, they can also help solve the not uncommon dilemmas of what to do for babies who have explosive liquid poop (most accurately referred to as blowouts) or those who pee so much during the night that they leak out of even the most absorbent of disposable diapers.

The Art of Diapering

Yes, believe it or not, there is an art to diapering. After all, who wouldn't be proud of the ability to diaper a moving target, save 5 cents per diaper, always be prepared for a blowout, or simply get the darn tabs to stick when and where we want them to? While as parents we all change a whole lot of diapers, the art of diapering involves doing it better, faster, and cheaper, and with less mess.

Choosing a Diaper

Whether you choose cloth versus disposable, brand name versus generic, or any combination thereof, you and your baby may develop some preferences for the diapers you use. Some babies are "well-contained" using a variety of brands and styles of diapers, whereas others may do best with one certain brand. Some require extra absorbency while others do just fine with the less expensive, less absorbent types. Some babies may be sensitive to particular materials in diapers and may be more prone to rashes when wearing certain brands. The bottom line: Each baby is different, more expensive brands are not always better, and finding a suitable diaper for less can clearly be a good way to save a lot of money. So don't be afraid to try something new!

Velcro Versus Adhesive

Deciding on the brand is not the only decision you'll need to make when it comes to choosing a diaper. Disposable diapers now come with a choice of Velcro or tape fasteners. While Velcro may be more expensive, it is easier to reattach—for instance, if you need to check for a wet diaper—especially if you find yourself doing it with water, lotion, Vaseline, or diaper rash cream on your hands. Additionally, the tape fasteners may stick steadfastly to themselves before you get a chance to secure them in the proper position and may also lose their adhesive qualities once detached. Once you become skilled in the fine art of changing diapers, however, it usually doesn't make too much of a difference one way or another under normal circumstances.

Diaper Sizing

The exact numbers vary from brand to brand, but in general, newborn diapers are designed for infants up until they reach about 10 pounds. Unless your newborn is particularly small (in which case, you might start out with preemie diapers for babies weighing less than 6 pounds), you may find yourself jumping up to size 1 diapers fairly quickly. Given that size 1 diapers are designed to fit infants between approximately 8 and 14 pounds, you may find yourself rounding up and bypassing the newborn diapers altogether.

Diapering Around the Umbilical Cord

Until a newborn's umbilical cord stump fully dries and falls off, it is recommended that you leave it exposed to air as much possible, as well as limit its exposure to pee- or poop-filled diapers. While newborn diapers usually have umbilical cord cutouts, you can also use diapers that don't and simply fold the front of the diaper down below the level of the belly button.

Buying Diapers

At an average of 25 cents per diaper for brand-name disposables and about 3,000 diapers, you can expect to spend around $750 during your first year of diapering—and that's not even factoring in wipes, diaper creams, and all the other diapering paraphernalia. With those figures in mind, we thought it would be useful to point out several potential ways you can save yourself some money in the diapering department.

- **Start small.** Start out buying diapers in smaller quantities. You'll want to make sure you've found a good match, but keep in mind that your newborn will be growing very quickly in the months to come. If at first you happen to settle on a more expensive brand, remember that as your baby gets older (and has less sensitive skin, less leaky poop, and pees less frequently), you may want to experiment with less expensive brands.

- **Divide and conquer.** Calculate your cost per diaper. This may sound obvious, but by simply dividing the cost of a pack of diapers by the number of diapers in the pack, you can figure out if what you're getting is really a good deal, or if it is just being advertised as one. You'll find that mega-jumbo packs aren't always the best bargain, and that one store's sale price doesn't beat the everyday price at another.

- **Cut coupons.** By checking such places as the newspaper and the Web, you can often find enough diaper coupons to make it well worth your while, especially at stores that double manufacturers' coupons.

- **Think big.** When you do find a sale or have coupons, buy extra diapers in advance to spare yourself a middle of the night run to the grocery store because you've used your last one. You might want to consider having your reserve supply be a size up from the one your baby's currently wearing so that you won't wind up with leftover diapers that don't fit.

- **Join the club.** Take note of frequent buyers' clubs. You know you're going to be in the market for diapers for a long time to come, and by simply collecting proofs of purchase (or "diaper points") many companies will reward you with baby clothes, toys, music, and other products. Similarly, some grocery store chains now tally up dollars spent on baby items and offer coupons each time you reach a certain total (eg, get a $10 store coupon every time you spend $100 on baby items at that store).

- **Consider your options.** Consider using cloth diapers and washing them yourself. While some people estimate that using a diaper service only lets you break even compared to paying for disposable diapers, washing cloth diapers yourself can cut your diaper costs by as much as half.

Wipes for Newborns?

It's not uncommon for a new or expectant parent to hear through the parenting rumor mill that wipes are not to be used during the newborn period. Like many parenting recommendations, we're not exactly sure why this one exists. After scouring the pediatric literature (which is not exactly extensive on the subject), it seems most experts believe wipes are safe to use on newborn skin, even if there is a rash or a break in the skin. In general, they are thought to be as mild as using a wet washcloth. In fact, the only report of skin problems we found was in parents with eczema who had skin reactions when their own hands came into contact with wipes (presumably caused by the fragrance or preservatives in the wipes). The best advice we have to give you on the subject is that if they seem to be causing a problem, don't use them. Otherwise, wipe away!

  NOT JUST FOR BABIES

Here's a little trivia that's sure to help you fit right in with the parenting crowd. In researching the subject of wipes, we also happened on an interesting and what we assume to be a little-known fact. There are companies now marketing wipes for adults, and apparently not without reason. A recent study showed that not only do many adults believe that moist wiping after toileting is more effective than using plain toilet paper, but 1 out of 4 adult respondents use moist wipes daily!

A Word on Wipes

Although we haven't officially counted, there have to be about as many brands and types of wipes as there are tennis shoes—environmentally friendly all-natural wipes, scented and unscented, with aloe and without, in round containers, in rectangular refillable containers, and packaged in reusable or disposable travel packs. And while they may only cost a few cents a wipe if you don't go for the top of the line or opt for fancy packaging, the cost can really add up. While the principles discussed in the "Buying Diapers" section generally apply to buying wipes as well, here are a few additional things to consider when buying and using wipes.

- **Packaging.** After one look at the shelves, you won't need us to tell you that when it comes to buying wipes, you pay for packaging. However, doing so is not always a bad thing. For example, someone who clearly had firsthand experience in the use of wipes on the go must have come up with the handy little plastic travel containers, and many parents find the added convenience well worth the extra money. That said, it is also useful to hang on to them, as well as to the full-size refillable plastic containers. By simply buying large refill packs and restocking the plastic containers yourself, you can save yourself the extra expense.
- **Don't flush 'em.** Enough said—almost. There are very few wipes on the market that don't have the potential to wreak havoc on your plumbing. Be sure to check package labels before buying if you are determined to find wipes that are flushable, because most of them are not.
- **The overuse of wipes.** Believe it or not, not every diaper change requires the use of wipes. This is not only because pee rarely irritates the skin, but also because today's super-absorbent disposable diapers effectively limit the amount of pee that even comes into contact with the skin. Reserving wipes for cleaning up poop can save you a considerable amount. Also keep in mind that a moist tissue, a wet washcloth, or even a quick rinse in the tub may be used in place of baby wipes when convenient.

Wipe Warmers

Believe it or not, they do make them. Seems that some people are convinced that warm wipes are less shocking to newborns. It sounds reasonable: Given that a baby's body temperature is 98.6°F and regular damp wipes are roughly 60°F or less, we're talking about a 40° difference. By heating up the wipes to just below body temperature, the wipe warmer can lessen the shock, so to speak. When it comes to the question of how hot is too hot, one manufacturer actually set an upper limit on its warmer; the warmer simply shuts off after reaching 105°F. On removal of a wipe from the unit and coming into contact with air, the wipe will be about 95°F.

In reality, however, most parents only briefly warm up cold wipes with their own hands, if at all, before using them on their baby. Those who do own warmers tend only to use the warmed wipes in the room where the wipe warmer is kept. And we have yet to meet a parent who actually carries their wipe warmer with them when venturing out of the house. Realistically speaking, most babies are not afforded this luxury and get used to cool wipes right from the start.

 TEMPERATURE TRIVIA

While we're on the subject of temperatures, we thought we'd point out that a toasty hot tub is set at 104°F and indoor swimming pools are usually around 84°F. And lest we leave room for misinterpretation, let us reiterate that we are not suggesting you take your newborn in either but simply offering you a frame of reference.

Changing Diapers

Location, Location, Location

Wherever you choose to change your baby's diaper—whether it's on your brand new changing table or next to you on your bed—you'll want to prepare the area so that everything you need (minimum: a diaper and some wipes) is accessible. While changing tables are clearly the norm when it comes to location, and some people, one of us included, even opt to have more than one around the house, you should be aware (if you aren't already) that they aren't inherently necessary. If you decide that you don't want your diaper changing to be limited geographically by where your changing table happens to be, then also consider keeping diapers accessible in convenient locations around the house (and in the car once you start to venture out). That way, you can limit how far you have to go to take care of business. Some people opt to use a simple diaper changing pad in lieu of the table, and the floor, bed, couch, or even the back seat of your car can easily serve the same purpose once you are comfortable with the routine. That said, some particularly messy episodes might require not only a new diaper, but also an extra pair of hands, a new outfit, and even a trip to the tub. On such occasions, you'll be much better off if you've chosen your "changing station" in close proximity to your supplies.

The Technique

Before starting to change your baby's diaper, keep in mind that some babies have a tendency to pee as soon as they are exposed to open air. By keeping them relatively covered as much as you can during the course of a diaper change, you can help keep yourself, your changing surface, and your baby's clothes from getting unnecessarily wet.

If your baby is cooperative, which most babies are at least until they learn how to roll (somewhere around 4 months), you can first lift her legs with one hand and place a clean diaper under her bottom with the other. Make sure you have the picture side of the new diaper in front and the side with the tabs underneath. *Then* unfasten the old diaper and wipe your baby's bottom with the front (inner side) of it as you remove it. While you clearly don't have to wipe with the old diaper before taking it off, doing so can often remove a significant amount of poop before you reach for your first baby wipe. If the old diaper isn't overwhelmingly messy, leaving it folded over on itself but still under your baby's bottom can help prevent her

still-dirty bottom from getting the new diaper soiled before
you've had the chance to clean her up, and also serve to
absorb any new pee that may present itself during
the uncovered stage of the diaper change.

Next, wipe your baby's bottom and surrounding dirty areas with a baby wipe,
moist tissue, or washcloth. Then remove
the old diaper along with the wipes from
underneath your baby (if you haven't
already) and find a "safe" place to set
them so that you don't end up with
your baby's foot in poop, or find yourself with a new mess to clean up after
accidentally knocking the diaper and
its contents to the floor.

Securing the new diaper simply involves
making sure that the front of the diaper is
centered between the legs and pulled up to at least the same level in the
back that it is in the front—usually around the level of the belly button.
Check to see that the tabs are evenly secured in the front so that there aren't
any gaps around the hips. Also, to help prevent leakage, make sure that the
fringe around the legs isn't tucked into the diaper's elastic edges.

A WORD ON THE PERILS OF LOOSE-FITTING DIAPERS

Many of you will know precisely what we are referring to when we suggest that
you use caution not to let the back of the diaper sit too low or loose on your
baby. This plumber-style method of diapering (no offense to plumbers intended)
leaves way too much room for less than desirable contents to escape your
baby's diaper. And even if you quickly become a master diaper changer
with impeccable technique and flawless fit, beware of those well-meaning
friends (and pediatricians) who are likely to pay less attention to the end
result of their diaper-changing efforts than you do!

Disposable changing pads (available in most drugstores and sometimes referred to as bed liners) can be helpful in protecting your changing table, crib, bed, floor, or wherever else you may choose to set up shop. These are especially good when you're away from home because they can be used first as a changing pad and then to wrap the dirty diaper for a quick and easy disposal. If you're at home and don't mind a bit of extra laundry, a towel can easily serve the same purpose.

🐣 DIAPER CHANGING 🔍 SAFETY CONSIDERATIONS

Never leave your baby unattended. Keep one hand on him at all times. Even though he may not even be able to lift up his head yet (much less roll over), it's a good habit to establish right from the start.

Avoid changing table falls by strapping your baby securely. If you use a changing table pad, make sure that it is secured to the table as well. These measures are not, however, substitutes for staying within arm's reach.

Talcum powder, when inhaled, can cause damage to a baby's lungs. If you choose to use baby powder, buy one that is talc-free. First carefully rub a little onto your hands and then apply it to your baby's bottom.

Keep plastic bags, safety pins, and any other potentially harmful tools of the trade out of your baby's reach.

A Word on Boys

Baby boys are notorious for indiscriminately spraying their parents, grandparents, and pediatricians. By simply being aware of this inherent hazard, in addition to holding your hand, a diaper, or a tissue over your baby's penis as much as possible during a diaper change, you can limit the amount of time you leave yourself vulnerable. If you do find yourself caught in the line of fire, take comfort in knowing that it happens to the best of us. While it may not help you much, those of us in the medical profession who have been peed on more than once find it somewhat comforting to also remind ourselves that urine is, after all, a sterile body fluid. If you can get the diaper on without being doused but find yourself nevertheless with urine sneaking out of your baby boy's diapers, also try aiming his penis downward before covering it with the diaper.

A Word on Girls

Baby girls obviously have more "nooks and crannies" to deal with in their diaper areas, and as a basic principle, you shouldn't forget to look in them for hidden poop. That said, it is not necessary to wipe vigorously in an attempt to remove all of the normal white discharge that is commonly found between the folds of the labia. In fact, doing so can cause undue irritation.

For many of you, this will be stating the obvious, but in hopes of promoting good hygiene and potentially decreasing the likelihood of urinary tract infections, we also feel compelled to remind you that baby girls should be wiped from front to back to avoid spreading poop into the region around the opening where the pee comes out (called the urethra). Sure, the poop may already have made its way there without your help, but at least you won't be adding to the mess.

UDOs: UNIDENTIFIED DIAPER OBJECTS

Many parents are at a loss when they first find clear or yellowish beaded gel-like particles in their infant's diapers, but you can rest assured that there is usually a simple (and harmless) explanation. Sometimes the materials used to make the inside portion of the diaper have a tendency to form little gel-like beads when the diaper becomes over-soaked. Simply changing your baby's diaper more frequently can stop them from appearing.

Also common are small harmless crystals that are made in the kidney that tend to appear during periods of relative dehydration. For this reason they are occasionally discovered along with pee in the diapers of newborn boys and girls. They too can be clear solid or gel-like crystals, or leave an orange- or pink-tinged stain on the diaper.

And finally, it is not uncommon for newborn girls to have some pink or even bloody stains appear in their diapers during the first few days or weeks. The bleeding, which is caused by exposure to mom's hormones before birth, typically resolves on its own but can really throw new parents for a loop in the meantime.

If you have any concerns about unidentified objects or discolorations appearing in your baby's diaper, be sure to consult your baby's physician.

Disposing of Diapers

Several manufacturers are in the market of selling diaper disposal systems designed to cut down on the odor associated with dirty diapers. These systems generally use built-in deodorizers, plastic bags, and airtight containers to seal off the smell. While many parents swear by them and love to use them, the main complaints some parents have about these systems include inadequate elimination of odor once things start to get smellier and the added expense of buying replacement bags. They also tend to be less useful for parents who choose to change diapers in a variety of locations around the house instead of at the official changing station where the disposal system is typically kept.

It comes down to a matter of personal preference (as well as how sensitive your nose is and how often you take out the garbage) whether a special odor-eliminating diaper disposal system is worth the extra money. Parents who conclude that mildly wet or soiled diapers don't actually smell too much may choose to use the disposal system to dispose of only the truly smelly diapers. Others find it just as easy (or easier) to toss the smelly diapers into one of the zillions of extra plastic grocery bags (or newspaper bags or bread bags or…) we all seem to accumulate. Doing so helps minimize the smell of the diaper enough that it can be placed in a regular garbage can in your house or in a trash container outside. Once your baby starts having more solid and stinky poops—which tends to happen when solid foods are introduced, if not sooner—you'll find it very worthwhile to dump any solid poop into the toilet first.

 IT'S A WRAP

If you haven't figured this one out yet, the simple technique of folding up a dirty diaper before disposing of it is actually quite useful. Simply take the old diaper and lay it flat with the inside facing up and the tabs out to the sides just as you would if you were spreading out a new diaper to put on your baby. Place any wipes you may have used into the (center) crotch area. Lift up the front portion of the diaper and roll it up like a sleeping bag. Once it is bundled up into a compact roll, take the side tabs and fold them over the rolled up part to keep it closed and its contents well contained. This technique not only saves space and decreases odor, but also limits your likelihood of spreading poop around.

The Medical Side

Diaper Rashes

Quite simply, anything that appears as an irritation or rash on the skin in the diaper area is a diaper rash. While there are several types and causes of diaper rash, they fortunately don't seem to show up too often during the newborn period. That said, the 2 types you are most likely to become personally familiar with are caused by contact irritation and yeast. Contact with pee or poop can sometimes be enough to cause irritation of the skin. In other instances, a type of yeast known as *Candida albicans* is responsible for causing considerable redness and irritation. *Candida* is very commonly found in moist, warm areas, which helps explain why it primarily targets the diaper area—one of the most likely spots on a baby's body to be excessively moist. When *Candida* finds its way into the inside of an infant's mouth, it also can cause white plaque-like spots, a condition that is referred to as *thrush*. Changing your baby's diaper regularly (every couple of hours during the day) and allowing her skin to air dry before putting on the new diaper can definitely decrease her likelihood of getting a yeast diaper rash.

 ## AN OUNCE OF POWDER

Baby powder serves the basic purpose of reducing moisture and potential irritation in skin folds, and is often used not only in the diaper area but also under arms and in double (or triple) chin folds. While some parents commonly use baby powder, others (ourselves included) have never bothered. If you do choose to combat moist creases with baby powder, be sure to apply it carefully so that your baby doesn't end up lying in the middle of a powdery cloud. And even more importantly, buy talc-free baby powder (the most common alternative being a corn starch-based powder) because talcum powder can cause a chemical irritation and pneumonia in the lungs of babies who inhale it.

Treating Diaper Rash

The treatment of diaper rashes depends on the underlying cause. If irritation is to blame, simply getting rid of or limiting your baby's contact with whatever is causing the irritation—whether it is a particular type of soap, detergent, or even just irritating poop—is often all that is necessary. Additionally, the use of zinc oxide creams, ointments, or petroleum jelly-type products that provide a protective barrier over the skin can help to limit the amount of contact and the severity of the resulting irritation. And lastly, mild over-the-counter anti-inflammatory steroid creams such as hydrocortisone can often help reduce redness and pain. Parents should always be sure to discuss the use of this type of treatment with their doctor before using it, in part because of the possible harm that improper or prolonged use of steroids can cause to the skin, but also because of the potential for steroid creams to worsen a rash if it is, in fact, caused by yeast. Yeast infections require specially medicated antifungal creams—some of which are over-the-counter and others that can only be purchased with a prescription.

CHAPTER 12

baby bath basics

While it is true that you are solely responsible for all of your newborn's nooks and crannies, you may be relieved to know that the task of bathing your baby does not necessarily need to be added to your daily routine just yet. The fact that you need to work around your newborn's drying-up umbilical cord stump actually gives you a bit of a "break-in" period—giving you a good reason to get used to sponge baths before trying your hand at more frequent and full-fledged baths. After all, it can be daunting and challenging to handle a slippery bundle of body parts that don't follow directions. As you get the hang of giving your baby a bath and no longer have to accommodate a crusty old umbilical cord, we hope you'll find that it becomes a less stressful and more enjoyable activity for everyone involved.

To Bathe or Not to Bathe

Contrary to popular belief, babies do not need to be bathed every day—especially as newborns. As we enter parenthood, we should all consider ourselves fortunate that we are given a few months in which to become comfortable with our baby-bathing duties before our children effectively figure out how to make themselves truly messy. It's really not until babies start crawling around in dirt, sandboxes, or even just on the kitchen floor (depending on how dirty yours is), and begin to explore baby foods—routinely ending up with more smeared on their faces than in their mouths—that they warrant frequent full-body washes. Until then, however, you have the practical option of focusing your attention on a relatively limited number of parts. Your primary area of focus predictably will be the diaper area—and, of course, the surrounding areas, the size of which will depend on whether your baby has taken to having blowouts (see "What Goes In Must Come Out" on page 59). Other areas to pay particular attention to: around the mouth and anywhere there are skin folds. While some of you may be looking at your newborn and thinking to yourself that there are few, if any, skin folds to be found—rest assured that they will soon appear. The present-from-birth and all-too-often-neglected armpit and groin folds are likely to be joined in mere weeks by double chins and thigh folds. If you make a habit of regularly spot-checking these hot spots and cleaning them as needed using a wet washcloth, you really won't have to bathe your baby every single day. In fact, bathing a couple of times a week is often enough. With that as a lead in, it's high time we move on to the practical details involved in achieving cleanliness for all.

The Bathing Part

Tub Timing

When it comes to deciding when during the day is best to sit down (or kneel or bend over) and give your baby a bath, it is simply a matter of personal preference and convenience. From a practical viewpoint, we suggest you consider timing your baby's baths around your work schedules, your baby's sleep schedule, your own bathing schedule, or before or after feeding (although if you do it after, you may want to wait awhile to let the contents in your baby's belly settle a bit and allow any spitting up, peeing, or pooping to happen preferably beforehand). One time-tested tip we have to offer you is that babies really do respond well to routines, and while you don't need to cling to a set schedule at all costs—there's definitely nothing wrong with accommodating a trip out of the house or visiting guests—over time you and your newborn are likely to benefit from a comfortable routine. Our personal favorite, and one we highly recommend starting sooner rather than later: offer breast or bottle first, follow this with a relaxing warm bath, and then take a few moments of cozy time curled up with a good book and your baby on your lap before bedtime.

Conditioning

This is not a reference to conditioning of your baby's hair (if, in fact, he has any, which we will address later), but rather conditioning newborns to water in general—the look, sound, and feel of water splashing around.

While there are certainly several bath-time safety measures we will address that you'll want to educate yourself about, you need not be timid about occasionally getting water in your baby's eyes or ears. Newborns are fully capable of blinking away splashed or even a bit of poured water. And to tell you the truth, few seem to actually mind it. That's why we have become convinced that there is such a thing as being too careful about splashing around newborns. From what we've seen, babies who grow up without ever being splashed with a few drops here and there, hearing the sound of the shower spraying, or getting a bit of water in their face every now and then are more likely to grow into toddlers who are afraid of water, put up a fight at bath time, and struggle through hair washing.

WATER IN THE EARS

As far as ears are concerned, your baby's ear canals dead-end at the eardrum (as do your own). What this means for bathing purposes: Water is conveniently blocked from getting into the middle ear. It also means that having a little water in one's ear canals every now and then doesn't cause middle ear infections (otitis media) and may even help keep them clean of wax.

Stocking the Deck

If you buy into our philosophy of parenting preparedness, a good portion of the thought you put into bath time will be in the form of forethought. It's important to have anything and everything you think you'll need within arm's reach before getting down to business. Never leave your baby alone in the bath even for a minute to get supplies, answer the telephone or doorbell, or any other reason. Whether the "deck" is the edge of your bathtub or the counter next to the kitchen or bathroom sink, you'll want to come equipped with the bath-time supplies you're going to need before, during, and after. Some of the more useful supplies to have on hand include

- **Water.** Seem obvious? Of course you need water, but we suggest you make a habit of filling whatever tub you choose to use *before* putting your baby in it. In general, we've found that a water level in the tub of about 3 or 4 inches is easiest to work with—full enough to get the job done but not so full that you (or your baby) are going to make waves.

You may also find that limiting the amount of water you put in the tub will make your number one job of keeping your baby's head above water logistically easier.

- **Soap and shampoo.** Washing your baby with plain water is fine, so long as you remember to adequately rub and rinse problem areas (the notorious diaper zone and skin folds). Many parents, however, opt for a foamier form of cleaning, in which case there are plenty of baby soaps, body washes, and shampoo from which you can choose.

- **Washcloth (or two).** We have found many an adult is unaccustomed to using a washcloth in his or her daily self-hygiene regimen. This is the reason we thought we would state what may be obvious to others of you: Washcloths are quite useful for sponge baths and baths alike. We like to use them wet for cleaning and dry for wiping off.

- **Towel (or two).** It's pretty safe to say that no one likes to step out of a warm bath or shower into the cold air. Babies are no exception. In fact, they are often the most vocal about their dislikes, and you're likely to be met with considerably more enthusiasm if you plan for your newborn's quick escape from the tub to a warm, dry towel. Feel free to use the cute little hooded baby towels if you are so inclined, or simply opt for a regular bath towel. We should point out that for newborn babies, many parents find adult-sized towels more difficult to work with for wrapping purposes than the custom-sized baby towels—just too much towel to work with and considerably more towel than you actually need. Other than that, we suggest you go with your intuition and use towels that are soft, absorbent, and cozy. Remember that if you're going to be laying your baby on a towel during a sponge bath, you'll definitely want to have a second one designated for drying off.

- **Moisturizer.** Despite the fact that most newborns have dry, peeling skin, most of them, if not all, don't need moisturizers. In fact, some moisturizers are likely to cause rashes when applied to the sensitive skin of a newborn. That said, if it makes you feel better to apply a moisturizing cream, ointment, or lotion to your baby's skin, don't hesitate to discuss with your pediatrician which ones are best. In general, it's thought to be best to use moisturizers that are hypoallergenic. When it comes to effectiveness, sticky, oil-based moisturizers tend to get the job done better than those that are water-based (see also "The Drying Effect of Water" on page 139).

- **Diapering supplies.** Remember that it is a newborn's prerogative to poop wherever and whenever they feel like it, and you may well be met with a mess just before or after putting your baby in the tub. Coming to the tub prepared means coming with baby wipes, a clean diaper (or two in case of diapering mishaps), and any diapering supplies you typically use.

- **Change of clothes.** Your newborn is likely to appreciate any extra effort you make to get her out of her damp towel and into a clean diaper and warm, dry clothes because we have yet to find a newborn who likes to lie around naked, especially when wet.

Bathing Around the Cord

Having to avoid getting your baby's umbilical cord stump wet is going to be a short-lived nuisance, because dried-up cords typically fall off within the first 2 to 4 weeks. To the best of our knowledge, there's no serious medical reason why you need to keep your newborn's umbilical cord stump 100% dry at all costs—there's no direct connection to anywhere and nothing to panic over if you should accidentally get it wet. What we can tell you, however, is that cords usually need to dry up before they fall off, and wet cord stumps can be quite messy and gooey: in other words, an all-around general nuisance. With that in mind, most parents find it easiest to stick to sponge baths until the momentous day of cord detachment arrives.

 PRELUDE TO A BATH

If your newborn is still the proud owner of a pesky little umbilical cord stump, has a healing circumcision, or even just for those days when you don't quite have it left in you to fit a full bath into your routine, you'll find that sponge baths make for a great alternative. With your baby lying on a towel spread out on a flat surface or placed in a baby bathtub with or without a little bit of water at the bottom, simply take a warm, damp sponge or washcloth, add a little bath wash if you like, and then gently dab or wipe—targeting especially those areas in most need of cleaning. Rinse with a clean, wet sponge or washcloth; follow up with a dry towel or washcloth; and voila—squeaky clean.

The Technique

Whether you choose to bathe your baby in an infant tub, bathtub, shower, or sink, here are some practical principles common to all.

- **Full support.** Once you've gotten yourself and your baby situated and your supplies ready, you'll likely find it easiest to use your nondominant arm and hand to support your baby's head and back as needed (eg, use your left hand for support if you're right-handed). By reaching behind/ under your baby and then holding on to his opposite arm throughout the bath, you will help to ensure that he will have your unwavering support, while you will still have your preferred/more functional hand free for cleaning. Using a plastic cup, washcloth, tub sprayer, or your free hand, you can then wet your baby's body from the head down with clean warm water.
- **Heads down.** When you work from the top down, it helps keep areas that were already rinsed clean from getting soapy again.

- **Focus on the face.** Wipe your baby's face with a clean, wet washcloth, using the corner of it to also clean the outer part of the ear and behind the ear.
- **Hair it is.** If your baby has any hair and you think it actually warrants washing, then add a small amount of all-purpose baby wash or shampoo to your palm or a washcloth and rub it into your baby's hair. When rinsing, simply tilt your baby's head back slightly to avoid getting soap or shampoo into his eyes or ears.
- **Lift and separate.** Remember to lift and separate as best you can any folds in your baby's neck, armpits, and groin.
- **Soap talk.** If you're going to use a mild soap or baby wash, put a small amount on the washcloth or your hand and gently rub it onto your baby's body from the neck down. For safety's sake, we highly recommend keeping your holding hand soap-free to prevent a slippery situation. If you get soap on your baby's hands, try to rinse them off fairly quickly before your baby decides he wants to rub his eyes or chew on his fingers.
- **Bend at the knees.** As you finish up, carefully hoist your baby out of the tub or basin without putting too much strain on your back. By bending at the knees and hips, or situating yourself comfortably on a stool or chair (or toilet, depending on the configuration of your bathroom), you can avoid unnecessary aches and pains.
- **No hands-free options.** For safety's sake, always keep at least one hand and both eyes on your baby (see "Undivided Attention" on page 140).

It's a Wrap
Especially if you are bathing your baby solo, you'll definitely want to have a towel set out within arm's reach before you start.

- **The lap wrap.** When you're ready to take your baby out of the tub, lay a towel across your lap or other firm surface (a plastic baby bathtub works well, assuming you didn't use it for the actual bath). Then carefully grasp your baby under the arms and support her head as you place her on her back just to one side of the center of the towel. Quickly flip the longer side over her, bringing the shorter end of the towel up around and under the back of her head, and then pat her skin dry.

- **The upright wrap.** Try holding your baby's towel vertically against your chest with part of it hanging just over your shoulder. Pick up your baby carefully and hold her up against your chest. Wrap her by bringing the bottom of the towel up over her feet and legs. Once you get comfortable with the technique, you can hold your baby against your chest facing outward, bring the towel up under her chin, and then use the excess cloth draped over your shoulder as a bath hood. You may find this technique easier to master while sitting down, although standing is also OK if you're comfortable with it. Once you've done the quick wrap and dry, you can move your bundle to a more convenient location to safely finish diapering and dressing.

THE DRYING EFFECT OF WATER

The fact that water itself can dry out the skin—yours and your baby's—
may come as a surprise, but it's true. The drying effect takes place when
wet skin is exposed to air and the moisture subsequently evaporates or
is rubbed off. You can counteract this drying effect by simply bathing your
infant less frequently, patting dry with a towel instead of providing a complete
post-bath rub-down, and applying a moisturizer to skin while it is still damp—
a technique which is thought to help lock moisture in the skin. Most
pediatricians will tell you to avoid the use of lotions, creams, and ointments
for dry newborn skin during the first month or so because baby skin tends
to be quite sensitive. If your young infant has dry, flaky skin, try your best to
ignore it and allow it to run its course (normally about a month).

Have Tub Will Travel

Baby bathtubs are quite popular these days, and you will undoubtedly have
plenty to choose from—from rigid, to inflatable, to collapsible and from
sponge-like to those made of soft or hard plastic. While it is entirely possible to live without a baby bathtub, most parents find them quite practical,
not to mention relatively inexpensive and multipurpose.

- They allow you to bathe your newborn on a counter, on the floor, in a
  sink, or in the bathtub (the tub-within-a-tub technique)—basically,
  wherever you are most comfortable.
- Even after your baby graduates from baths in the baby bathtub, it can
  still prove itself useful as a towel wrapping station or as a safe place to
  set your wet or towel-wrapped baby after a bath.
- Once you become comfortable with the nuts and bolts of baby bathing,
  you may decide to take baths or showers with your baby—a somewhat
  risky business (see "Caution: Slippery When Wet" below) but cases in
  which baby bathtubs prove to be very logistically convenient, safe, and
  waterproof places to set babies before, during, and after.

Caution: Slippery When Wet

It is definitely not our nature to scare new parents. Instead, we want to
introduce and reinforce a few simple but extremely important bath-time
safety measures that will keep you and your baby from getting in over your
heads. It probably goes without saying that the reason bathing an infant

can sometimes seem like a daunting prospect is because there are some definite (albeit avoidable) risks involved. It's hard to miss the fact that babies are slippery when wet, much less ignore the occasional evening news story about an infant or child being unintentionally scalded or drowning unattended in mere inches of water. The good news is that most childhood injuries in general are preventable, and those related to bathing are no exception. In the committed spirit of tub safety, there are several hard-and-fast rules well worth committing to memory and putting into practice from day 1.

Hot Tubs

- **It's a matter of degree.** The ideal bath water temperature is thought to be somewhere between 95°F and 100°F, while water warmer than 105°F is considered to be too hot and cooler than 90°F too cold. In contrast, many water heaters are installed at 140°F to 150°F. *At 140°F, it only takes 3 seconds for a child to get a third-degree burn.* Before you christen your baby's tub, we suggest you pay a quick visit to your water heater and make sure that the upper temperature limit is set no higher than 120°F—a temperature at which you should be able to hold your hand under a running stream of hot water without getting burned. While most parents have heard this advice at least once, very few actually follow through. We suggest you make yourself one who does.

- **Fill 'er up first.** Run the bath water first. Turn off the water, and *then* put your baby in it. Having water flowing directly into the tub when your baby is already in it is an unnecessary risk because the temperature of running water can be inconsistent and hot water controls can be bumped.

- **Know what your baby's getting into.** Make it a habit to always test your baby's bath water on your own skin (preferably on a more sensitive area such as your wrist or elbow) *before* putting your baby in it. That way you'll be sure to know exactly what you're both getting into.

Undivided Attention

Regardless of how much or how little water you have in your newborn's bathtub, you'll need to offer him at least one hand of support at all times and ideally keep 2 eyes focused on the task at hand.

CHAPTER 13

clothing and accessories

The Big Picture

We all tend to have one thing in common as parents when it comes to baby clothes. Whether you're the type of parent who is looking forward to shopping for baby clothes or you happen to have very little interest in infant clothing beyond having it fit and adequately serve its purpose, you will inevitably dole out a sizable amount of money on your child's wardrobe. For a glimpse of the big picture, consider that the average parent in the United States spends an estimated $10,000 to $15,000 to outfit his or her children—an amount that equals 6% to 8% of the total estimated cost of raising a child to the age of 17.

This chapter is especially meant for those of you who haven't had much, if any, experience outfitting and dressing infants prior to becoming a parent. Even if you have picked out baby apparel as gifts for other people's children before, let us just say that you're likely to find that you take a hugely different approach once you're faced with choosing (and paying for) your own infant's attire.

Learning the Layette of the Land

We wanted first to include a basic run-down of what's available in the world of baby wear and help you get a sense of what your baby might realistically need in the days and weeks ahead. The term layette itself comes from the French word for drawer or trunk and, technically speaking, it describes a baby's full clothing wardrobe, bedding, and accessories. Nowadays, the term is actually used much more loosely. You'll find that newborn sleeper gowns are sometimes called layette gowns, and many manufacturers market coordinated sets of baby clothing—often accompanied by matching accessories (such as hats, booties, and blankets)—as layettes. These coordinated set versions of a layette are especially useful as a quick gift. While there's no reason you can't buy some for your own baby if they catch your eye, be aware that you'll probably pay a premium for items you could most likely purchase individually for less.

With that in mind, here is a description of some of the more commonly found items in the baby clothing department, and our opinion on their usefulness.

ONESIES DEFINED

As far as we know, credit for the term Onesies goes to Gerber, the baby product manufacturing company that first used it to describe their baby undershirts that snap at the crotch. Just as many other brand names—Kleenex, Xerox, and Coke to name a few—seem to have taken on lives of their own, Onesie is often used generically to describe all brands of snapping undershirts, and sometimes even entire 1-piece outfits (which we consider to be more accurately called rompers when worn as outdoor wear or sleepers when used for nightwear).

- **Undershirt Onesies.** These are handy in cooler weather as undershirts during the day and at night, and can also double as stand-alone outfits in warmer weather. Some look quite a bit like undershirts, while others are fancier and come in a variety of colors or complete with patterns. We suggest using the same rule of thumb as many adults do when buying themselves underwear: Buy enough to last you at least as long as it will take you to do laundry…and then buy a few extra for good measure.

- **Pajamas/sleepers.** While your baby is still young, you may find that you don't venture out of the house all that often, and even when you do, dressing your baby in sleepwear (as opposed to a fancy outfit) is not only convenient, but also socially acceptable. Most parents of newborns don't end up making much of a distinction between their babies' daytime and nighttime outfits. If you plan on using sleepers as your baby's primary clothing, then we again suggest you take into account leaky diapers, spitting up, and other common mishaps when calculating how many to buy.

- **Sleep sacks and gowns.** Sleep sacks typically zip up the middle and look like long- or short-sleeved shirts at the top and sleeping bags at the bottom. Gowns are similar but often come in lighter weight material— sometimes with buttons instead of zippers up the front and often with an open elasticized bottom. Either type can prove useful in the early weeks for easy access, for keeping your baby covered if you would rather not use a baby blanket, or if your baby repeatedly wiggles out from underneath her covers.

- **Socks.** There's not a whole lot of enlightening information to share with you about baby socks that you don't already know from your own sock experiences, so we'll just point out a few quick considerations. When you do go shopping for baby socks, consider how many of your own socks you lose over the course of a few months. Then picture them smaller and with a much greater tendency to disappear or fall off tiny feet and you'll realize why we suggest buying quite a few. If you find that you like using them under (or even over) pajamas and footed outfits in addition to covering bare feet, then add a few more to your shopping list. Until your baby starts walking, you won't need to search for no-skid bottoms, but you will want to make sure you buy socks that are well elasticized to minimize how many fall off and get lost.

AN OUTFIT A DAY...

...is rarely enough for most babies. If you buy baby clothes with the expectation that your newborn will only wear one a day, then we predict that you will be doing laundry very frequently. What with spit-up and leaky diapers alone, you may find yourself going through at least 2 (if not 3 or maybe 4) outfits on any given day.

Size Matters

After preemie and newborn sizes, just about all baby clothes come with relatively age-specific size labels starting with 0 to 3 months and continuing up in 3-month increments throughout the first year. This approach to sizing seems very straightforward—until you actually have a child of your own and start putting the labels to the test. You'll quickly find that one manufacturer's idea of newborn doesn't always match another's, and that many newborns don't fit in newborn-sized clothing at all. Some may fit into size 0 to 3 months from day 1 and size 3 to 6 months within weeks of being born. While it's theoretically possible to take a baby into a fitting room and try clothes on to see if they fit, the thought of actually doing so is fairly comical and we have yet to meet someone who has ever done it! If you want to come away with a few practical pieces of sizing advice, we suggest you consider the following:

- If a label reads 3 to 6 months, an average-sized baby is more likely to fit in it around 3 months of age so we don't recommend holding your breath for it to fit at 6 months of age.
- Look for tags that offer weight and height guidelines as well as age ranges.
- Remember that sizing varies by brand. Just as with adult clothing, some brands run big and others run small. Once you become familiar with one or several brands, you'll have an easier time gauging what size your baby needs relative to the specific brand.

SUPERSIZING

Right from the start, you'll discover that you're able to get longer wear out of your baby's clothes if you supersize them—or, in other words, buy big. Onesies are well suited for being worn big, especially if you use them as undershirts because there's no law that says they have to fit perfectly. Well-elasticized cuffs at the wrists and ankles of rompers, shirts, and leggings help keep sleeves and pant legs from hanging way over your baby's feet and/or hands, allowing him several inches' worth of room to grow (which translates into extra months' worth of wear). Outfits or pants with attached footies can also be worn big if you simply put socks over the footies—a simple but ingenious way to keep your baby's feet snugly inside them.

Profiles in Color

As a quick comment on color, we suggest you give some brief thought to whether you consider yourself color casual or a color conformist before buying a lot of clothes for your baby. If it's all the same to you, then you may as well limit the number of outfits you buy in baby blue and pastel pink in favor of more gender-neutral colors (pastel yellows and greens and primary colors)—especially if you don't know whether you're having a boy or a girl (or if you intend to have more children and hope to use your baby clothes more than once). On the other hand, if gender-neutral clothing is unappealing to you and the mere thought of an onlooker mistakenly referring to your baby boy as a beautiful little girl horrifies you, then you may be better off opting for the more gender-definitive pinks or blues.

Principles of Practicality

Think back to your pre-parenting days and the last time (if ever) you purchased a cute little baby outfit. Did you opt for one with cute little ribbons? Splurge on matching dress shoes or the color-coordinated hair bow (which, on a side note, we have decided should more appropriately be called a head bow because most babies are significantly lacking in actual hair)? Well, many of these eye-catching features may be cute, but also tend to be impractical. We're not by any means saying that we haven't succumbed to temptation and bought adorable but inconvenient outfits for our own infants, or that there's no place for them in your baby's closet. As you find yourself faced with the reality of day-in and day-out dressing, not to mention coping with changing weather, frequent diaper changes, and even more frequent washings, you are likely to find that practicality is a priority. With that in mind, in the spirit of practicality, here are several fundamental principles to consider.

Easy Access

It's exceedingly easy to disregard the access factor the first couple of times you set out to buy clothes for your baby, but the moment you're faced with dressing and undressing your baby several times a day—including as a result of the middle-of-the-night blowouts (you know, the occasional explosions that defy even the most absorbent and well-secured diapers)—you'll instantly gain a new appreciation for easy access.

- **One piece or two.** There are definitely benefits to both 1- and 2-piece outfits. In terms of easy-on, easy-off, many parents find that 2-piece outfits are more convenient. This is especially true for those late-night diaper changes that end up requiring a full wardrobe change. Once you've tried to remove a soiled 1-piece outfit over your baby's head without making more of a mess, you too may decide to go for 2 pieces instead of 1. A benefit of 1-piece outfits is the fact that they involve, by definition, fewer pieces to coordinate. One-piece outfits also generally keep babies more reliably covered. Bottom line on 1 versus 2: personal preference prevails.
- **Zippers, snaps, and Velcro.** These are generally easier to do than buttons—especially in the middle of the night or when you're on the go.

 ZIPPITY DOO OW!

If you think it hurts to zip your own skin, think about how you'll feel if you accidentally zip your *baby's* skin. Get into the habit of lifting the fabric and zipper away from the skin while zipping up or down. To be extra careful, we recommend putting your fingers under the zipper whenever you zip.

Newborn Dressing for the Beginner

If you haven't had any experience holding and handling babies before, it's quite understandable that figuring how to get arms and legs going in the right direction while properly supporting your newborn's head and getting everything snapped and secured may take some practice. We've come across enough new parents who are embarrassed to admit they aren't comfortable dressing their babies that we decided to include this step-by-step tutorial on the subject.

1. **Positioning.** Lay your baby down on her back, as if you're going to change her diaper.
2. **Head support.** Gently put one hand behind her head and neck for support.

3. **Over the head.** With your other hand, put the neck opening over your baby's head and gently pull the clothing down over her head and your supporting arm. Then let her head rest on the changing area while you remove your arm from underneath.

4. **Limbs.** One by one, guide each arm through the armholes. For sleepers and rompers with zippers or snaps down one leg, it is generally easiest to put the leg in the side without the zipper/snaps in first (because it tends to be a tighter fit) and then put the other leg in.

5. **Securing.** Fasten any zippers, snaps, or buttons. If you've chosen an outfit with back snaps or buttons, consider picking your baby up against your shoulder or laying her on her belly to access them.

🧺 REMOVING SOILED ONESIES 🔍 WITHOUT ADDING INSULT TO INJURY

If you find yourself faced with a massive blowout—the kind where poop is up your baby's back and onto his clothes—we suggest you first place your baby on a towel, changing table, or disposable pad. Next, put a washcloth, wipe, or paper towel against the area of dirty skin and leave it there. Roll up the soiled piece of clothing so that the mess is well contained inside, away from your hands. Then carefully remove each of your baby's arms and lift the rolled-up outfit over your baby's head. For some outfits, you may actually find it easier to pull the clothes down over your baby's waist and legs instead of up and over. Once undressed and having done your best to minimize the mess, you can finish cleaning and redressing your disrobed baby.

Comfort Is Key

It shouldn't come as a surprise to you that your newborn is just as likely as you are to appreciate soft fabrics and well-designed clothes that don't scratch, poke, twist, or irritate when worn. On the surface, decorative collars, frills, bows, and lace can definitely add to the appeal of an outfit, but cute isn't always what it's cut out to be. Be sure to consider whether added frills might get in the way or, worse yet, irritate your baby's skin. Additionally, the more ornate an outfit is, the more challenging it will probably be to clean.

Keeping Hands Covered

Newborn outfits often have fold-over sleeves that allow parents to keep their babies' hands covered during the period when infants have a disconcerting tendency to scratch themselves on the face with tiny yet rapidly growing fingernails (a problem we'll cover in more detail in "Head to Toe and in Between" on page 221). Their usefulness is generally limited, however, to the first couple of months at most. Once your baby begins to try using her hands and gains control of the flailing movements typical of her first few weeks, you'll definitely want to uncover her hands and let her explore.

Safety Considerations

You'll want to always take safety into account when choosing baby clothes. Fortunately, there aren't too many hazards lurking out there when it comes to baby clothing, and there is an organization called the CPSC (Consumer Product Safety Commission, www.cpsc.gov) that provides safety standards for clothing (as well as other consumer products) and issues recalls for potentially unsafe items. In addition to identifying specific products as potentially unsafe, we've listed below some good general baby clothing safety considerations.

- **At sleep.** Sleepwear for babies should fit snugly, as any loose material may cause tangling or suffocation. Pajamas usually come with a flame-resistant or flame-retardant finish, but check the labels to be sure.
- **No strings attached.** Simply put, anything in which a baby could potentially become entangled is best left on the rack. While prevention measures have made it far less likely to find potentially dangerous outfits in the stores, items with strings or large, loose hoods should be carefully scrutinized before purchase. The CPSC recommends that no strings whatsoever be used in the neck or hood region and advises shortened drawstrings (measuring no more than 3 extra inches at either end) at the waist.
- **Loose object liability.** Get in the habit of evaluating baby clothes for small and potentially removable objects. The most obvious, of course, are buttons. It's amazing how many small 3-dimensional objects you can find attached to baby clothing in the name of fashion these days. If it isn't securely fastened, be sure to avoid or remove anything your child could choke on should it come loose.

Cleaning Baby Clothes

Washability is definitely something to consider. Be sure to look at the labels not only for size information but also for washing instructions. Unless you relish the thought of hand-washing a lot of baby clothes and frequently replacing those that don't hold up well, we suggest you give some serious thought to the durability and washability of the baby clothes you buy—especially your baby's everyday outfits, Onesies, and sleepers.

- **Washing.** Because newborns tend to have sensitive skin (and because you don't know who has handled the clothing and with what before it made its way into your possession), it's generally a good idea to wash all clothes prior to using them. An exception might be outerwear such as coats and jackets that don't have much contact with the skin (and tend not to wash and dry easily). As a helpful hint, consider putting small items such as socks in a mesh bag for washing and drying and remember to fasten any Velcro tabs (such as on bibs) to avoid snagging other clothes.

- **Detergents.** It is a common recommendation that baby clothes should be washed separately, using special "baby" detergents that supposedly leave fewer residues and are therefore less likely to cause skin irritation. In reality, we've found that many if not most parents simply toss their baby's clothes in with the rest of the family's laundry without causing any problems. That said, it is worth paying attention to the fact that detergents in general don't strip away the flame-retardant properties of sleepwear, but soap flakes can. Given that information, you can choose your detergent as we do—buy one that smells good and gets the dirt out, and only consider a milder "baby" detergent (or hypoallergenic/fragrance-free "adult" detergent) if your baby develops any signs of skin irritation.

- **Stain removal.** The best approach to managing stains made by breast milk, formula, spit-up, or poop is to try wiping or rinsing off the offending substance as much as you can while it's still relatively fresh. We realize that this may be easier said than done—especially if you find yourself in the middle of a diaper change or feeding with a clothing stain that is settling itself in for the long haul—but if you can remove even some of it with a baby wipe or soak the clothes in some water and detergent, you'll be glad you did. We also suggest stocking your laundry room with a good stain remover and designating a place for soaking stained or soiled clothing.

NEW MOMS DON'T WEAR SILK

OK, so maybe some do, but as for us, we sure stuck to plaid (flannel pajamas, that is); sweats; and other practical, comfortable, easily washed, no ironing or dry cleaning required clothes for several months after our babies were born. We have put together our own quick list of things to consider and watch for when laying out your own new-parent attire so that you too will be dressed for success.

Dress like your baby. Especially during this time when you're spending most of your waking (and non-waking) hours tending to your newborn, we highly recommend choosing soft, comfortable clothing over frills and fancy duds. As you make your selections, remember to keep an eye out for inopportunely placed zippers, buckles, snaps, or any other adult clothing accessories that could end up scratching, poking, or irritating your baby. And remember, unless you want to devote extra time, attention, and money to keeping your own clothes stain-free and clean, we strongly suggest adding "machine washable and dryable" to your own clothing checklist.

Easy access. This is especially applicable to you breastfeeding moms. Whether you opt for specially designed (and accordingly priced) breastfeeding attire or simply a loose-fitting shirt and an accommodating bra is up to you, but it's a safe bet you'll find yourself more at ease with your new role if you aren't at the same time wrestling with your wardrobe.

Comfort. We can't emphasize this enough: Make yourself comfortable. Now is not the time to worry about snapping up pants and zipping up jeans if drawstrings or elastic waistbands feel better.

Personal style. Bottom line advice: Don't expend any more time and effort on pulling your outfits together than you need to to make yourself feel good. Some of us feel just fine about how we're handling new parenthood even as we lounge around for the first few weeks in ponytails, sweats, and T-shirts. Others, we have found, find themselves feeling further removed from the life they used to lead and more like they aren't rising to the challenge of new parenthood unless they get up and make themselves outwardly presentable. Either way, whatever works for you, wear it!

As Good as New

Having told you it's a good idea to wash your baby's clothes before using them, let us point out one important caveat. Instead of washing them all well in advance (which many parents do before their babies are even born), we suggest you wash a couple and leave the tags on the rest until you are ready to use them. By getting into this habit, as well as keeping all your baby-clothing receipts in a convenient place, it will be easier for you to return those you end up not using. Believe us when we tell you that there's probably not a parent out there who hasn't bemoaned the number of outfits that have gone unworn in their baby's closet. Even if you're not able to return or exchange an outfit at the store where you bought it, unused clothing that have their tags still on retain a significantly higher value at resale or consignment shops, on eBay, when donating to charity, or—dare we say it (lest we be perceived as publicly admitting to it)—if you are tempted by the thought of re-gifting.

These Shoes Weren't Made for Walking

Because most babies don't walk before their first birthdays, you may be wondering why one might need shoes as an infant. The fact of the matter is that you really don't. Until your baby reaches the point where she's pulling up to a standing position (which probably seems impossible to imagine at this point), the only reasons we can come up with for needing shoes are to keep socks in place, help keep feet warm, and look good in pictures (if you or your family consider bare baby feet to be unacceptable in an otherwise "formal" portrait). If you do decide to buy shoes for your newborn, we suggest soft, roomy ones that are easy to put on and allow for plenty of wiggle room without falling off.

CHAPTER 14

taking care of yourself

Have you ever noticed that flight attendants routinely recommend that adults traveling with small children take a moment to strap on their own oxygen masks first before tending to their child(ren) when faced with a loss of cabin pressure? Well not unlike this standard announcement, we make a point of telling all new parents we encounter (which now includes you) that you shouldn't expect to do a perfectly wonderful job of tending to someone else's needs (namely, your newborn) if you completely neglect your own. We're not suggesting regular days at the spa and weekly pedicures here (although we think one of the all-time best presents to receive as a new mother is a gift certificate for a relaxing massage). No, we're talking the basics—as in hygiene, food, and sleep. While we're well aware of the fact that many of the take-home messages we've included in this chapter have been said before (including several suggested elsewhere within this very book), we think they're worth drawing your attention to as much more than side comments or afterthoughts in the grand scheme of newborn parenting.

Tending to Your Own Activities of Daily Living

Try to allot time for your own activities of daily living, not the least of which include such seemingly simple tasks as brushing your teeth, bathing or showering, and getting dressed in the morning. Those of you who have yet to have your babies may be laughing at this advice and wondering "how hard could the completion of such basic tasks possibly be?" We are quite confident in telling you that we are not the only ones who found ourselves routinely going on upwards of 36 hours with bad breath, wearing the same clothes, and in need of much more than a quick deodorant application. Unless you sincerely don't mind sitting around in pajamas all day with fuzzy teeth, attending to your own basic hygiene each day, getting a bit of fresh air, and offering yourself a change of scenery or a little extra time to do some grooming every now and then in lieu of housekeeping or doing dishes, for example, often works wonders in helping new parents feel accomplished and in control.

Supplying Yourself With the Strength to Carry On

It's unreasonable for you to expect yourself to keep up with the pace of new parenthood without providing yourself with adequate nourishment, regardless of whether you're asking your body to nourish your newborn as a breastfeeding mom. Anything you can do in the early weeks (if not months) to make mealtime easier and less effort-intensive, the better. If you don't exactly have someone volunteering to do all your grocery shopping, prepare you gourmet meals, and bring you breakfast in bed, we highly recommend considering the following time-savers:

- **Hydrate.** Remembering to actually sit down and drink can be a bit of a new-mom challenge. We recommend building this necessary habit into your daily routine by simply grabbing a bottle of water or drinking a glass of whatever healthy fluid you choose each time you sit down to feed your baby. Now we're not saying that you can't indulge in your caffeinated and/or alcoholic drink of choice every now and then, but when it comes to keeping well hydrated (especially as a breastfeeding mom), you'll be better served by keeping a good stock of water, milk, and juices close at hand.

- **Splurge.** Whether splurging means buying more prepared foods (fresh or frozen) or indulging in take-out (better yet, home-delivered) meals, it's entirely possible to do so without overindulging in a lot of fried fast foods. You most likely will pay a bit more, but you may also find it seems like a small price to pay for the convenience of getting the tasks of food shopping and preparation off your plate.

- **Stock up.** Accept and even suggest the gift of freeze-and-heat casseroles or other premade meals from friends and well-wishers. If no one is offering and you have not yet had your baby, then now is the ideal time for you to prepare a few (dozen) of your own. It's also useful to keep plenty of relatively healthy "adult" snacks around the house, as well as having them available to take with you if and when you find yourself on the go (see "Thinking Outside of the House" on page 159).

- **Streamline.** Consider using disposable (or very easy to clean) plates and utensils whenever possible, and try to enlist the help of others to take over any preparation and cleanup involved, regardless of how much or little there is to do to get meals on and off the table.

In Search of Sleep

Getting rest is a great way to help your outlook on life, not to mention your physical condition and general sense of well-being. It is therefore an unfortunate and sometimes even painful fact of new parenthood that getting an 8-hour stretch of sleep quickly becomes a distant memory and your nights will undoubtedly be interrupted for the next few months. Nevertheless, we want to reassure you that it is possible to compensate, at least to a certain extent.

- **Get your priorities straight.** Start by making sleep a priority—ranking well above entertaining and doing dishes or housework—on your to-do list.
- **Partners in sleep.** Make every attempt to follow the age-old adage to sleep when your baby sleeps. Granted it's not going to be 8 hours at a time, but then again, beggars shouldn't be choosers. Besides, it's amazing how good it can feel to get an extra hour or two of sleep when you're functioning under conditions of relative sleep deprivation.
- **Set the mood.** If you're the type of person who can sleep anytime, anywhere if you're tired enough, then you can skip this tip. For the rest of us who need peace and quiet to fall (and stay) asleep, do whatever you can to create a sleep-conducive setting for yourself, whether it's simply finding a quiet room with a door you can shut while someone else takes over baby duty for a while or investing in light-blocking shades.

PART IV

thinking outside of the house

Looking for a Way Out

Having a new baby around the house tends to make even the most routine of pre-parenthood tasks require a bit more forethought. Many of you will find yourselves perfectly content to head home and remain there until you feel you've mastered the primary new-parent challenges of feeding (yourself and your newborn), sleeping, diapering, clothing, and maintaining a healthy state of household hygiene, to name but a few. Don't be surprised if homeward bound starts to feel just that—a bit binding. Looking at the same 4 walls has a way of making some new parents start to get a little stir crazy, leaving them longing to get out of the house—somewhere, anywhere, just out. Whether you decide to venture out of the comfort zone of your own home early on or weeks down the road, of your own free will or out of necessity, and with or without your newborn in tow, we wanted to put together a set of basic considerations to help you feel properly prepared.

Dressing for the Occasion

Yes, your baby's relatively large head is a surefire source for heat loss. No, you shouldn't take your baby out of the house without bundling him appropriately. And no, you won't want to venture out and expose your newborn to direct sunlight. Before you spend all your time memorizing the endless "don'ts" involved in stepping out, we suggest you focus on a few general wardrobe issues and pieces of advice. By becoming familiar with and then applying them, you will significantly reduce the number of "don'ts" you need to commit to memory before safely and comfortably exposing your newborn to the outside world.

- **At a loss.** Whether you're headed outdoors or in, your newborn is going to benefit from a covered head for several weeks to come. That's because relative to the rest of their bodies, newborns have impressively large heads—a characteristic that not only makes them completely dependent on parental head support, but also leaves them prone to significant loss of body heat from their uncovered heads.

- **Anticipation.** It's next to impossible to go anywhere and be able to rely on predictable climate control. Regardless of how much faith you have in weather forecasting or the person in charge of the thermostat, your best bet will be to come prepared with several layers of easy-on, easy-off clothing.
- **Overshadowing.** Ideally, you'll want to keep your newborn out of direct sunlight. Additionally, we suggest you provide some guaranteed shade by dressing your baby in a thin layer of clothing even in warm weather.

All Dressed Up but Now Where to Go?

You're certain to find a lot of advice regarding taking your newborn out of the house with you. In reality, there are really only a few basic principles in action here, with the rest tending to be a matter of opinion as opposed to expertise.

- **Less is more.** You are going to be better off if you choose to go to places with fewer people around. Close contact with a lot of people tends to be one of the most predictable hazards when it comes to the spread of germs. Enough said, at least until you reach the "Fever: Trial by Fire" chapter (page 251).
- **An easy out.** Our advice to you—consider starting small when you first leave home. A walk around the block is a great example of a doable first choice (weather and neighborhood permitting). Not only does it tend to be a relaxing way to get back on your feet gradually, but babies often like the soothing motion, you're less likely to find yourself in close quarters fending off unwanted well-wishers, and it leaves you an easy out should you need to abort the mission and retreat back home for any reason—diaper blowout; fatigue (your own); or a hungry, crying, or otherwise unappreciative baby.
- **Overwhelming success.** Heading out of the house can be quite an adventure for a newborn. And depending on your newborn's temperament and tolerance of stimulation in general, you may find yourself with a crankier-than-usual baby at the end of the day. For some newborns, a trip to the grocery store can be like a day spent at the amusement park. Any routine you may be working toward stands a

chance of being thrown off kilter a bit by such stimulation. We by no means want to imply that heading out of the house is the wrong thing to do. Instead, we want you to set your expectations appropriately, test the waters, and plan your approach accordingly. It is entirely possible to end up with an overwhelmed baby but still feel the outing has been a success.

- **Timing your travels.** This is a subject we've addressed specifically as it relates to airplane travel in "Flying the Family-Friendly Skies" on page 189, but it really is a concept you'll want to apply whenever you choose to leave the house—with or without your newborn. Have faith that what now seems like orchestrating a grand production will soon become a routine you fall into.

 IT'S ABOUT TIME

You may increase your odds of being met with success when you head out by taking into account a few time-tested recommendations. They include

Just after a feeding. This doesn't always work, given that we've spent many pages telling about how unpredictably and frequently newborns tend to eat. Nevertheless it's worth a shot.

Off-hours. Go where the crowds aren't, or at least to places at times when it's not as crowded.

When you're well rested. You're probably now thinking this means we recommend no outings in the foreseeable future. To clarify, we don't mean well rested in the pre-parenthood sense of the phrase, but rather in a relative sense. You're bound to have good days/nights and bad ones. We simply suggest giving yourself time to catch up if you've just finished a bad one.

You've got coverage. Venture out when someone can cover for you at home or go along with you and lend a hand with logistics.

Don't Leave Home Without Them

Despite the catchy heading, technically speaking there aren't many items that we consider a must-have before taking your baby out of the house, especially if you're not planning on strolling far from home. There are, however, definitely some useful items we've found best to have on hand,

and others that we feel have earned their characterization as modern-day conveniences. Here are a few thoughts and suggestions for when you're ready to get on the go again.

- **Diapering supplies.** These definitely warrant the recommendation to not leave home without them. It's Murphy's Law of Newborns that if you don't have a diaper within arm's reach, they are guaranteed to poop the first chance they get.

- **Accommodating change (of clothing).** Expect to need at least one complete change of clothing—definitely for your newborn, but quite possibly for yourself as well. Blowouts, leaks, and spills are far less stressful if you've planned ahead.

- **Food for thought.** Newborns don't care how recently they've been fed before setting out on an adventure. The minute you and your newborn step out the door, any semblance of a feeding schedule you may have achieved within the confines of your home has the distinct possibility of flying right out the window. In short, you'll never regret being prepared to feed your baby on the go. With that in mind, we suggest you flip to our "Into the Mouths of Babes" section (page 1) for a more in-depth look at what supplies you might want or need for either feeding option—be it breast or bottle.

- **Baby carriers.** Right off the bat let us tell you that we love baby carriers. They offer new parents a comfy, cozy, baby-friendly, hands-free option. While there are many, many options readily available (including carriers that go in front of you, backpacks that go behind you, and slings), we are going to narrow our discussion a bit to issues that apply specifically to newborns.

  - **Weight limits.** Some baby carriers aren't designed for use by small infants. If you plan on using one early on, double-check the lower weight limit first.

  - **Support.** As we've mentioned elsewhere in this book, babies are born with poor head control and neck support. Be sure to choose an appropriate carrier for your baby's development and motor abilities.

  - **Comfort level.** Not all baby carriers are created equal when it comes to comfort. You'll want to consider ease of use—how comfortable you are strapping it on and putting your baby in it—as well as how comfortable you find the carrier to be. Remember to factor in how much you plan on using the carrier, because some are perfectly comfortable at first but quickly become less so when put to the test by heavyweights.

- **Price points.** Factor in cost to determine if you're getting what you pay for. This really is a personal preference. Some parents consider the more expensive, Cadillac-equivalent baby carriers to be well worth the price they must pay for them—especially if they are easy to use and end up being put to good use. Others find that the more economical models serve their purposes just as well.

- **Strollers.** From the basic umbrella stroller to a top-of-the-line double jogging stroller, parents these days have nearly unlimited options to meet their needs—whether it's transporting your baby in a shopping center, going on a daily jog, or strolling a colicky baby through the hallways of your own home (a "remedy" that, in some parents' minds, even justifies the purchase of an extra stroller specifically for use indoors!). You may ultimately find that having a few different strollers is worthwhile—a lightweight umbrella stroller for quick trips or to use when traveling, a sturdier stroller for outdoor errands, and a jog stroller if you're the athletic type (or want to look or feel the part)—but for the time being, you'll want to narrow your scope a bit and look for newborn-appropriate strollers.

  - **Rate of recline.** In general, newborns need strollers that offer a fair degree of recline because their development does not yet allow them to sit upright and hold their heads high. Some stroller seat backs even recline completely to aid with napping—a feature whose usefulness extends well beyond the first few weeks and months. Most jogging strollers, on the other hand, aren't recommended for use during the first 5 or 6 months because they aren't designed for recline (although some have secure enough harnesses and positioning for younger babies).

  - **Canopies and covers.** Whether it's windy, rainy, or sunny out, some type of stroller canopy is guaranteed to prove useful in protecting your baby from the elements. Some cover more than others, so consider the weather variations in your area. These may also help your baby sleep while in the stroller.

- **Travel systems.** A car seat and stroller may come as a matching set, or a special attachment can allow car seats of various makes to hook on securely to a stroller. Each of these options allows for easy transfer of your baby from car to stroller and back without requiring you to remove her from her seat. If you don't plan on keeping your baby in her car seat while strolling, this option is unnecessary. If you do plan on taking advantage of the convenience of (potentially) uninterrupted slumber in the car seat, just be aware that there is growing concern among experts that allowing infants to spend extended amounts of time in their car seats (and seats in general) may not be good for infants for a variety of reasons. What counts as "extended amounts of time"? Unfortunately, we don't have an answer for you (because there isn't one yet), but we suggest that in addition to never leaving your infant unattended in a child safety seat, you don't get into the habit of relying on it as a prolonged sleep site.

 SIT BACK AND STAY A WHILE

You may find it interesting to know that traditional Chinese and Indian cultures actually dictate that new moms not leave the house for about a month after childbirth. This gives mothers time to slow down and recuperate from childbirth—something that can be healthy for mom and baby (but in our opinion, would lead us to develop a serious case of cabin fever).

Taking Your Own Sweet Time

Now that you've read about the preparation that can help with venturing outside the home, you may actually decide that you're not quite ready to do so. That's OK too. In fact, there may be days where you don't even feel like showering or changing out of sweats or pajamas. If you have the luxury of being able to hang out at home (and perhaps let others come to you), enjoy it while you and your baby can.

Leaving Home Alone

Want to know where I (Laura) went the first time I left home without my newborn when she was only about a week old? Target. Want to know what I needed to get there? Nothing. I, like many new parents, just started to feel a gradually increasing need to get out of the house and get some time to myself—if only for a brief while. Whether you're more likely to be enticed by the thought of a walk in the park than a visit to a nearby retail establishment, we strongly recommend seeing what you can do to make it happen if and when the urge strikes you. Start by finding and enlisting trusted help to take over baby duty and give you a chance to do whatever it is (within reason, of course) that you think will help make you feel like you're not trapped or missing out. You may well find that getting some occasional alone time out of the house is invaluable in refreshing your perspective and outlook on your new life.

CHAPTER 15

car safety

Buckling Up So You Can Enjoy the Ride

Buying an infant car seat has become an integral part of the official entry into parenthood—ranking right up there with getting a prenatal ultrasound and picking out nursery furniture. Knowledge about how to keep our children safe in cars has improved dramatically since our own parents were faced with the same task. After all, we've come a long way from the days when new babies were brought home secured in nothing more than a parent's loving arms. Only a generation ago, parents had to be convinced to even buy a car seat, much less use one, while today few of us would dare leave home without it. As you join the ranks of proud parents, you will inevitably become well acquainted with car seats. Not only are they guaranteed to be part of your everyday parenting routine for many years—long after teething, colic, strollers, and diapers have all come

---

 HOW TIMES HAVE CHANGED

A quick historical look at the evolution of automobile safety may help you understand why there is a generation of grandparents (and even parents) out there who still need to be convinced to buckle up!

1965: Lap belts first required in passenger vehicles
1971: First federal standards for child restraints (car seats)
1973: Lap/shoulder belts required in front seats
1989: Lap/shoulder belts required in both outer positions of the back seat
1996: Phase-in of air bags and requirement that all seat belts come with a locking mechanism
2002: All new vehicles and child seats equipped with universal tethers and anchors—a system referred to as LATCH (more on LATCH at the end of the chapter)

and gone—but making sure your child is always secured properly in a car seat constitutes one of the most important measures you can take to help ensure your child's safety. You may notice that we have temporarily put aside our joking tone a bit in this section—something we did intentionally for the sake of offering you a serious, useful, and hands-on look at how to do it right.

Before Leaving the Hospital

Buying a car seat for your baby will certainly be one of the most important purchases you'll make, and one that you will need to make before your big day arrives—or at least before you leave the hospital. All 50 states now have laws requiring the use of infant safety seats in the car, and it has become standard hospital policy that parents must have one in their possession before taking their new baby home. Showing up with an infant seat, however, is not the same as using and installing it correctly. We strongly recommend that you plan ahead, take time to educate yourself, practice installing the seat in the car and, if possible, schedule a time before your due date (or as soon as you can after your baby is born) to have the seat checked by a certified child passenger safety technician in your community (more on this at the end of the chapter).

 THE "CAR SEAT CHALLENGE"

For infants born more than 3 weeks prematurely, the American Academy of Pediatrics recommends that they be monitored in their car seat before leaving the hospital. Taking this simple precaution helps to ensure that the car seat's semi-reclined position won't cause the newborn to experience breathing problems or slowing of the heartbeat. When it is a problem, doctors may recommend that an infant use a car bed, as described on page 174.

Selecting the Perfect Seat

Although you may be hoping that this is the part of the chapter where we tell you exactly which make and model of car seat to buy, we're actually going to tell you a bit about what your options are and then give you the information you need to make the choice best suited to your needs.

Your take-home message in a nutshell: *The seat you should buy is the one that meets or exceeds all federal standards, is the right size for your child, you can securely install in your vehicle, and you will use every time you take your baby in the car.*

While manufacturers work very hard to appeal to parents' sense of convenience and style, safety should still be your number one priority when choosing a car seat. All child safety seats made and sold in the United States must meet certain federal safety standards (Federal Motor Vehicle Safety Standard 213)—a fact that must be referenced on each car seat label. If only ensuring your baby's safety were as easy as reading the label, but there's clearly more to it than that. Your next step will be to determine if the seat you select is the right one for your baby, and if it can be installed properly in your particular car. It would be nice if all car seats fit well in all vehicles, but incompatibility is unfortunately not uncommon. And while some stores gladly accept returns or allow exchanges, others are not so accommodating, so you'll want to explore your options.

An Overview of Your Rear-Facing Options

Infant-Only Seats

This type of seat is designed for use *only* in the rear-facing position and may be used only until your baby reaches the seat's upper weight limit (which is almost always 20 or 22 pounds), or until the top of his head is within 1 inch from the top of the seat.

Advantages

- Carrying handles allow you to carry your baby around in the seat conveniently.
- Once installed, detachable bases remain in the car so that you don't have to reinstall the seat each time you take it out—simply click it back onto its base. Many seat manufacturers offer the option of purchasing additional bases if you want one in each car.
- The infant seat can be installed and used without a base. While the seat is not always as easy to install correctly when used alone, some actually fit better in the vehicle seat without the base. Having this option can be quite useful when traveling so you don't have to lug the base around.
- Many come with stroller travel systems, where the car seat fits interchangeably with the base and with a stroller (which can also be used alone). This allows for the much less disruptive transfer of a sleeping baby from stroller to car seat and into the house (see "Travel Systems" on page 166).

Practical Considerations

- Most babies reach the upper weight or height limits before their first birthdays and must be moved to another type of seat that has higher rear-facing capabilities (see "Convertible Seats" on page 173) to allow infants to remain rear-facing as long as possible.
- As your child gets heavier, carrying her around in an infant car seat is likely to become less of a convenience and more of a physical challenge.

 CARRYING HANDLES

One of the most common mistakes parents with infant-only seats make is leaving the carrying handle up while driving in the car. Whether it's simply out of convenience, because the bar makes a good place to hang toys, or because parents think it is designed to function like a roll bar, the fact is that the hard plastic handles on these seats are not designed to withstand the force of a crash. When used in the car, unless instructions say otherwise, carrying handles should always be put down behind the head of the car seat to prevent potential injury.

Convertible Seats

Convertible seats are so called because they can be used not only as rear-facing infant seats, but then "converted" to forward-facing toddler seats later on. Perhaps one of the most important things to consider when purchasing a convertible seat (in addition to what it offers in safety and compatibility) is its rear-facing upper weight limit. While a few are similar to the infant-only seats in being limited to 20 to 22 pounds, most now offer the advantage of much higher rear-facing limits—some as high as 35 pounds.

Advantages

- Higher rear-facing weight and height limits allow for longer use rear-facing.
- They have greater potential longevity because they can later be used forward-facing.

Practical Considerations

- Newborns and small infants sometimes don't fit as well in these seats, because they are designed to accommodate a wider range of sizes.
- They lack a carrying handle, detachable base, or stroller attachment.
- They are generally bigger and bulkier than the infant-only seats.

 THE AAP WEIGHS IN

The current recommendation by the American Academy of Pediatrics, published in March 2002, states that infants should not only remain rear-facing until at least 1 year AND 20 pounds—whichever comes later—but that they should in fact remain rear-facing *as long as they are able within the limits of the seat*. This upper limit is determined either by the upper weight limit of the seat, or when the top of a child's head comes within an inch of the top of the seat.

One Seat Fits All: Birth to 80 pounds

This type of seat can be used from birth (rear-facing, usually 5–30 or 35 pounds) through toddlerhood (front-facing from 20 or 22 up to 40 pounds), and all the way through booster seat age (with a lap/shoulder belt from 30–80 pounds). Forward-facing only combination toddler/booster seats (2 seats in 1) are also available but cannot be used in the first year or below 20 pounds.

Advantages
- Longevity—One seat fits all.

Practical Considerations
- Longevity—Some parents see little to no benefit in being stuck with the same seat for more than a year or two—especially those of us who have witnessed the wear and tear that apple juice, spit-up, and worse can cause to a car seat over the years. Additionally, as improvements are made in children's car seats, you may find yourself wanting the latest newfangled seat long before your child outgrows this one.
- Even more so than with convertible seats, some parents and safety advocates are hesitant to use all-purpose seats for newborns and small infants because, they argue, these large seats do not fit as well as infant-only seats.

Car Beds
We've chosen to mention this particular type of child safety restraint because some of you may come across one on the shelves of your local car seat retailer, and a few of you may even find yourself needing one. It's worth pointing out that car safety seats—"regular" infant car seats—are recognized to provide excellent protection for infants positioned rear-facing and are the preferred method of transportation. Car beds are not considered to be as safe as the standard rear-facing infant car seats and *are not recommended for general use.* Rather, they are meant for those infants who cannot be safely restrained in a regular infant car seat and must be transported lying down. Most commonly, this applies to very small and/or premature infants. Car beds should never be bought secondhand or reused unless you are advised to by a child passenger safety professional. Unlike car seats, most car beds are designed for one-baby use—even if only used for a few days or weeks.

Used Car Seats—Considerations and Common Pitfalls
We'll admit it, buying a car seat secondhand seems at first glance like a very good way to get a great deal at a fraction of the cost. Before you decide to use one, we want to offer you a little cautionary food for thought. Unless you get a used car seat from someone you know and trust, you will have no

way of determining whether it has been involved in a crash. Fact is, not all seats show outward signs of damage from a crash, but any seat that has been involved in a significant crash is considered to be unsafe for use. And if you don't send in the original registration card or later call or write with your contact information, the manufacturer of the seat will have no way of notifying you if there is (or has been) a recall. The take-home message when it comes to used seats? We strongly recommend out with the old, in with the new if you don't know the seat's history. The money saved by buying used may not be worth the potential price you'll pay.

REPLACING CAR SEATS AFTER A CRASH

While no one ever plans to get in a crash, it happens. In the event that you ever find yourself in one, you will not only want to repair the damage done to your car, but determine whether you need to replace your car seat(s). Up until early 2004, the National Highway Traffic Safety Administration (NHTSA) recommended that all seats that were in use at the time of the crash, as well as the seat belts used to secure them, be replaced. Given that evidence now suggests that minor crashes do not generally cause damage significant enough to warrant a new seat, NHTSA put together new criteria to help parents determine which crashes can be considered minor. These criteria are

1. There is no visible evidence of damage to the car seat when carefully inspected. This includes uninstalling the seat and taking the padding off to look for any cracks or otherwise hidden damage.
2. The vehicle is in good enough condition to be driven away from the scene of the crash.
3. The vehicle door nearest to where the child safety seat was installed at the time of the crash is undamaged.
4. None of the vehicle's occupants were injured.
5. No air bags deployed in the vehicle containing the child safety seat.

Because these guidelines are quite new and not universally agreed on, it will be up to you to determine whether you replace your child's car seat after a crash regardless of the severity or using the above criteria. Either way, we've found that most parents are not only unaware of this safety recommendation, but don't realize that their insurance is likely to cover the expense!

The Key to Keeping Safe

The key to keeping your baby safe in the car lies not just in buying an appropriate car seat, but also in using it properly. Properly installed infant car seats have been shown to dramatically reduce the number of deaths in children younger than 1 year—by some estimates more than 70%. Yet *9 out of 10* car seats are not installed correctly. If you've already tried your hand at the task of installing one, you may have discovered that mastering this necessary task of modern-day parenthood is not exactly easy.

4 Rs of Installation

Just as with the 3 Rs of reading, 'riting, and 'rithmetic, the 4 Rs of maximizing your infant's safety in the car are not all there is for you to know—as is obvious by the rest of the information we've included in this chapter—but reading, rear-facing, recline, and recalls are definitely a good start.

Reading

Yes, we realize that actually sitting down and reading an instruction manual is not exactly human nature (we plead guilty as well), but becoming a parent inevitably involves many changes, so just consider this one of them! There are so many car seats and so many different cars these days that it is virtually impossible to give you all of the information you need to install your own properly. While we intend to help you become well informed on basic safety principles, it is still essential that you take the time to read through your car seat instruction manual and your vehicle manual for the exact details that apply to you.

Rear-Facing for the Long Haul

One of the most misunderstood concepts relating to car seats is the recommendation that all infants must be kept rear-facing until they reach at least 1 year of age AND 20 pounds. Parents and pediatricians alike misinterpret this advice, not waiting for both requirements to be met. The fact is that if we could all ride around rear-facing in the middle of the back seat with a 5-point harness, we'd be a lot safer. While this is obviously not realistic for adults, the American Academy of Pediatrics now recommends that children remain rear-facing as long as possible within the height and weight limits of their child safety seats. Fortunately, car seat manufacturers are rising to the occasion, and most convertible seats now on the market have rear-facing size limits as high as 30 or 35 pounds and 30 inches, allowing many infants to safely remain rear-facing well past their first birthdays.

 ## BUT HER FEET TOUCH THE SEAT

It may seem a long ways off right now, but one of the most common concerns that parents seem to have about keeping their infants rear-facing is that their legs eventually grow long enough that their feet press up against the back seat. While we'll hand it to you that this may seem somewhat uncomfortable, based on what we now know about crash dynamics, it does not seem, in fact, to be a significant safety risk. In our estimation, and in keeping with the opinions of our child passenger safety–trained colleagues, it is a concern that should not take precedence over your goal of protecting your baby's brain and spinal cord— a goal that is best achieved rear-facing.

The reason for the rear-facing position is as follows. We know that most crashes involve frontal collisions. During a frontal collision, the crash forces are spread over a rear-facing infant's entire body as she is pressed into the back of her car seat. This is in contrast to the forward-facing child whose head and body are thrust forward with the full force of the crash. As we noted before, infants have very large heads in proportion to the rest of their bodies. They lack the muscle strength and the reflexes that allow older children and adults to resist whiplash-type forces, so the rear-facing position is crucial in preventing brain and spinal cord injuries. Bottom line: If your car seat's height and weight limits allow your child to be rear-facing until well past a year, we strongly recommend that you leave her that way for safety's sake.

BUT I CAN'T SEE HER FACE

Even though it is clearly safest to keep your baby rear-facing as long as you can, we empathize with parents who find it difficult to comply. Nevertheless, we want to stress that there really aren't many, if any, activities related to child care that you can safely undertake while driving. Many children's safety advocates even discourage the use of back seat mirrors because they inherently require drivers to take their eyes and attention off of the road. Our best recommendation: If you are so inclined, sit in the back seat next to your infant while someone else drives. Otherwise, take comfort in knowing that your baby's car seat is properly installed, focus your attention on what lies ahead, and pull over to a safe spot if and when you feel that your baby's demands truly warrant an immediate response.

Recline

Rear-facing car seats should ideally be installed at a 45° recline—or halfway back from upright—especially when your newborn lacks the head control necessary to prevent serious injury. Knowing that you need to install a seat with 45° of recline is one thing; actually getting the seat installed in this position is another (see page 171). Many vehicle seats are not level and cause rear-facing car seats to sit too upright. Because of this problem, many infant-only seat bases come with an adjustable reclining platform for securing the seat at the appropriate angle. Convertible seats that sit too upright may need to be adjusted into the recline position (because the upright setting is for later, when the seat is used forward-facing). For seats that do not have these options and remain too upright, placing a rolled-up towel, newspaper, or foam swimming pool noodle (cut to size) under the foot of the infant seat is often all that is necessary to compensate for the slope of the vehicle's seat. Many car seats come with recline indicators designed to show you if you've placed the seat in an acceptable position, but it's worth also looking at your infant in the seat to make sure his head doesn't look like it will easily flop forward and that he is halfway from upright. And remember—more of a good thing is not always better because too much recline could allow an infant to be forced up and out of the seat in the event of a crash.

REAR-FACING TETHERS

As of late 2005, only a few car safety seats used in the United States have top tethers that can be used in the rear-facing position—a feature that not only secures the head of the seat, but also can make it much easier to get the seat appropriately reclined.

*R*ecalls

If you are like most of the population, you rarely (if ever) fill out manufacturers' product registration cards. Once you buy a car seat, however, it is very important that you do so because supplying the manufacturer with your seat's make and model number, along with your contact information, allows them to contact you in the event of a recall. And despite manufacturers' best efforts, recalls do occur. If you've already misplaced your registration card, be aware that there are other reliable ways to find out about recalls as long as you remember to look. You can refer to Web sites for the National Highway Traffic Safety Administration (NHTSA, www.nhtsa.gov, 888/DASH-2-DOT) and the Consumer Product Safety Commission (CPSC, www.cpsc.gov). You can also call in your car seat details and contact information to the manufacturer.

Making Your Efforts Last

We want to emphasize that an important determining factor in keeping your baby safe is not just how secure you are able to make your car seat at installation, but rather how secure the seat is *at the time of a crash*. All too often, well-installed seats are able to work themselves loose because they are not properly locked into place. To avoid this, take a look in your own car and ask yourself how you're going to get the seat belt to secure the car seat. The following advice is meant to help you figure out the answer to this question.

And You Thought You Knew Seat Belts

Buckling your own seat belt is a task that we hope you do without much thought and one that requires little effort or understanding. When installing a car seat, however, a little more thought is generally required—hence our primer on vehicle seat belts.

Lap/Shoulder Belts

If you're using a lap/shoulder belt, you'll notice that it can be easily pulled out and then spooled back in again on what is called a retractor. When lap/shoulder belts were first introduced, they could be pulled out; however, once slack was allowed to spool in, the retractor automatically locked the lap/shoulder belts in so that they could not be pulled back out again. Consumers did not like the inconvenience of these automatically locking retractors, and as a result we now have lap/shoulder belts that only lock up in an emergency. While most adults enjoy the comfort, there's a potential problem with installing car seats using seat belts that have only emergency locking retractors: They allow car seats to move just as freely as they do adults until the event of a crash.

Fortunately, 2 locking mechanisms have since emerged to address this problem. The first is a *switchable retractor*—one that affords an adult the comfort of a free-sliding seat belt that only locks up in the event of a crash, but that can easily be switched into the automatic locking mode by simply pulling the seat belt all the way out to the end. Once this seat belt is fully tightened and set to lock, it can't be pulled back out until the seat belt is first allowed to spool in completely. The second mechanism is a locking latch plate (the metal and plastic part of the seat belt where the lap belt threads through and becomes the shoulder belt), which has the ability to lock the seat belt in place. If you have a relatively new car, it should come with either a switchable retractor or some type of locking latch plate. In the event that your car does not have either feature or you are simply unable to get them to work properly, only then will you need to figure out how to use a locking clip.

Locking Clips Explained

Locking clips are the small, metal, H-shaped objects that now come with all infant car seats. Quite often, parents use locking clips when they don't actually need them simply because they are not familiar with their seat belt's built-in locking mechanism as described previously.

1 inch

- To effectively prevent seat belts from loosening up, locking clips should lock the lap and shoulder belts on the buckle side of the seat belt, *within an inch of the latch plate.* More often than not, locking clips are incorrectly used to secure the shoulder belt to the lap belt on the side of the car seat opposite the buckle and latch plate.
- The trick to getting a tight installation using a locking clip is to buckle in the car seat, get the seat belt snug, and then pinch the lap and shoulder belts together to prevent them from slipping as you unbuckle the seat belt. This allows you to slip the locking clip on in the appropriate location and then you can re-buckle the seat belt. If re-buckling requires some effort, then chances are good that when you're done, you will have installed your seat securely.

 ### SEATS WITH BUILT-IN LOCKING CLIPS

A few infant and convertible seats have locking clips (also called lock-offs) conveniently built right onto the sides of the seat—an added feature that helps ensure that they can be properly secured by just about any type of seat belt without the need for an additional metal locking clip.

Lap Belts

Lap-only belts are generally found in the middle of the back seat, as well as in additional seating positions of older cars. While they offer older children and adults no upper-body protection, they can safely be used to install infant car seats, which all come with internal harness straps. Some newer models of cars have lap belts that ratchet in and out on automatically locking retractors, whereas others function like airplane seat belts—with a locking latch plate that allows the length of the seat belt to be manually adjusted and then locked in place. Thread your lap belt through the guide slots provided on the car seat and secure it into the vehicle as tightly as possible.

Getting It Right Means Getting It Tight

Once installed, you should not be able to move your baby's car seat more than an inch from side to side (at the path of the seat belt) or away from the vehicle seat. The trick to getting seat belts extra tight is to put your weight on the car seat base (if you're using one for an infant-only seat) or the car seat itself (while your baby is not in it, of course) and then give the already buckled seat belt an extra pull to remove any additional slack. As you take your body weight off of the seat, it should be sufficiently secure.

    SEAT BELT TIGHTENERS

These devices, marketed as the easy solution to the challenges of securing car seats with seat belts, are unnecessary and have been noted on occasion to damage the seat belt (tearing or fraying the nylon webbing). In general, safety experts consider them to be potentially dangerous and at best unnecessary.

LATCH—The Future of Car Seat Installation

When it comes to the future of car seat installation, the future is now. All new child safety seats and vehicles manufactured after September 1, 2002, must be LATCH-compatible. LATCH stands for Lower Anchors and Tethers for Children, and the driving force behind its creation was a desire to standardize the installation of all child safety seats to make it simpler and quicker and leave less room for error. LATCH involves the use of a top tether for forward-facing seats for older children and 2 lower attachments that can be used to secure rear- or forward-facing car seats to universal anchor points located in the car. While LATCH may ultimately make the use of seat belts to install car seats (and most of the preceding information in this chapter, for that matter) unnecessary,

Top tether

it's going to be many years before everyone has access to this system. In the meantime, if your car is not equipped with top tether anchors, check in your owner's manual and with your local dealer to see if they can be installed well before your infant is ready to be positioned forward-facing. If so, the actual installation is often quick and, if you're lucky, done at little or no cost.

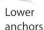

Lower anchors

Securing Your Infant

After you have put time and effort into installing your infant's car seat, it is equally important to make sure that you know how to secure your infant in it. All infant car seats come with harness straps. There are small variations between brands, but the basic principles are the same. While harness straps should be threaded through the lowest level of harness slots for all newborns, you'll notice that most infant car seats have more than one pair of these slit-like openings. Because the harness straps must be at or below your baby's shoulders when in a rear-facing car seat, you'll want to remember to move the straps when her shoulders are at the level of the next opening.

Getting to the Points

All infant car seats come with harnesses. Some are 3-point—meaning that they attach to the seat at each shoulder and one between the legs—while others are 5-point—attaching at the same 3 points, but additionally at the hips. While both types are considered safe when properly positioned, safety advocates (and race car drivers) all choose 5-point.

3-point harness   5-point harness

Once your baby is placed in the car seat and buckled in, the harness straps should not be twisted. They should be adjusted snugly enough that you can only run one finger between the straps and your baby's collarbone. Any extra slack simply leaves your infant more room in which to move (and, therefore, more susceptible to injury) in the event of a crash. The clip that holds the 2 harness straps together is called a harness clip and should rest across your baby's chest at armpit level.

A Word on Accessorizing

If you look in any baby store, you'll find an impressive array of products with which to "adorn" your infant's car seat. Before you find yourself lured into buying any, there are a few safety considerations to keep mind. Whether you've got your eye on a cute little car toy or a suction cup mirror, any items that are hard, rigid, and can't be secured well are best left on the shelf of the store or reserved for use outside of the car. The reason is simple—the potential for objects to become dangerous projectiles in the event of a crash far outweighs their possible usefulness or entertainment value.

UFOs: UNRESTRAINED FLYING OBJECTS

At the risk of causing a flashback to high school physics, it is worth refreshing your memory about Newton's First Law of Motion, which states that things in motion stay in motion until acted on by an opposing force. Applying this concept to the context of car safety means that any and all loose objects in your car can easily become projectiles. It's well worth glancing around at what you have lying around, and then ask yourself what it would feel like to be hit with it at 60, 40, or even 20 miles per hour. You're likely to find that even the tissue box on your back dash looks a little more threatening in this context.

Padding the Seats

Specially designed and readily available baby headrest cushions help prevent young babies' heads from flopping around in their seats, and are therefore especially popular among parents of newborns. That said, you shouldn't place any additional padding (including blankets and winter clothing) between your baby and the back of the seat or his harness straps unless it came with the car seat, lest it interfere with the seat's ability to protect your baby. Cushions and padding sold separately to fit around the sides of your baby's head are acceptable, but if you would rather spare yourself yet one more purchase, then just roll up 2 towels and place them along either side of your baby's head instead (see picture on page 185). As your baby grows, remember that when any of these items become a nuisance or unnecessary, simply stop using them. If you feel your baby needs another layer of warmth and that your choice of clothing seems insufficient, you can secure him in his car seat first, then tuck a blanket or coat over him.

Location, Location, Location

Infants and Front Seat Air Bags

You're probably familiar with the golden rule that *infant car seats should never be placed in front of front seat air bags.* As a point of future reference, neither should young children. That's because air bags deploy at such great force that they can cause great harm, if not death, to children placed in front of them. Granted, there are a few exceptions—such as trucks with air bag turn-off switches—but we want you to think long and hard and enlist the expertise of someone trained in child passenger safety before deciding that you qualify as an exception to the rule.

The Back Seat

It is recommended that all children under the age of 13 years sit in the back seat. The reason is quite simple—because it is almost always safer than the front. While the middle of the back seat is generally felt to be the safest and most protected location in the car, not *all* infant seats can or should be installed there. If the center back seat does not work, the next question many concerned parents ask is which side of the back seat is considered safer—the driver's or the passenger's? Statistically speaking, the passenger side fares slightly better in crashes, but it often ends up the side of choice out of convenience. It's not uncommon for a rear-facing infant seat to get in the way of the vehicle seat in front of it, and most parents would rather have the inconvenience of having to scoot the front passenger seat farther forward than the driver's. When parallel parked, it also tends to be easier to remove a baby from the car if she's on the same side as the curb.

 GOING PRO

As you near the end of this chapter, we hope that you feel a bit more knowledgeable and confident in your abilities to keep your child safe in the car; but don't feel like you are now on your own. There are now more than 20,000 certified technicians across the country trained in child passenger safety. You can locate one in your area by simply contacting your state's department of transportation, local fire or emergency personnel, or a nearby children's hospital, or by looking for listings by ZIP code on the National Highway Traffic Safety Administration's Web site (www.nhtsa.gov) or the National Safe Kids Coalition's Web site (www.safekids.org). You can also watch for local car seat checkup events advertised in your community. These services are usually offered at no cost, and just about all parents who take the time to have the techniques we've discussed presented in a hands-on setting find the experience to be invaluable.

A Little About Lots

As a parent, what you consider to be the most convenient spot in the parking lot may not just be determined purely by the distance from car door to store door, but also what lies between. Unless you are one of the lucky few who consider valet parking or a chauffeur as viable options, here are some thoughts to ponder when parking as a parent.

- **Curbside check-in.** Whenever possible, park along the curb so that you won't have to cross a busy parking lot and you'll be able to load and unload without another car pulling up beside you.
- **Last in line.** For those of you who have never considered the option before, parking at the end of the row and away from the crowds can offer you more space for unloading and loading babies, bags, and strollers. However, be aware that others may follow suit or cut across the parking lot from any direction while you attempt to manage your goods.
- **New parent parking.** Take advantage of "new parent parking" if any of your local area merchants have been so kind as to designate special

parking spaces for new parents along with their disabled and "stork" (expectant mother) parking.

- **Out of harm's way.** If you can find a spot between 2 parked cars that has more than squeezing room on either side, you'll be better able to keep yourself, your bags and, most importantly, your baby tucked relatively safely out of the way of traffic.

- **Corralled.** Parking next to the cart corral not only allows for quick transfer of baby and goods from car to cart and back, but also lets you return your cart without leaving your infant unattended or in harm's way. However, we feel obliged to add that our husbands do not like this choice of parking spots—if only because it puts the cars at risk of being bumped, dented, or otherwise damaged by stray and misplaced carts.

  JUST SAY YES!

In some parts of the country, "Do you want help out with that?" is one of the most common questions asked in grocery stores these days—second only to "paper or plastic?" Before you selflessly decline the offer, take into account that an extra pair of hands to unload groceries will allow you to focus on securing your child in the car, and you'll undoubtedly be offered the luxury of having someone else put your shopping cart away free of charge.

Mr Carr's Words of Wisdom

Believe it or not, one of us had a driver's ed teacher whose real name was Mr Carr. Of all his "take home and remember until parenthood" messages, one stood out above the rest—and that was to always, without exception, walk all the way around your car before getting in and driving off. Even before children are able to crawl or walk themselves into precarious positions, the potential tragedy of an infant left in a car seat on top of or behind a car is unfortunately not hypothetical. As a rule to live by, never set your baby in front of, on top of, or behind your car. And if you have to set aside the car seat or stroller momentarily while loading or unloading, consider opening a door and placing it in a spot where the open door will shield your baby from and deter oncoming cars.

Keeping Your Wits and Keys About You

Having experienced it firsthand, believe us when we tell you that getting locked out of your car with a hungry, crying infant can be a very traumatic experience—one that's even more traumatic if the baby is inside the car along with the keys! Acknowledging that parenthood often makes it harder to keep one's wits about them, much less stick to a routine, we strongly suggest that you make it a habit always to check for your keys before shutting the car door rather than randomly tossing them in a purse, in a diaper bag, or onto the seat of the car.

Maintaining a Perfect Attendance Record

As parents, we've gained a new appreciation of drive-thrus. Sure, they were convenient before we had children, but we never fully appreciated them until we were faced with all of the loading and unloading involved in even the most simple—and what used to be quick—errands. It's no wonder that parents are tempted to quickly run into a store, bank, or gas station without taking their infants along with them. Before you do, stop and ask yourself if you'd consider leaving a million dollars in the back seat of your car in plain view, even if the windows were cracked for air.

 IN THE HEAT OF A FEW MOMENTS

The inside of a closed car on a 75°F day can reach temperatures well above 100°F in less than half an hour. In direct sunlight on a day when the temperature is in the mid 80s, it takes less than 5 minutes. Combined with the fact that a baby's body temperature increases 3 to 5 times as fast as an adult's, the heat of a few moments shut inside a car can lead to serious if not lethal consequences.

While we don't need to tell you (although we've found all parents like to hear it) that your child is priceless, we do feel obliged to reinforce for you the fact that carjacking-turned-kidnappings, heat stroke, and even worse calamities do happen in cars where children are left unattended. It is for these reasons that we urge you never to get in the habit of leaving your baby alone in the car, however briefly. It is as much a part of keeping your child safe as having a properly installed car seat!

CHAPTER 16

flying the family-friendly skies

In this age of upward mobility, a large number of new and expectant parents find themselves faced with what we consider to be an altogether new form of travel: airplane travel with a baby. As with just about every other aspect of parenting, this undertaking will inevitably involve a lot more advanced planning than the trips you used to take alone. In this section, we've included insights that apply specifically to flying with your baby—a topic we've found to be especially useful during the early weeks of parenthood when you're laden down with diapers, strollers, and car seats and still settling into sleep and feeding routines.

Timing Your Ticketed Travels

Most parents who find themselves planning airplane travel with their newborns wonder about the age at which it's safe and easiest (relatively speaking), not to mention which time of day generally works the best with a newborn's "schedule." First let us say that planning flight times around a young infant's sleeping and eating schedule is a noble idea and one worth pursuing, but be aware that things do not always proceed according to plan—even for those babies who settle into predictable routines conveniently early in life. This is definitely where the phrase "even the best laid plans…" comes to mind. While we have found from personal and professional experience that there isn't one right answer to the question of when it's safest and easiest to travel, the fact of the matter is that newborns and young babies generally adapt pretty well to changes in sleep and eating schedules.

First in Flight

We have found no wiser advice than to take it easy on yourself after having a baby and devote your time and energy to establishing a comfortable routine. In this regard, airplane travel is not exactly conducive to rest and recuperation. Yet it is surprisingly common how often new parents end up faced with taking their newborns or young infants on an airplane. Whether you find yourself traveling by choice or because of a hard-to-cancel and far-away obligation, it should be reassuring to know that healthy term babies generally do just fine flying anytime after the first week or two. Parents, on the other hand, don't always fare so well. We recommend you think through your travel plans carefully before embarking on yet another journey, because setting out on your journey through parenthood is likely to require a great deal of planning and adjustment in and of itself. Especially during the time when your baby is younger than about 4 months, it's worth stopping and asking yourself whether the trip you are contemplating is optional. If it's not, then jump right ahead to the rest of the chapter for practical advice on how to go about it successfully. If you're unsure, then it is up to you to decide how fatigued you are from your recent and ongoing induction into parenthood, how much you like (or dislike) to travel, and whether your baby is likely to be accommodating. For young infants, this generally means considering whether they have become relatively skilled at eating and sleeping in unfamiliar surroundings or whether they tend to be very sensitive to stimulation.

 FLYING PREMATURELY

While commercial airliners are pressurized and the oxygen level in the cabin is carefully controlled during flight, premature babies whose lungs are not fully developed may be more sensitive to the effects of high-altitude travel. We haven't found a definitive answer as to when it is OK to travel with a premature infant, and therefore recommend you double-check with your baby's doctor before flying (or going to the mountains, for that matter) where the altitude's effect on oxygen concentration may be a factor.

Parting Gifts

Even if you're ready to take on the challenges of air travel, consider the fact that airplanes are notorious for their close quarters and recirculated air. Even a good many adults who fly the friendly skies find themselves with the lovely parting gift of fresh colds soon thereafter. As discussed in the chapter we devoted to the subject, fever in newborns is more than just an inconvenience and needs to be taken seriously—requiring not only the involvement of health professionals but also the possibility of tests and treatment. In general, avoiding closed-in spaces—especially those filled with recirculated air and people who have the sniffles—is definitely in your baby's (and your) best interest.

Sleeping en Route

Over the years, we've been asked or told about many home remedies rumored to be effective in getting babies to sleep on planes. As nice as it would be to have a calm, quiet, and sleeping baby throughout an entire flight, we simply haven't found any ingestible remedy that we can bring ourselves to recommend. Common sense, never mind our medical training, tells us that giving babies even a tiny spoonful of an alcoholic beverage or a sampling of a sedative is a very bad idea, however tempting it may seem under duress. The use of sedating over-the-counter children's medications (most notably antihistamines used to treat allergies and itchiness) in hopes of inducing sleep is also not recommended for young infants. For those of you who are still tempted, let us also forewarn you that some children actually have the opposite response and become hyperactive and irritable instead. If you are determined to use something to get your child to sleep on the plane—during infancy or in the years to come—then be sure to talk to your baby's doctor about it first to double-check that it's safe and you know the correct dose. Then do a trial run at home so you know ahead of time how your child will respond.

Late-Night Flights

We have found that babies tend to sleep more reliably at nighttime than they do during naptime travel once they've mastered the concept in the first few weeks. If you and your baby can sleep on the plane, a late-night flight may be the way to go. Before you book a cross-country red-eye, give it your best guess as to whether your baby actually will sleep through the night if he's on a plane instead of in a crib, not to mention whether you'll be able to sleep as well. Then factor in some extra time for getting yourself *and* your baby settled in safe and sound once you arrive at your destination, because the additional tasks of child care—not the least of which include installing a car seat and setting up a crib—can add a fair bit to your overall travel time. If nothing else, having a baby along all but ensures that you won't have time to sleep in after a late night or early morning arrival, especially if your baby is well rested and raring to go.

Booking Your Flights

To Buy or Not to Buy

Yes, it's true…the Federal Aviation Administration (FAA) does not require the purchase of an airline ticket for any child younger than 2 years, and we openly acknowledge that from a budgetary standpoint, the option of traveling with a lap child (as the airline industry calls unticketed infants and toddlers) can be financially appealing. You should know, however, that safety experts across the country unanimously agree that forgoing the purchase of an assigned seat for your baby is not an ideal way to save money. Even if the FAA doesn't make it mandatory for parents to purchase infants their own tickets in the near future, we want to strongly encourage you to save up and pay for the extra seat anyway if at all possible. Believe us when we say that we wish there were a good alternative, but knowing what we do about safety and airplane travel, we can't come up with one. Instead, we suggest you look around and take advantage of the discounted seats many

 DISCOUNTS FOR THE UNDER TWO JET SET

Before purchasing your tickets, be sure to check with the specific airlines you intend to fly to see if they offer any discounted fares for children younger than 2 years. You may be pleasantly surprised with purchase prices of up to 50% less than the published adult fare. International flights may offer even larger discounts for "underage" fliers. In fact, these fares are not always limited to children younger than 2 years; some are even offered for children up to the age of 12 years.

airlines offer for infants and get in the habit (if you aren't already) of making use of frequent flier mileage programs to soften the blow to your budget.

Safety First

Securing your infant in a seat of her own in an FAA-approved car seat is an important step in committing yourself from day 1 to the idea that your baby's safety comes first. We're not saying that you can't unbuckle to change a diaper or take care of other baby business while in flight, but be aware that turbulence poses the greatest safety risk to passengers of all ages, and is not always predictable. Before you set out, you'll also want to keep in mind that not all car seats are FAA approved for use in aircraft, and those that are may still not fit in the airplane seat if they are wider than about 16 inches. Check for a label on your car seat that says it is FAA approved, and check with your airline if you're concerned about whether the seat will fit. You can also search around on the FAA Web site (www.faa.gov) for more details.

 STATISTICALLY SPEAKING

The chance of injury from an automobile crash is much higher than that from airplane crashes or in-flight turbulence, yet in some states, babies are not required to be secured in car seats if they are riding in the back of taxis, limos, buses, etc. You'd be amazed how many parents throw the car seat in the trunk of the taxi with the luggage, thinking, "It's just a short ride to the airport." We advise you to buckle up your baby on the way to the airport as well as on the plane!

Sitting in the Lap of Luxury

Even if you love to hold and cuddle with your baby when you're at home, you may find that doing it for an entire airplane flight is somewhat uncomfortable. Also, many babies who would otherwise be content to sit in their car seats and entertain themselves or sleep tend to have much greater expectations when they are held.

If You Don't Opt for the Extra Seat

There are definitely those out there who would matter-of-factly tell you that if you can't afford to pay for an extra seat for your infant, you shouldn't be traveling. We too feel strongly about keeping children safe, but we also intend to live up to our claim that this is a book about the realities of parenting—and we know full well that not all of you are going to buy your babies airline tickets. If you still find yourself looking for tips about traveling with an infant on your lap, we have some useful ones to offer.

- **Playing the odds.** Even if you haven't purchased your infant a seat, it is possible on occasion to get one. Some regularly scheduled flight times are notoriously less popular than others. If you are traveling with a lap child, consider booking yourself in a window seat on one of these typically less than full flights (such as overnight red eyes) and take your chances that there will be open seats left. When you check in at the gate, ask the ticketing agent if there are any seats still available. If there are, chances are good that they will be middle seats, and you may be allowed to secure your infant's car seat in the window seat you had reserved for yourself and then sit in the adjacent middle seat without paying extra. If your flight does end up being oversold, however, you'll be asked to check your baby's car seat and proceed with your original plan.

- **Picking a seat on a full flight.** If finding an open seat is out of the question, then you'll want to decide which you think is going to be the lesser of 2 evils—a window seat that is out of the way but with less easy access to the aisle, or an aisle seat where you'll need to pay attention to a second set of body parts (your baby's, that is) to make sure that heads, feet, and limbs don't get bumped by service carts or passers-by. In the aisle seat, you may also have to accommodate your middle- and window-seat neighbors' need to access the aisle. When traveling with your baby and another person, we suggest you book the aisle and window seats. Chances are better that the middle seat between will remain unoccupied (in which case you can secure you infant's car seat in the window seat as described above). If someone else does get assigned to the middle seat, you can virtually guarantee that person won't mind switching from the middle to an aisle or window seat, allowing you and your travel companion to sit next to each other with your baby on your lap.

- **Baby carriers.** Baby carriers (including slings) are very popular among flying parents, but they by no means offer the same degree of protection as placing your baby in a secured car seat during the flight, and the FAA does not approve them for use during take off or landing.

Other Seating Rules, Regulations, and Recommendations

Before your days of flying with your baby, your seat preference was probably based on proximity to the front of the plane, a desire for extra leg room, or an interest in seeing the sights out the window. Not so anymore. If nothing else, you will now be required to install your infant's car seat in a window seat so as not to block passengers from exiting the row, and opting for the exit row is no longer a possibility, because families traveling with small children aren't exactly the ideal people to perform the necessary exit-row duties in the event of an emergency.

As for the choices you do have when it comes to seat assignments, many parents vie for the opportunity to sit in the bulkhead rows located at the front of each section of the aircraft. These seats typically offer more space than is allotted between the rest of the rows and ensure that rear-facing infant car seats won't be in a position to interfere with the ability of the passenger in front of your baby to recline his seat. As an added benefit, you also don't have to go far to reach them. Now that we've extolled the virtues of bulkhead seating, let us point out that the odds of getting assigned to bulkhead seats are not that great, and you will likely have to sacrifice the convenience of stowing your diaper bag under the seat in front of you (because there is usually no allotted space) and store it in the less-accessible overhead compartment instead. If you find yourself in the likely position of considering your second choice in seat selection, you may find that there are benefits to the front and the back. Sitting toward the front of the plane is particularly useful if you're loaded down, whereas the back of the plane will get you tucked out of everyone's way once you make it back there, and is often just loud enough (from the sound of the engines) either to soothe your baby with background noise or to drown out his crying for all but those sitting closest to you.

Navigating the Airport

Arrivals

As the rules of 21st century air travel changed and airport security heightened, so did the challenges of navigating the airport with an infant. There was a day when we would have recommended that you simply pull up to curbside check-in before parking, leave one person stationed at the car with the baby, and have the other stand in line to check in. For obvious reasons, those days are long gone. Figuring out how to get everyone and everything checked in and to the gate on time takes a little more forethought these days. We've found that the easiest solution to this problem is to avoid the prospect of parking altogether and get dropped off whenever possible.

Divide and Conquer

If you do end up driving yourselves to the airport, you might want to consider the divide and conquer approach (assuming that you are not traveling solo). Drop off one adult with photo ID and ticket in hand at curbside check-in with all of the bags, including the carry-on(s). This leaves the parking parent less encumbered and more easily able to park the car expeditiously and hurry back with the baby to check in. If your parking prospects look particularly grim, you may want to consider dropping off your baby as well—especially if you don't have a stroller or baby carrier. That way, if you find yourself heading to the remote corners of the economy lot, you'll avoid the frustrating dilemma of how to secure your baby safely on the shuttle, because quite often you just plain can't. The final key to success with the divide and conquer approach is to be sure to set a clearly defined meeting place before parting ways.

Security Checkpoints

Many airlines now require that even infants without a paid ticket receive a boarding pass. This helps with their inventory of passengers and weight estimates of each airplane load. Be sure to let the airline agent know, at the time of booking and when checking in, that your infant is traveling with you. The security personnel will check that each passenger has a boarding pass and photo ID if applicable.

LET SLEEPING BABIES LIE

As inconvenient as it may seem, safety regulations now require that you lift your baby out of her car seat so that the seat and your baby can be properly inspected—even if your baby is sleeping contentedly. When walking through the metal detector, you may even be asked to carry your baby at arm's length in front of you to prove you are not concealing any objects (other than your nursing pads) between your bodies.

Leave the Pointy Objects Behind

Most adults have become quite accustomed to leaving potentially dangerous objects (tools, weapons, flammables, and even butter knives) at home as but one of the post-September 11th security changes—but don't forget that this "absolutely no sharp objects on board the airplane" principle may apply to your baby's nail clippers and other grooming supplies as well. By substituting a cardboard emery board for a pair of sharp-pointed metal nail scissors, for example, you'll avoid having them confiscated. Fortunately, most baby supplies are not considered to be security risks. Check the Transportation Security Agency's Web site at www.tsa.gov for full details.

Ease on Down the Terminal

When making the seemingly endless trek through airport terminals with an infant in tow, it's best to make the most of modern-day conveniences such as rolling luggage, Smarte Cartes, and your baby stroller or baby carrier. Smarte Cartes typically run $2 to $3 and in most airports can be rented using cash or a credit card. Unfortunately, in some airports, Smarte Cartes are only allowed up to the security checkpoints, at which point parents are left to their own devices to find ways to get their belongings gracefully to the gate. In a bind, we've been allowed to use a spare wheelchair to hold carry-on bags and free our hands to hold our babies, tickets, and ID—just make sure to ask permission first and leave the wheelchair at an acceptable location. If you have a long way to go to reach the gate, are really heavily loaded, or especially if you have a lightning layover, by all means request to be picked up by one of the airport's indoor electric carts.

GETTING THINGS ROLLING

Rolling backpacks make for a perfect example of a relatively simple but well thought out design that we can only assume was invented by a parent. Even if it wasn't, we recommend that you consider investing in one for use during travel. Many are big enough to hold the same amount of stuff as a rolling carry-on suitcase, but the added hands-free feature of the shoulder straps can be invaluable—especially if you're going it alone.

Gate Checking Baby Gear

Gate checking is an option well worth knowing about as a parent. If nothing else, it allows you to use your stroller to make your way through the entire parking lot and airport, right up until the time you're about to set foot on the plane. At the gate you will be given a claim ticket for your tagged stroller and then asked to leave it at the end of the Jetway as you board. If everything works the way it is supposed to—which it usually but not always does—your stroller should be waiting for you immediately outside the plane as you get off or shortly thereafter. We've found gate checking to be so convenient that we make a habit of checking even the small umbrella strollers that can fit in the overhead compartments for the simple reason that doing so gives us one less item (or 3) to lug on board.

All Aboard

Walking up to the gate with a baby and all of your travel accessories should be enough to cause everyone but those we consider to be truly cold-hearted to offer sympathetic glances, in some cases assistance, and—in what has become less common but no less appreciated—the option to pre-board. The privilege of getting on first used to be a luxury that was granted to anyone and everyone traveling with children. It seems, however, that not all airlines believe in pre-boarding anymore and when they do, it feels a lot more like a 2-second head start than a luxury. The good news is that you do have some options.

- **Boarding last.** Your first option is to pass on pre-boarding and instead wait until last to get on the plane. This works especially well for parents who aren't going to require a lot of overhead space, find it stressful to be solely responsible for blocking 100 other passengers from their seats, or who simply don't relish the idea of entertaining their infants in a confined seat on the plane for any longer than they have to.

- **Send ahead or go your separate ways.** This is what we like to think of as the (relatively) hands-free option. Whether you are traveling with another adult or need to seek the assistance of an airline employee working at the gate, consider sending someone ahead with the car seat, carry-on suitcase, stroller, and any other bulky items without which you can manage until closer to flight time. The 30 extra minutes or so that this is likely to afford you and your baby in the gate area instead of being stuck in your seat(s) can make quite a difference—especially for an awake and demanding baby.

- **Stand up for pre-boarding.** If you definitely want to get on the plane and get settled in, then don't be shy about broaching the subject of pre-boarding even if it seems to have been "overlooked" by the gate attendants. While a few airlines seem to have lost a little bit of their family-friendly charm, it is still challenging to find a ticket agent who is comfortable turning away a loaded-down parent and infant at the front of the line just because their row number has yet to have been called.

Please Remain Seated

You already know our strong bias toward having a purchased seat for your baby. If you have followed through and chosen to buy one or just lucked out and taken over an unused seat, then by all means make sure to use it during as much of the flight as possible. Quite often, babies decide to voice their disapproval of having to sit in a car seat loudly enough that their parents feel obliged to remove them to stop the crying. Before you give in too easily, try to treat flying in an airplane as you would a trip in the car. Just as (we hope) you wouldn't dream of setting out for a drive without first securing your infant safely in his seat in the car, use the same approach on the airplane. Your baby will be safer and you'll increase the likelihood that, as he gets older, it won't occur to him to complain about being restrained on the plane.

TURBULENCE

According to the Federal Aviation Administration, turbulence is the most common cause of nonfatal injury in passengers and flight attendants—about 60 people per year are injured by turbulence while not wearing their seat belts. It is most likely to occur when the aircraft is above 30,000 feet and tends to be worse in the winter than in the summer.

Dressing for Success, Not a Flight of Fancy

Those of you who are frequent air travelers are undoubtedly well acquainted with the concept of dressing for the occasion. For one, there's the unpredictability of cabin temperature. We highly recommend dressing yourself and your child in easy-on, easy-off layers so that you are prepared for whatever in-flight conditions you may find. In making your selections, remember that easy access and comfort are key—even for you, but definitely for your baby. If you consider this an opportunity to show your baby off in a frilly new dress or a fancy new outfit for this venture out into the real world, it will quickly become apparent that function was meant to overrule fashion when it comes to infant airplane attire. Simply put, elastic-waist pants, zip-up outfits, or easy-snap crotches are far easier than tights and lace or button-up-the-back Onesies when it comes to diaper changing—especially when faced with doing it in cramped quarters.

Carry-on Contents

One of the major differences in traveling with kids is that you inevitably lose claim to almost all of the space in your carry-on suitcase—at least until several years down the road, but believe us when we say it's well worth it to pack with your baby in mind. The basic goals underlying your suitcase-stuffing efforts should be that when you're done, you will be well prepared but at the same time weighted down by as few carry-on bags as possible. If everything you choose to bring along as carry-ons fits easily in your bag(s) it will significantly decrease the likelihood that you will leave a trail of belongings in your wake. That said, there are quite a few supplies that you probably won't want to board without—several of which we have listed for you on the following page.

- **Diapering supplies.** When it comes to changing diapers on airplanes, expect the worst and don't assume the airline will have the supplies you need. If your baby usually poops twice a day, expect the pleasure of 3 or 4. And if they're usually semi-formed, expect liquidy leaky ones— just because good old Murphy said so. We highly recommend giving priority in your carry-on or diaper bag to plenty of extra diapers, a hefty supply of wipes, and some small plastic garbage bags (grocery store plastic bags work quite well). If you don't end up needing them, that's great, but carrying them along with you is a small price to pay for not being caught empty handed. Remember that flight attendants should not be expected to touch or discard diapers (out of politeness and for sanitary reasons, because they are the ones handling everyone's food). You can either dispose of the diapers in the lavatory—preferably tied up to minimize the odor—or pack them in your diaper bag to toss when you land. If you run out of plastic bags, the airsick bags work well as backup. Also consider bringing an antibacterial hand sanitizer in case you are unable to get to the sink.
- **Change of clothing.** Think about how many outfits your baby typically goes through in a day, double it, and make room for them in your carry-on. And then consider doing the same for yourself, because you aren't likely to enjoy sitting in clothes that bear the fresh stains of parenthood any more than your baby would. Also remember to leave space in your carry-on for any extra layers you and your baby may shed during the trip.
- **Additional supplies.** You will undoubtedly know your baby well enough to know whether leaving home without a pacifier is going to spell disaster. Making room for a favorite blanket, stuffed animal, or other attachment object is also a good idea if your infant is old enough to care about them. Be sure to tuck in an adequate supply of tissues and paper towels, and then proceed to pack anything you might actually want for yourself in whatever space you have left.

THE IN-FLIGHT CHANGING CHALLENGE

Some airplanes come with pull-down changing tables above the toilet in the lavatory that can be logistically helpful for in-flight diaper changing (although you'll still need to beware of precariously placed diaper-changing supplies). These handy lavatory accessories are, however, far from universal.

Changing your baby's diaper on your lap is a handy skill to master in anticipation of an airplane flight, whether you find yourself faced with having to stay in your seat or the sometimes greater challenge of changing a diaper in what seems like a 2-foot by 2-foot room at best. While the underlying principles are essentially the same as those described in the diapering chapter (page 115), there are a few extra considerations that will make diaper changing on your lap go more smoothly. Practice laying your baby on your lap with her head resting near your knees and her bottom toward your stomach. It is a particularly good idea to use the method of slipping a new diaper under your baby's bottom before taking the old diaper off when your lap is serving as the changing table. Now more than ever, you'll also want to keep "things" covered as much of the time as possible to avoid being caught in any crossfire. Have wipes and a bag readily available for quick cleanup and sanitary disposal. As a side note, solo lap changing is entirely possible, but an extra pair of hands sure is nice for expediting the process and reducing the likelihood of a mess. Based on the rules of airplane etiquette, however, we don't suggest you seek assistance from any of your in-flight neighbors—unless, of course, they happen to be traveling with you. Most importantly, for the sake of your fellow travelers, we suggest that you make every effort to limit your lap changes to wet diapers and save the smelly ones for the lavatory.

In-Flight Feeding

As hard as it already is to eat a meal comfortably on a tiny tray table if and when you're offered one, traveling with your baby will likely add to the mealtime challenge. The first challenge is managing to eat your own meal; the second is feeding your infant in cramped quarters with the likelihood of onlookers 6 inches away. You may find that this is all the more reason to get your baby his own seat, freeing up space for your own meal and having a place to either secure or hold him while he's eating. Be aware that tray tables rarely, if ever, can be put all the way down flat in front of a car seat.

Breastfeeding in 6 Inches of Personal Space

Breastfeeding on airplanes presents its own unique set of obstacles. If your baby's car seat is in the window seat, you are in the middle seat, and a complete stranger is on the aisle encroaching on your shared armrest (which, as you know, is not just hypothetical), nursing comfortably may seem like an oxymoron. Here are a few suggestions that can help.

- **One-sided.** If the flight is short, nursing on just one side while saving the other for later when you get off the plane may be an acceptable option.
- **At an angle.** The close quarters greatly limit a breastfeeding mother's chance of privacy. Simply angling your body so that you're facing the window before trying to breastfeed can help minimize the degree of exposure.
- **Covering up.** For the sake of modesty or convenience, it may be well worth your while to wear a breastfeeding shirt or a loose-fitting top layer over a button-down or untucked shirt.
- **Layering.** Use your outer layer, a blanket, a magazine, or even the back part of your baby carrier as a practical way of obstructing the view.
- **Stalling.** Nursing in the lavatory may seem like a reasonable last resort, but suffice it to say that it generally poses a huge inconvenience for fellow passengers and isn't exactly hygienic. In other words, we don't really recommend it.

In-Flight Formula Preparation

Short of taking along the more expensive but ready-to-feed formula, the best way to have plenty of easily prepared formula on hand is to put premeasured amounts of powdered formula into several of your baby's bottles complete with nipples and lids. As an important forethought, be sure your bottles are completely dry before putting the formula in them, because a few drops of water left inside a bottle can make the powder stick to the sides in a manner reminiscent of cement. Needless to say, this can make future bottle cleaning a much more challenging proposition. Once the premeasured powder is sealed in dry bottles, tuck the bottles into your carry-on bag (or purse or diaper bag). Whenever it's time to feed your baby, simply add the appropriate amount of room-temperature water to each bottle.

And even though airlines still reliably offer beverage service on just about all flights, you can't always count on the timing. That's not to say that most flight attendants aren't quite accommodating, but there are inevitably going to be times (during take-off and landing, for example) when they are going to be unable to respond to your baby's urgent insistence. Instead, play it safe and bring along at least one extra bottle of water of your own. That way you won't have to worry about refrigeration, heating, or the timing of beverage service to be able to appease your suddenly starving child.

In-Flight Troubleshooting

As frequent fliers, we have often received wary looks from fellow passengers as we board a plane with a baby (or 2 or 3) and take our seats. We're not sure which is more stressful: being the passenger who first realizes he will be seated next to someone else's crying baby, or being that baby's parent. Fortunately for all involved, however, many young babies actually do travel well in flight; quite often it tends to be the crawlers and toddlers who get antsy and upset when confined, but that's a different book altogether.

High-Altitude Crying

Babies of all ages do cry for various reasons, so in the space constraints of aircraft, try to be resourceful when trying to calm your crying child. As you do, take comfort in knowing that the drone of the engines usually limits how far a crying baby can be heard. Keeping your own cool can go a long way when you're trying to soothe your baby and have to remain seated. Check the usual suspects and respond accordingly: Is your baby hungry, wet or dirty, cold or warm, bored? If it's bright, try closing the window shade; if your baby wants a view, show her the one outside the window or in the pages of the airline's magazine. Sometimes changing the scenery is all it takes to stop a little crying, so if the seat belt sign is not illuminated, you may want to get up and walk the aisles. If all else fails, try not to let a few dirty looks bother you and be assured that most people sympathize with the parents of a crying infant. After all, everyone was a baby once, many have had to try to quiet one in a public place at some time in their past, you're unlikely to have to face any of these people ever again and, lastly, they'll get over it.

The Ears Have It

Before we discuss ear pain on airplanes, let us first offer you the reassurance that a great many babies never show the slightest signs of discomfort. Until you know that your own child (and you) will be spared, the thought of a baby screaming because of ear pain is easily and understandably one of the most dreaded aspects of air travel. And from firsthand experience, we can tell you it tends to be all the more disconcerting when that baby happens to be your own. Any of you who have flown before know that ears can be quite sensitive to changes in pressure. Switching to pediatrician mode for a moment, this is because the outer ear is separated from the middle ear by a thin membrane (the tympanic membrane, or ear drum). Experiencing a difference in pressure across this membrane causes a sensation that as many as 1 in 3 passengers (children more so than adults) experience as temporary muffled hearing, discomfort, or even pain. Unfortunately, having a stuffy nose or a head cold can increase a child's chances of ear problems. For an adult, chewing gum or yawning is often all that is needed for the middle-ear pressure to equilibrate with the outer environment and make plugged-up ears pop. Perhaps part of the reason that babies tend to complain more about their ears than adults is because chewing gum is simply not an option and we have yet to meet an infant who can yawn on command. If your baby has a cold or ear infection, discuss with your pediatrician whether you can give him an infant pain reliever, some decongestant (which some pediatricians do recommend and some parents swear by, but which nevertheless has not been clearly proven to help), or whether it's best to postpone flying. In most instances, travel plans are not flexible enough to cancel because of a cold, but be aware of your increased odds of dealing with ear pain when you do hop aboard.

Sucking Away One's Sorrows

Once on board, it's useful to know that there is a practical and realistic alternative to gum chewing (which, for obvious reasons, is absolutely contraindicated at this age regardless of your level of desperation) that works very well for babies when it comes to relieving ear pressure—and that alternative is sucking. Pediatricians, flight attendants, and seasoned parents alike commonly suggest offering a bottle, breast, or pacifier during the times when the pressure changes in the cabin are likely to be greatest—during takeoff and initial descent. You'll notice we said *initial* descent, not landing. That's because the pressure change is typically most noticeable as much as a half hour or more before landing, depending on a flight's cruising altitude. The higher up you are, the earlier in the flight the descent usually starts. If you generally don't tend to notice your own ears popping and the captain doesn't announce plans for the initial descent, you can always ask a flight attendant to let you know when it would be a good idea to try to get the sucking started. If sucking doesn't cut it and your baby seems to be bothered, stay calm and try rubbing his ears and singing a soothing song. Even if you find that nothing short of reaching solid ground (and normal air pressure) works to calm him down, remind yourself that you've done everything you can, and that most babies who have difficulty with ear pain on airplanes tend to outgrow it.

OUT OF EARSHOT

Airplane cabin noise hovers around 100 decibels, and is even louder during takeoff. Using cotton balls or small earplugs may help to decrease the decibel level your baby is exposed to, and as a result make it easier for her to sleep or relax.

These Shoes Were Made for Wearing

As you make your way through airports and on and off airplanes, one thing's for sure—you'll be very grateful for comfortable shoes. And for those of you who were recently pregnant—just when you thought you'd seen the last of swollen feet, think again. Sitting for hours on a plane is a well-known cause of sluggish blood flow and swollen feet. Also misleadingly referred to as economy class syndrome, poor circulation and blood clots (called deep venous thrombosis, or DVT) resulting from air travel can affect people sitting anywhere in the airplane, not just in the coach cabin. As you focus your attention on changing, feeding, soothing, and entertaining your baby, remember to keep your shoes on (lest you're unable to get them back on) and stretch your feet and legs frequently throughout the flight.

PART V

just for the health of it

INTRODUCTION

No newborn parenting book worth its weight in diapers would be complete without an explanation of the most common medical aspects of newborn care, including a basic overview of the working parts and important signs of illness. The fact that we are both parents and pediatricians puts us in the relatively unique position of understanding what you are likely to want to know about ensuring the health and well-being of your precious new baby and what information pediatricians want all newborns' parents to be familiar with before they head home—most notably fever and jaundice. Having already included the obligatory disclaimer that we cannot and should not take the place of your own pediatrician, and having read far too many superficial parenting magazine checklists and questionnaires in parenting magazines on how to find yourself the "perfect" one, we decided to start out our Just for the Health of It section by offering you some practical (and more in-depth) "insider" advice on how best to approach the task of picking out a pediatrician you will be happy to call your very own.

CHAPTER 17

finding the right baby doctor—
a view from the inside out

As pediatricians and parents, we wholeheartedly agree with the current trend in which parents "interview" pediatricians to find the one that best suits them. After all, you can expect to pay a visit to your chosen health care provider at least 6 times during your baby's first year—and that's only accounting for the standard well-baby visits. It's worth starting out on your "mission" to find just the right one by keeping in mind that pediatrics, just like parenting, isn't always an exact science. When it comes to the art of pediatrics and parenting, you will undoubtedly come across a wide range of styles and opinions on what's best—whether you're discussing the use of antibiotics, feeding, approaches to colic, or how to handle sleep problems. Beyond finding someone who is well trained in the science of pediatrics, it will clearly be to your advantage to make sure that the person (or group of providers) you choose shares your own personal parenting philosophy and style.

Your Quest for the Best

We have every intention of including the specifics of what you can and should look for in your search for the "perfect physician." Before we do, we thought we'd toss in a little reality check: There's no such thing. That's because physicians are people too, and to date we have yet to meet a person—ourselves included—without quirks and flaws (real and perceived). Just like everyone else, doctors have good days and bad. Some are superb communicators and others are men and women of few words.

Some have families and children, some don't. Some have breastfed while others don't have breasts (which, for clarification, is not a commentary on breast size but on the difference between the presence or absence of a Y chromosome). Some work part-time while others put in unbelievably long hours and take call 24/7. Yet none of these traits alone guarantees you that you've found a model of perfection. Instead, we recommend that you take all of them into account and then factor in personality so that you end up finding someone you can really relate to. Remember—the doctor that seems perfect in the eyes of other parents may not be at all right for you. On a personal note, one of the hardest parts about beginning in private practice after finishing our pediatric training (aside from being bombarded with questions to which we were never taught the answers and trying to stick to some semblance of a schedule) was coming to grips with the fact that not everyone who came to see us was going to like us or our parenting philosophies. Over time we came to realize that it's just plain unnatural to see eye to eye with everyone—whether you're a parent or a pediatrician! The key is finding a good fit for everyone involved.

Let the Search Begin

The third trimester is an ideal time for you to start considering whom you want to serve as your baby's health care provider. Ask around to find out who in your area is well liked, well trained, and conveniently located. You'll find that in addition to friends, neighbors, and family members, obstetricians are often a great source for recommendations. So are the nurses in labor and delivery and the newborn nurseries—most of whom interact with area pediatricians on a regular basis and know which ones are the most skilled and which have the best bedside manner. Other reliable sources include the American Academy of Pediatrics Referral Service at www.aap.org/referral, the American Medical Association's Doctor Finder at www.ama-assn.org, or your local medical society.

BACKGROUND CHECK: THE AAP

Now is as good a time as any to familiarize yourself with the AAP because you're bound to come across these 3 letters at just about every turn in your search for reliable information and all-around parenting enlightenment. AAP stands for the American Academy of Pediatrics—a professional organization of about 60,000 pediatricians, pediatric medical subspecialists, and pediatric surgical specialists throughout the United States, Canada, and Latin America. If you happen to spot the letters FAAP after a doctor's name, it tells you that he or she is a Fellow of the American Academy of Pediatrics—a title bestowed on just over half of the AAP members in recognition of passing the pediatric board exam (which we can tell you from personal experience is no cake walk). As the authoritative source on health issues for children, the mission of the AAP is to attain optimal physical, mental, and social health and well-being for all infants, children, adolescents, and young adults.

Choosing Among Health Care Providers

You will find that we tend to refer to babies' health care providers as pediatricians in this chapter (and throughout the book) as a matter of convenience. It's important to note, however, that there are several types of health professionals who are qualified to care for babies and children.

- **MD and DO.** If doctors have an MD after their names, it simply tells you that they attended a "traditional" medical school. Others have the initials DO after their names—a designation that tells you they are graduates of osteopathic medical schools. MD and DO medical schools train physicians, and both types of doctors can go on to do pediatric residency training specializing in the care of children. While there are some differences between these 2 types of physicians, both are educated about normal human health and disease conditions.
- **Board-certified pediatrician.** Board-certified pediatricians are physicians who have graduated college, completed 4 years of medical school, and have at least 3 years of "on-the-job" training (residency) in pediatrics. To become board certified, pediatricians must also pass a rigorous 2-day examination given by the American Board of Pediatrics. To remain board certified, most physicians have to pass a board

exam every 7 years and maintain ongoing education in pediatrics to help ensure that they remain up to date on how best to provide quality care for children.

- **Family physician.** Family practice doctors can be either MDs or DOs and, like pediatricians, also complete medical school and at least 3 years of "on-the-job" training (in a family medicine residency). Like pediatricians, family physicians must also pass an examination to become board certified and then renew their certification (ie, pass a board exam) every 7 years. Unlike pediatricians, however, family physicians do not limit their practice to the care of children from birth through adolescence. As their titles imply, they care for patients of all ages.

- **Nurse practitioner.** In some instances, you may find that your baby is scheduled to see a pediatric or family nurse practitioner. These health care providers are registered nurses with additional education. Those who specialize in pediatrics generally have specific advanced training in caring for children. Nurse practitioners may work in your doctor's office in conjunction with or under the supervision of physicians.

Whomever you choose, you'll want to make sure that they have the training and/or experience to offer guidance on the health- and illness-related matters you may encounter—many of which are unique to childhood.

The Selection Process

Once you have found one (or a few) possible doctors, call the office(s) to see if it is possible to schedule a prenatal or "meet the doctor" visit. You might want to also ask if the visit is offered free of charge (because some doctors' offices do charge) or see if it's covered by your insurance. While just about all of the parenting books and magazines we've read suggest bringing along a standard set of questions for the doctor, we have found that most parents are left not knowing exactly what to do with the answers. Furthermore, you may find that the specific answers you do get are in reality less important in your decision-making process than the physician's personal style and whether you felt like you've clicked. That is why we have included several points to consider under each commonly asked question that follows. Remember that you are not necessarily looking for the smartest doctor in your area, or the one with the most patients, but one who is a good match for you, your family, and your parenting style. If at any point you feel this physician-patient relationship is not a good fit, even after you've already brought your baby home, we encourage you to discuss your concerns with your doctor, and if need be, to find another one.

The Issue of Insurance

Q: *Does your office accept my insurance?*

This question is worth asking even before you set up an interview because the reality of managed health care these days is that your insurance carrier may well dictate which physicians and practices you can take your child to and which ones you can't. Given the ever-increasing costs associated even with routine doctor visits, it's a rare parent who decides it's worth going outside of the system and paying out of pocket to see a particular doctor.

 INSURANCE ASSURANCE

As you plan for the arrival of your newborn, don't forget to check with your insurance company to find out what you need to do to have your baby added to your insurance policy, and be sure to have any and all necessary forms submitted within the required number of days (usually 30) after your baby is born.

How Privileged Is Your Provider?

Q: *Do you have hospital privileges at the place where we plan to deliver?*

While this information is worth knowing, we've found that it rarely factors into a parent's decision about their baby's health care provider unless they feel very strongly about seeing that particular person in the hospital. If you decide to take your baby to a health care provider who does not have hospital privileges where you plan to deliver, your baby will still be seen and evaluated by a qualified physician at the hospital. On discharge from the hospital, you can proceed to arrange all of your well-baby visits with your chosen provider.

Q: *Where do you admit infants and children in the event that they require hospitalization?*

The answer to this question is important only if you (or your insurance company) have a strong preference for one hospital over another because your baby's physician will naturally admit your child to the hospital at which he or she has privileges. Some physicians have privileges at multiple hospitals, which may give you some flexibility.

Asking About Availability

Q: *What are your office hours and location(s)?*

While you're probably like most parents in that you'd be willing to drive to the ends of the earth for your unborn or newborn child, chances are good that when given the choice, you'd rather not have to drive across town much less all over creation every time your baby needs to see the doctor. As with nearly everything from real estate to diaper pails, location will most likely play some role in your decision. You'll also want to find out whether the practice you're considering has office hours that actually suit your needs. If your schedule is flexible, extended hours may not be such an important factor. For those of you who can barely make it to the post office during banker's hours, much less set up camp in your doctor's waiting room on a work day, you may want to look around for a practice that offers weekend hours and/or stays open late on weekdays.

Q: *How does your office handle scheduling appointments, answering patient phone calls, and after-hours emergencies? How difficult is it to get an appointment for a sick visit? For a routine checkup?*

Don't cross doctors off your list simply because they are not always available to answer your questions personally and in a timely fashion in the middle of a busy work day—so long as qualified members of their staff are ready, willing, and able to help you during regular business hours. The office should have a well-defined mechanism to contact the doctor (or clear instructions as to where to go directly) in case of an after-hours question or emergency. Again, this is some good basic information to have about your chosen (or considered) practice, but it's not likely that you'll be told something that makes you decide to look elsewhere. In reality, you're more likely to find out after you've started going to a particular practice whether your wait time is unacceptably long, whether you're able to get advice by phone or schedule appointments relatively easily, and if you're happy with the overall workings of the office.

Q: *Is Timeliness Next to Goodliness?*

Being a punctual pediatrician is *much* easier said than done. That's because pediatricians never really know how long any one visit is going to take until they are in the room, which makes scheduling a best-guess attempt. Having said that, factoring a doctor's visit into your own less than predictable and very demanding schedule is not any easier. That's why you and your doctor should each do your best to show up on time, and yet be willing to cut each other some slack every now and then in acknowledgment of the strenuous jobs you both have. That said, if your doctor routinely runs late—not just 15 to 30 minutes every now and then but regularly more than an hour—then it's worth considering if there is something wrong with the way your doctor is setting up the schedule.

Tricks of the Scheduling Trade

To give you your best shot at avoiding the pediatric practice rush hours, traffic delays, and peak travel days, we suggest

- **Be the first out of the gate.** Ask for the first appointment of the day, or pick a time right after lunch whenever possible. These are the times when traffic is less likely to have backed up. We have no insider knowledge to share with you about how to avoid those days when your doctor arrives late in the morning or takes an extended lunch break; in those situations all bets are off.
- **Schedule mid-week.** Mondays and Fridays are notoriously busy in the doctor's office because parents either come in anticipation of a weekend without convenient access, or come in as soon as they can after going it alone with a sick child over the weekend.
- **Avoid holidays, vacations, and predictable events.** Rush-hour traffic on the road may slow down considerably on national holidays and during vacation times, but this is often a time when parents can opt to

bring their kids into the doctor without having to take a day off from work. It's not that you shouldn't set out to visit your pediatrician on, say, President's Day—you are just not likely to be alone. On holidays when your doctor's office is open, hours may be reduced and they may be short-staffed—both factors that increase your likelihood of a longer wait. For future reference, there also tends to be a bit of a mad rush at the end of the summer when kids all but flood in for school physicals.

• **Anticipate extended visits.** If you anticipate needing extra time with your baby's doctor, ask if you can be scheduled additional time for the visit, and consider taking the last appointment of the day when your doctor won't feel the pressure of lots of other parents stacking up behind you.

Training and Experience

Q: *What is your training background and level of experience?*

Our first response to you on this one is to figure out how much you really care. As practicing physicians, we all have diplomas hanging on our walls and have had to go through the careful scrutiny of the state licensure board before hanging a shingle. And to be board certified in pediatrics, everyone has to pass the same test regardless of where he or she trained. While some new parents conclude that the older and more experienced a pediatrician is, the better, plenty of others find themselves interested in taking their babies to a younger provider— one that they feel shares more of their contemporary attitudes or perhaps has children of a similar age.

Going Solo?

Q: *Will other physicians in the practice see my baby?*

This is a perfectly legitimate question, but it shouldn't surprise you if the answer is yes. While there are still a fair number of solo practitioners out there, there has been a definite trend toward group practice. If you are considering a group practice, you may be better off asking how many days a week the practitioner you're interested in seeing works and if you'll be able to request visits with that person whenever he or she is in the office. Given that pediatricians are just like everyone else and occasionally take days off, get sick, or go on vacations, you'll also want to make sure that you are comfortable with the other practitioners in the group who will take over when yours is not available.

Seeing Eye to Eye

Q: *What is your philosophy about particular medical treatments such as circumcision, the use of antibiotics, or giving routine vaccines? What is your approach to breastfeeding? Sleep problems? Colic?*

If you don't have strong feelings about child rearing or definite opinions regarding your child's medical care, then you'll be able to focus your attention more on other factors such as those listed above when selecting a pediatrician that's right for you. More often than not, however, parents and pediatricians alike have strong feelings about certain approaches to raising children. If you are dead set against using formula or pacifiers, for example, you will definitely want to find out which providers in your area are the most supportive of and experienced in the practicalities of breastfeeding. Similarly, if you are a big believer in cosleeping and the family bed, then you might consider asking potential providers their thoughts on the subject ahead of time.

Personal Characteristics

Your search for a pediatrician need not be scientifically based or entirely logical. It is perfectly reasonable to take into account personal qualities in your quest. Depending on your own comfort level or the gender of your child, you may prefer a male pediatrician instead of a female (or vice versa). It may be a priority for you to have your child treated by someone who has firsthand experience as a parent, shares your cultural or religious background, or has an authoritative style instead of a collaborative one (or again, vice versa).

A Room of One's Own

It's worth discussing the feature of separate waiting rooms (separating those who are sick and those who are well) if for no other reason than because it seems to have become standard for magazines and parenting books to recommend finding a practice that has them. We wholeheartedly agree that in an ideal world (or at least in an ideal doctor's office) it would be very nice to keep those who happen to be coming to the doctor because of an illness away from those who have yet to catch one—especially when those who are well include you and your baby. We want to point out that it's not exactly realistic to think you can successfully dodge all illnesses—either in or out of the doctor's office. After all, people tend to be most contagious *before* they develop symptoms, and we all live in a world full of bacteria and viruses. To be honest, we've never actually known a parent to choose a practice based on whether it had one waiting room or two. In our experience, parents are usually more concerned with how long they have to wait to be seen than where.

Our thoughts on the matter: Ask if it's possible for you and your newborn to wait in an empty examination room if you're not comfortable with the waiting room arrangement. Other than that, we suggest using common sense just as you would when taking your baby out anywhere in public, limit the amount that others are allowed to come in direct contact with him, shield him from the direct line of fire if someone nearby is coughing or sneezing, and use criteria other than architectural design to determine if a particular pediatrician/practice is right for you.

In the End

When it comes to the bottom line and making a decision, we hope we've persuaded you that there's more than one "right" answer to each question, and that you are well-equipped to figure out your own right answers. When all is said and done and you've weighed all your choices, remind yourself that while you're not exactly searching for a new best friend, you certainly want to find a doctor whose style best suits your own needs and who is going to be a supportive partner in your exciting and educational journey through parenthood.

CHAPTER 18

head to toe and in between

Ever wish that parenthood came with a tour guide and your new-born came with an instruction manual? Given that we are determined to serve as helpful tour guides and this book is, in many ways, meant to play the role of an instruction manual, we certainly don't want to neglect any of the nuts and bolts of baby care. The following is an up close and personal look at all of the involved parts—a handful of which are unique to infancy, such as the shriveled up umbilical cord and the soft spot on the top of every newborn's head. Others we discuss not because they would otherwise be unfamiliar to you, but because the context has changed. Chances are good you've never paid so much attention to or been solely responsible for some-one else's fingernails, tear ducts, or noses before. Without any further ado, we'll get on with the tour.

From the Beginning—How Far Things Have Come

A Quick Glance Back

You may find that part of the wonder of your beautiful new child is trying to comprehend just how he or she could possibly have come to be. Not just the birds and the bees stuff, but the fact that a single fertilized egg can grow and develop into a newborn baby in a matter of a few short months. When you think about it, becoming a parent is nothing less than miraculous. Yes, we know that referring to the many long weeks of pregnancy as "relatively short" may lead you to question whether we've actually experienced the joys of pregnancy before, but we assure you we have. It's just that in the grand scheme of things, the reality of what was once a microscopic blur now taking the form of a newborn represents the fastest rate of growth that we as human beings ever experience over the course of our entire lifetimes. As you prepare yourself for what lies ahead, here's a quick look back at how far you (and your baby) have come.

- 4 weeks: your baby probably measured no more than a large grain of sand
- 9 weeks: about the size of an olive
- 14 weeks: about the size of a fist
- 24 weeks: around 1 pound
- 32 weeks: half of his ultimate birth weight
- Newborns: an average weight of 7 pounds 5 ounces and roughly 20 inches long.

Sizing Up the Situation

Many parents are greatly relieved to find out that it is perfectly normal for newborns to lose weight—up to 10% of their birth weight, in fact—before they start gaining it back again. This characteristic weight loss tends to be more pronounced in newborns who are breastfed (see "Breastfeeding" on page 5) than for those who are bottle-fed. In either case, all newborns are expected to turn the corner, stop losing weight, and start gaining back ounces all within the first week or so—ultimately regaining or even exceeding their birth weight by 2 weeks. Monitoring day-to-day weight changes (and even comparing before- and after-feeding weights) serves as a rela-

     WEIGHT LIST

In the first few days, most newborns lose several ounces, but usually not more than 10% of their birth weight. That means that a baby who weighs 7 pounds at birth may well drop the scales instead of top them—reaching a weight as low as 6 pounds 4 ounces or so before turning things around.

In the first few weeks, babies gain up to an ounce per day, or as much as a pound per week.

Your baby is likely to double her birth weight by 4 months of age and triple it by the time her first birthday rolls around.

In the spirit of looking ahead, you can estimate your baby's adult height by doubling her height at age 2 years.

tively good indicator of whether newborns are getting enough to eat. You'll therefore find that your baby's pediatrician pays close attention to your baby's day-by-day numbers in the hospital and in the days after discharge. This will be especially true while you are waiting for your milk to come in and if your newborn gets off to a sleepy start, is uninterested in eating, or is simply a poky eater.

Parts Is Parts

Taking It From the Top

As you've undoubtedly noticed, newborns have little to no head control—at best mustering up their resolve to briefly pick up or turn their heads. In part, this is because it requires a fair bit of strength and the muscles involved simply need time to develop. Babies also have another factor working against them when it comes to holding their heads up high, and that is their sheer size. While your baby's head may not seem all that big to you, take a moment and compare it to the size of the rest of his body. Now make the same comparison between your own head and body. Your baby's head is proportionately much bigger, making him unquestionably top heavy. On a practical note, we thought we'd point out a point of parental interest: Newborns' big heads don't require extra attention just by new parents. Clothing manufacturers have also taken note and subsequently figured out how to accommodate them as well, designing infant clothing with expandable and stretchy wide collars or adding snaps, zippers, or buttons to narrower necklines.

 HEAD HANDLING WITH CARE

On a more serious note, head size along with a distinct lack of head control leave babies very susceptible to injury. This is why it is so important never to shake a baby. Doing so has the potential to cause much more serious harm than it would in older children or adults. As for the soft spot, it's not as vulnerable as one might think, but it still warrants being handled with care (see "The Soft Spot" on page 225).

Room to Grow

The fact that the bony plates that make up your baby's skull won't join together for many months is quite fortunate. By remaining open and expandable, they allow your baby's brain to grow. You will find that your pediatrician routinely monitors this growth by measuring your baby's head circumference (the distance around the largest part of your baby's head) and recording it on a head circumference growth curve right alongside her weight and height. On average, your newborn's head should

- Increase in circumference by as much as 2 inches over the next 2 months
- Reach about 90% of adult head size by the time your child turns 2 years

 ## A BIG HEAD USUALLY MEANS... A BIG HAT

While there are certainly some instances when a big head can signify an underlying medical problem, it's reassuring to keep in mind that the most common cause of a big head is genetics; the tendency toward having a big head simply runs in the family.

The Shape of Things to Come

This topic is particularly directed toward those of you who have been mistakenly led to believe that all newborns are born picture perfect with pretty little round heads. Let us just say that for anyone who has gone through or will experience vaginal delivery, it is nothing short of a blessing that a baby's skull is made up of soft bony plates that are capable of compressing and overlapping to fit through the narrow birth canal—a process referred to as molding. For some babies—such as those who "drop" well in advance of being born (in other words, settle themselves head first deep into their mother's pelvis well in advance of delivery), or those who must endure long labors and narrow birth canals—the result is often a newborn head shape that more closely resembles a cone than a nice round ball. If you run your fingers over your baby's skull, you may also find that you can feel ridges along the areas where the bony plates of the skull have overlapped. In short, cone heads are quite normal. Fortunately, over the next several weeks the bones of your baby's skull will almost assuredly round out and the ridges will disappear.

The Soft Spot

You will notice one if not 2 areas on your baby's head that seem to be missing bony protection. These soft spots, referred to as *fontanelles* (anterior for the larger one in the front, posterior for the smaller, often less noticeable, one in the back), are normal gaps in a newborn's skull that allow your baby's brain to grow rapidly throughout the next year. In the meantime, many parents are afraid to touch these soft spots, but you can rest assured that, despite their lack of a bony layer, they are well protected from typical day-to-day baby handling. Other things to know about the soft spot(s)

Fontanelle

- In young infants, a sunken soft spot (when combined with poor feeding and dry diapers) can suggest dehydration. Our advice to you: Don't read too much into this because it can be a subtle finding or sometimes be present in normal babies. Instead, make sure you have a good grasp on how to recognize dehydration (see "What Goes In Must Come Out" on page 59) and check with your doctor if you have any concerns—with or without a sunken soft spot.
- In some instances, the soft spot on the top of your baby's head may seem to be pulsating. There is no need to worry—this movement is quite normal and simply reflects the visible pulsing of blood that corresponds to your baby's heartbeat.

Cover-Up

Ever wonder who was in charge of determining what's the latest style in newborn head wear in the newborn nursery? Well before you spend too much time laying blame, we figured we'd point out that those typically unattractive polyester knit newborn caps aren't given out just for looks.

Newborn babies not only have proportionately bigger heads, but they don't regulate their body temperatures as well as adults or even older infants do and therefore stand to lose a significant amount of heat from their heads if they are left uncovered. This is the real reason that it's generally recommended that you put a hat on your baby's head during the first few weeks—especially in cool weather or drafty rooms.

Bumps and Bruises

In addition to molding, it is not uncommon for newborns to have a bit of swelling or bruising of the scalp immediately following delivery. The swelling usually is most noticeable at the top back part of the head and is medically referred to as a caput (short for caput succedaneum). When bruising of the head occurs during delivery, the result can be a boggy-feeling area, called a cephalohematoma. Bruising and molding are usually harmless and go away on their own over the first days and weeks of life.

Gone Today, but Hair Tomorrow

Sure, babies are sometimes born with full heads of hair, but it's far more likely for them to be born with little to none. And those with hair today are likely to find it gone tomorrow, because any hair your newborn is born with is likely to thin out significantly over the next few months before ultimately being replaced with "real" hair. It is also entirely possible that whatever hair your baby does have will change color by several shades and several times over his lifetime.

Cradle Cap

Although seborrheic dermatitis is the technically correct term for cradle cap (the baby dandruff equivalent), parents faced with scaly newborn scalps tend to agree that it is more appropriately called cradle "crap." Although harmless, flaky scalps tend to drive some parents nuts. That's most often because cradle cap can be a nuisance to get rid of—especially for those babies who have a lot of it. While you can certainly try the standardly recommended approach of massaging affected areas with a little baby oil or olive oil and then gently removing the flakes with a soft brush (some use soft-bristled toothbrushes), we strongly suggest you don't lose any sleep over it. Your pediatrician can give you additional advice if you're looking for it, but we've found that quite often it's best simply to let cradle cap run its course.

The Eyes Have It

Do You See What I See?

When it comes to baby vision, the eyes don't really have it all until 4 or more years down the road—about the time when 20/20 color vision is thought to set in. That does not mean, however, that your newborn can't see anything. Here's a glimpse of what your newborn can see.

- **From a distance.** Because of their limited range of vision, newborns tend to pay closest attention to objects near their faces. At birth, your newborn should be able to see a good 12 inches in front of him fairly clearly—the perfect distance at which to gaze at your smiling face.
- **In contrast.** Early on, babies are rumored to prefer items with contrasting colors. While this serves as a good explanation for the popularity and marketing of red-white-black infant toys, the truth is that you really don't need to go out of your way to offer your newborn a healthy daily dose of visual stimulation. Your everyday interactions and commonplace baby objects (such as books, pictures, or rattles) should suffice.
- **Gaining control.** While it is relatively common for babies younger than 4 months or so to appear cross-eyed on occasion, they should develop better eye-muscle control relatively quickly. Normal eye alignment and the ability to focus are key factors in developing normal eyesight, so you should be sure to mention any unusual eye movements you notice to your baby's pediatrician.

 NO MORE TEARS...YET

Newborn babies don't typically shed tears in the first month or two of life. This is because the tear ducts aren't fully functional yet—but never fear, they will be up and running soon enough.

Duct Work

Your newborn has tiny tear ducts located in the inner corner of each eye that drain into the nose and, when functioning properly, play an important role in draining tears. We liken this drainage system to a sewer system; if and when babies become stuffy, those that happen to have been born with narrower than usual (or blocked) tear ducts may experience a noticeable backup in the sewer system.

Tear duct

Unable to adequately keep up with the normal ebb and flow, tears back up—resulting in a more watery and/or goopy eye (or eyes). If you and your pediatrician determine that your baby has a blocked tear duct or two, you can clean off any goop that accumulates around your baby's eyes by gently wiping the lids with a warm, damp, clean towel or tissue. We should point out that eye goop often seems to bother parents much more than it does newborns. When the going gets goopy, we recommend you resist the temptation and keep your wiping in check—limiting it to when things get really nasty. Although its usefulness is debated, some pediatricians also

 PINK EYE

While blocked tear ducts end up being solely to blame for a good many goopy eyes, it is nevertheless going to be important for you to be aware of and on the lookout for pink eye. Although pink eye generically refers to any eye that appears pink (or red) regardless of cause, the term is often used to describe actual eye infections. Although it's easy enough for us to tell you that true infections often have a thicker yellow or greenish discharge and are more likely to be accompanied by some degree of swelling and/or redness, distinguishing between the two is easier said than done. It is very important for eye infections to be diagnosed and treated without delay, so any suspicions you may have should promptly be followed up with a phone call to your pediatrician. If your baby has already been diagnosed with a blocked tear duct, you'll still want to watch for signs of infection, because infants who have blocked tear ducts are more prone to developing eye infections than those who don't.

recommend lightly pressing and then gently massaging the area between the corner of the eye and the nose downwards—presumably to help relieve any obstruction in the duct and get things moving. Most blocked ducts get better by the first birthday. Those that don't clear up on their own generally necessitate a trip to see a pediatric ophthalmologist, who may deem it necessary to use a small probe to carefully open up the uncooperative duct(s).

What's Going to Make Those Brown Eyes Blue?

What you see when you gaze into your newborn's eyes is not always what you'll ultimately get when it comes to eye color. Not only are the genetics of eye color quite complex, but predicting a baby's future eye color before birth is relatively unreliable. We can tell you, however, that a baby's eye color depends on how much of a particular pigment there is in the colored part of the eye, or the iris. The more of this pigment—called melanin—there is, the darker brown a baby's eyes will appear. Conversely, babies with blue eyes have very little melanin. Anywhere in between results in varying shades of brown, hazel, or green. With that in mind, it will probably make more sense to you when we tell you that if your baby is born with brown eyes, nothing short of colored contact lenses is likely to change her eye color to blue. However, babies who are blue-eyed at birth have the potential to produce more melanin over time and end up with eyes of a different color (usually by 6 months of age or so) than those they were born with. Interestingly, some older kids and adults also continue to see changes in their eye color as they age (even without the help of fashionable contact lenses).

Seeing Red

Ever end up with red eyes in photographs? If so, then you're already familiar with exactly the same reflex your pediatrician is looking for when he or she shines the light from an ophthalmoscope into your newborn's eyes—the red reflex. What may be a nuisance to photographers happens to be a very reassuring sign for pediatricians when it occurs in newborns. The red reflex not only reflects the presence of normal retinas at the back of your baby's eyes (appearing red because of the many blood vessels located there), but also tells us that light can make its way all the way in and back out again unobstructed. An absent (or white) reflex, in contrast, may mean there is a problem with the eye.

We're All Ears

Setting the Sound Stage

Did the latest music CDs for yet to be born babies catch your attention? Perhaps you came across parents-to-be who religiously read books to the bulging belly that was soon to become their child. Well, as tempting as it may be to get a head start on a baby's education, we suggest that expectant parents sit back and relax during their pregnancies because there will be plenty of time for teaching later. Now with that said, if your idea of relaxing happens to include listening to a little classical music or taking a few practice runs through *Goodnight Moon* before bed, your efforts are not likely to fall on deaf ears—at least not after your sixth or seventh month. That's because the parts of the ear involved in hearing generally finish developing by 24 weeks, and by 28 weeks fetuses have been shown to respond consistently to sound in utero.

  SOUND ADVICE

Whereas an adult can typically hear sounds at around 13.5 decibels (the level of a soft whisper), a fetus between 27 and 29 weeks is able to detect sounds at a level closer to 40 decibels—the average sound of a running refrigerator or the flow of light traffic. By the time a baby reaches full term, his ability to hear will have matured to such an extent that he can hear sounds similar to those heard by adults. While the American Academy of Pediatrics recommends that *all* newborns have their hearing checked prior to discharge, this universal approach to newborn hearing screening is only presently mandated in 38 states. You may want to check and see what your hospital's policy is, because some hospitals only routinely test the hearing of newborns that meet certain criteria (eg, whether they have a family history of deafness, were born prematurely, or were treated with certain antibiotics). Even if your newborn's hearing isn't officially evaluated before you head home, you should remember to take note of whether you notice your newborn responding to sound—turning toward the sound of your voice or startling in response to loud noise. If you have any doubts, your pediatrician can help you determine if a hearing test is recommended or if one has already been done, and whether a follow-up hearing evaluation is necessary.

Accessorizing

It may (or may not) surprise you that one of the most frequent ear-related questions we get is "How soon can I get my baby daughter's ears pierced?" Our response: If you can wait until your child is several years older—an age when she will be less susceptible to infection, better able to care for her own ear piercings, and much less likely to swallow the tiny (and not generally size-appropriate for children younger than 3 years) parts inherent to wearing earrings—we highly recommend doing so. If, however, you feel compelled to have your infant's ears pierced during infancy, then you'd be well-advised to wait for at least 2 weeks after she gets her 2-month shots, one of which will be an immunization against tetanus. Then try to find an experienced piercer who uses sterile equipment and, if possible, has experience piercing baby earlobes. As with many things, you'd be wise to check with your pediatrician first. A few actually provide this service themselves, while others may be able to steer you in the direction of someone they feel is careful and trustworthy.

Your Baby's Nose Knows

Despite the fact that mouth breathing seems as though it should be a perfectly reasonable alternative, newborns are, for the most part, "obligated" to breathe through their narrow little noses for a good 5 months or so. Knowing that, it should begin to make sense to you why many newborns develop noisy breathing with the slightest amount of stuffiness or dryness. Add a snotty-nose cold and congestion to the picture and the effects

---

 THE AIR MOVES IN,
THE AIR MOVES OUT

Every now and then, a baby's nasal passageway doesn't develop and open up the way it's supposed to. A quick and easy way to determine whether air is able to make its way in and out of your newborn's nose normally is to take a thin piece of cotton (stretch out the tip of a cotton swab or part of a cotton ball) and hold it just in front of one nostril while lightly pressing the other nostril closed. You should see the cotton move gently each time your baby breathes out.

become much more noticeable and inconvenient—especially at feeding time. Below we have included some of the basic techniques recommended for ridding your baby of unwanted snot and congestion in the hopes of keeping everyone breathing easy.

- **Nose drops.** Often referred to as saline nose drops, they work by simply moistening and loosening up mucus. They are inexpensive, sold over-the-counter, and readily available just about anywhere that sells basic baby supplies. They can be used alone (to moisten or loosen things up) or followed by a bulb suction. If you are so inclined, you can even make your own by mixing 1/4 teaspoon of salt in 1 cup of warm water. Use just a few drops at a time.

- **Bulb suction.** We've included this option not because we think it always works, but because some new parents are quick to reach for their bulb suctions when in search of fast relief. While we readily admit that they can and do serve a definite purpose for babies (and parents) in their more snotty times of need, we suggest you take a moment to consider what it feels like to have a piece of rubber or plastic shoved, however gently, up your nose. After factoring in this not-so-comfortable thought, we recommend that you limit the use of a bulb suction to those times when your baby not only seems to be truly congested and has a big blob of mucus in clear view, but when the snot actually seems to be interfering with your baby's ability to eat and/or breathe. If, on the other hand, the goober is just hanging out minding its own business and not really bothering anyone (save for its appearance), consider giving your bulb suction a rest and grab a tissue instead.

 SUCCESSFUL SUCTIONING

If and when you do need to use a suction bulb to remove mucus, it's generally a good idea to limit your attempts to about 3 times a day, as more frequent use can irritate your baby's nasal lining and make him even more congested. For best results, press down lightly on one nostril to hold it closed while you gently suction the other side, keeping in mind that the middle part of each nostril tends to be the most sensitive to probing.

- **Vaporize.** Running a vaporizer or a humidifier in your baby's room is almost a knee-jerk reaction of parents everywhere when faced with the challenges of a baby with a stuffy nose cold. While, to be perfectly honest, we don't generally see a hugely noticeable response, there are definitely times (such as when your baby won't sleep or eat because she's congested and irritable) when you'll probably agree that every little bit helps. Adding moisture to the air is certainly one small step in the right direction. You may find that running a hot shower with the door closed and then sitting in the steamy bathroom with your baby can also help improve the drainage.

Sneezing

Newborns typically sneeze a lot. You can save yourself a lot of unnecessary worry if you remember to chalk the sneezes up to sensitive reflexes rather than over-interpret them as a sign of illness. Most babies outgrow this tendency to sneeze in response to the slightest little tickle within a few months—at about the same time as they begin to gain control over their other reflexes (see "Reflexes" on page 248).

Mouth to Mouth

Most new parents have few, if any, concerns about their newborns' mouths—that is, unless they see something that they think doesn't belong there. If you find anything in your baby's mouth that surprises you or that you're just not sure about, be sure to bring it to the attention of your pediatrician. Typical in-mouth sightings can include everything from

- **White/clear bumps.** Whitish bumps are sometimes found or appear on the gums, lips, or roof of the mouth. Generally harmless, they often serve to fool parents into thinking that a tooth is erupting months before one pokes its way through the gum.
- **Newborn (or natal) teeth.** On rare occasion, infant teeth decide to erupt way ahead of schedule—sometimes even showing up right at birth. If your doctor doesn't notice them first, you'll definitely want to point them out because they may need to be removed.
- **Sucking blisters.** Babies can develop blisters just from sucking—something they obviously do a lot of in their first weeks and months. They

appear most often on the lips, but sometimes on fingers or even toes as well, if and when newborns manage to reach them and get them to their mouths. Sucking blisters generally require no treatment and end up going away on their own.

- **White coating.** If you start to see white on the inside of your newborn's mouth, you'll want to consider 2 major causes—either lingering breast milk/formula or thrush. The white of thrush (a yeast infection found in the mouth) tends to appear most often on the tongue and hidden in the nooks and crannies of the mouth—commonly tucked between the cheeks and gums. Thrush is often overlooked or written off as residual formula or breast milk until it persists and spreads. As a rough rule of thumb, any white spots or patches in a newborn's mouth that don't easily wipe off with a cotton swab should be evaluated for thrush and treated accordingly.

Thrush Attack

Thrush is caused by a type of yeast *(Candida)* that commonly lives in the intestinal tract and is also responsible for some diaper rashes. Unlike the red spots and patches it is known to cause on a baby's rear end, *Candida* forms spots and/or patches of white in the mouth that don't easily wipe away and slowly spread. While many parents consider thrush to be a pain in the butt, in most instances it is fortunately not a pain in the mouth—simply a nuisance. Your baby's pediatrician can help make the diagnosis and set you up to remedy the situation. Good ways of treating thrush include

- **Liquid yeast medication.** This comes as a prescription solution suitable for putting in your baby's mouth. While you'll want to follow your doctor's recommendations—typically putting one dropperful in each cheek 4 times a day—the underlying approach to treatment is even more straightforward: Look for white spots and try to get your medicated solution on them (we prefer to use a clean cotton swab).
- **Thinking outside the mouth.** You aren't likely to rid your baby of thrush unless you address the problem outside of her mouth as well as in it. It takes a good boiling to kill the yeast that hangs out on pacifiers and baby bottle nipples. And for those of you who breastfeed, be forewarned that *Candida* doesn't limit itself to artificial nipples. If your baby has thrush

and/or you experience a burning, irritated feeling on your nipples, check with your doctor about treatment for yourself as well (see "What's Behind Burning Nipples" on page 20).

- **Persistence.** Thrush isn't always easy to get rid of. Not only does it hide out in hard-to-reach places, but it has an annoying habit of popping back up again just when you think you, your bottle of yeast medication, and your boiled pacifiers have conquered it. Even when the coast seems clear, keep your guard up and watch for any new white spots to appear.
- **The purple approach.** If your baby's thrush is widespread and/or persistent despite your best efforts, your pediatrician may suggest the use of a purple-staining, yeast-killing solution called gentian violet. While effective, we strongly suggest you anticipate a bit of a mess and be prepared to postpone baby photos for several days after gentian violet is applied to let the purple staining in and around your baby's mouth fade first.

Tongue Tied

We're all born with a little tissue called a frenulum that connects the bottom of our tongues with the floor of our mouths. Babies occasionally are born with a frenulum that extends as far out as the tip of the tongue—seeming to "tie" a newborn's tongue, limit its ability to stick out past the lips, and interfere with sucking and feeding—but most are harmless and require no treatment. In the past, doctors were quick to snip that tissue to help with feeding or speech, but nowadays all but the most extreme cases are left well enough alone.

Smiling

No one knows exactly why newborns first begin to smile when they are sleeping—waiting a few weeks until they carry over to the daytime. Nor is it easy to say exactly when during the first month your baby's smiles will become more intentional. If you ask us, does it really matter? We don't find it very worthwhile to spend much time debating the meaning of a smile because we think any newborn smile is enough to melt a parent's heart.

Chest

A Breath of Fresh…Fluid?

Take a moment and consider the fact that babies actually practice breathing well before they're born. It is not exactly intuitive, given that their lungs are filled with amniotic fluid right up until the day when they decide to leave their cozy surroundings, enter the outside world, and take their first big breath of fresh air. This fluid, found in all babies' lungs throughout pregnancy, is essential for normal lung development. So is time. For the first month and a half of pregnancy, fetal lungs take on their basic shape and structure. If you think of the lungs as a tree, this is the period where the trunk and major branches are formed. Up until the 25th week, smaller branches form and then the smallest "leaves"—known as alveoli—start to develop and take on the structure ultimately necessary to breathe in oxygen. By the time a baby reaches full term, he is estimated to have anywhere from 50 to 150 million alveoli. This number actually continues to increase over the first several years of life, burgeoning to a total of about 300 million alveoli in adulthood.

Baby Breaths

For anyone not already familiar with some of the notable differences between the way adults and newborns breathe, some of the characteristic newborn breathing habits may make you more than a little nervous. In the interest of sparing you unnecessary angst, we wanted to familiarize you with 2 of the more common tendencies.

- **Picking up the pace.** Perhaps one of the most common questions we get about the newborn breathing style is if it's normal for them to breathe so fast. The answer is yes—even at rest, infants breathe considerably faster than adults in addition to having faster resting heart rates.
- **Taking a break.** The tendency of newborns to take several breaths in rapid succession followed by a few seconds of rest—referred to as periodic breathing—is common and often disconcerting to parents caught previously unaware. As long as newborns remember to limit their pauses to no more than a few seconds and experience no accompanying color changes, then periodic breathing is considered a normal, harmless habit.

Breasts

We're willing to bet that there are many of you out there who were hoping that there were going to be at least a few body parts that you could put off thinking about until puberty. In addition to recommending a great book for you to read when you aren't quite so sleep deprived (called *From Diapers to Dating: A Parent's Guide to Raising Sexually Healthy Children* by Debra Haffner), we wanted to be sure to mention that baby girls and baby boys alike are, on occasion, born with enlarged breasts. That's right, the swelling of one or both breasts can vary from subtle to fairly pronounced and is thought to be the result of babies' exposure to their mothers' hormones during pregnancy. Some newborns even have some milky white breast discharge to go along with the swelling—something you may have heard referred to as witches' milk. The good news: You don't need to do anything about the swelling or discharge. Swollen newborn breasts generally disappear on their own within a few weeks to months.

 "IT'S A NUBBIN"

Nubbins, extra nipples, supernumerary nipples, accessory nipples—whatever you want to call them—these so-called third nipples are extra breast tissue found on the chest below the level of a baby's 2 normal nipples (and as low down as on the abdomen). Brought into the national spotlight on an early episode of "Friends" (Chandler had one), they're hardly ever of any medical significance, rarely change during puberty, and in most cases are small enough and flat enough either to go unnoticed or to look like birthmarks. Some babies, however, are born with a third nipple that more closely resembles a normal nipple. If they become a source of embarrassment later in life, they can be removed.

The Care and Keeping of the Cord

The umbilical cord is one of the new-baby body parts that seems to get the most attention. After serving for so many months as a vital connection between mom and baby, it quickly becomes unnecessary once your baby is born and starts breathing and eating on her own. You can expect your newborn's umbilical cord stump to dry up and fall off within a few weeks (anywhere from 1 to 5, to be more precise). In the meantime, you may be relieved to know that the blood vessels that once ran through it are now closed off, and your baby's umbilical cord and belly button are no longer a direct connection to anywhere.

Letting Go

Many new parents are very tentative when it comes to caring for their newborn's umbilical cord. For the most part, dealing with the umbilical cord actually means waiting for it to fall off. While some health care professionals apply a special infection-preventing purple dye after birth and others recommend gently applying rubbing alcohol to the umbilical cord stump to help it stay clean and dry, it has become routine in the past few years for pediatricians to recommend doing absolutely nothing. When left alone, most umbilical cords will just fall off by themselves. Even if you're not going to apply rubbing alcohol, we've found that it still helps to speed up the drying process by intermittently pushing down the skin surrounding the

---

 UNCOOPERATIVE CORDS

Some of you may benefit from a little forewarning: Not all cords cooperate according to plan. Some of the more common inconveniences we come across include

Hanging on. Some cords are persistent, clinging on for dear life despite daily encouragement to fall off. While the range of normal is as long as 5 weeks, it's worth discussing an obstinate cord with your pediatrician to see if there's something that can be done about it (see Oozing).

Oozing. After the umbilical cord stump falls off, the belly button tissue may take its own sweet time to heal. If it continues to ooze or develop a little pink moist bump that doesn't dry up, your pediatrician may apply a touch of a chemical called silver nitrate to quicken the healing process. Rarely, pus may ooze from the belly button and/or the surrounding skin may become red and swollen. If this happens, show your baby's doctor without any delay because any and all potential infections warrant immediate attention at this age. True infections of a newborn's umbilical site generally require medical management, antibiotics, and close observation.

Bleeding. When your newborn's cord comes off, don't be surprised if there is a little bleeding to go along with it. The best way we've found to explain the bleeding: It's like when a scab comes off and pulls a bit at the normal skin as well. There's bound to be a little short-lived bleeding.

umbilical cord so that the base of the stump gets some exposure to air as well. In case you're worried about hurting your baby, you'll be relieved to know that there are no nerve endings on the cord itself, and babies don't feel any pain or discomfort with careful wiping or handling. Of course they may startle or react to the feeling of cold, but you can think of it as similar to the sensation you get when removing polish from your nails: maybe a little cool, but definitely not painful. No matter what cord-tending technique your pediatrician recommends and you ultimately choose to adopt, the most useful approach to cord care is to avoid undue moisture to the cord (see "Prelude to a Bath" on page 135).

Innies Versus Outies

Ever look at your own belly button and wonder why it was that your doctor didn't do a better job of giving you a cute little innie when you were born? Well you'll soon discover, if you haven't figured it out already, that the innie versus the outie status of your newborn's belly button is completely out of anyone's control. Ultimately, how much or little your newborn's belly button sticks out depends on how the umbilical cord scar heals.

Back to Basics

Sacral Dimple

It's adorable to see babies with dimples on their cheeks, but on occasion they show up on a baby's backside in the area just above the buttock crease, called the sacral area. Most sacral dimples, when present, are very shallow and simply look like a little indentation in the skin. They are still quite cute, but it is well worth making sure they're carefully evaluated by a health professional because every now and then they serve as a sign that what lies underneath didn't develop quite according to plan, because they have the potential to extend deeper below the surface.

Sacral dimple

Genitals

Now to get down to business and address those parts of your newborn's body that new parents tend to have questions about but often hesitate to ask. When it comes to learning about your newborn's genitals, we strongly believe that 1) "down there" just won't suffice (for long, anyway) and 2) there's bound to be information that's new to you regardless of whether you have a baby of the same or opposite sex as you.

 BOY OR GIRL

Along with pregnancy comes the inevitable question, "Are you going to find out?"—a question that refers to the modern-day luxury of being able to find out months ahead of time by ultrasound, or even more definitively by chromosome testing, whether you're destined to have a boy or girl. Even though you may not be, the early period of genital development is, for good reason, referred to as the "indifferent" stage. That's because there is no difference in the appearance of the external genitals between boy and girl fetuses until around the 14th week. So if you, like we, are among those who couldn't wait to get a sneak peak, rest assured that your obstetrician was not just trying to teach you a lesson in patience by making you wait until somewhere between your 16th to 20th week to get an ultrasound.

Baby Girls

Keeping Clean

Unless poop is involved, there is no need to scrub thoroughly in all the nooks and crannies that make up your newborn girl's vulva. In fact, when cleaning your baby girl, soap is not necessary and you can use plain water or a baby wipe to gently remove any pee, poop, discharge, or blood. Try to wipe from your baby's front to her backside. Too-vigorous cleaning can irritate the labia and actually cause the flaps of skin to stick together.

Vulva

Labia

LABIAL ADHESIONS

Infants and young girls sometimes develop what are called labial adhesions. This is a condition where the folds of the labia minora fuse together. This usually starts from the bottom and extends up. In most instances, a large enough opening remains to allow pee to come out normally. Labial adhesions are caused by irritation of the labia with subsequent fusion of the tissues during the healing process. This condition usually goes away on its own once a girl reaches puberty because the higher estrogen level helps to lubricate the tissues. For newborns, your pediatrician may advise you to apply Vaseline or a prescription estrogen cream to help separate fused labia.

Vaginal Discharge

Newborn girls often have clear or white discharge from the vagina. This discharge helps to protect the vaginal area from sticky poop and the like. During diaper changes you can gently wipe away excess discharge, but you don't need to dig deep or scrub hard to get rid of it all. Call your pediatrician if the discharge becomes yellow or green or develops an odor because such changes may suggest the need for further evaluation and/or treatment.

Vaginal Bleeding

Many newborn girls seem to have mini-menstrual periods with bloody discharge from the vagina. This is a normal effect of mom's hormones and usually goes away within a few weeks.

Baby Boys

Penis Care

Whether you decide to circumcise your baby boy, the routine newborn care is the same—gently clean the penis during baths, pulling the foreskin back only as far as it will go. In uncircumcised boys, you will only be able to see the opening at the tip of the foreskin. It will be a few years before the foreskin will loosen enough to pull behind the head (or glans) of the penis for cleaning. For circumcised boys, your goal is to keep the head of the penis clean and prevent any foreskin from causing adhesions by sticking to the glans.

 HYPOSPADIAS

In this condition the foreskin won't look quite right, and the opening of the urethra (the meatus, where the pee comes out) may not be where it's supposed to be right at the tip of the penis. Recognizing hypospadias at birth is especially important for parents who plan to have their newborn sons circumcised, because the circumcision procedure should be delayed and performed by a urologist at the same time as the correction of the hypospadias.

To Circumcise or Not to Circumcise

Because there is no medical necessity to circumcise an infant boy, the decision to remove the foreskin of the penis should be made based on your personal, religious, and cultural beliefs. While there are reports that circumcision may further decrease the already low risk of cancer of the penis, urinary tract infections in men, and spread of sexually transmitted diseases, the American Academy of Pediatrics has weighed in by stating that you need not base your decision to circumcise on health benefits or concerns. Good hygiene can usually prevent these conditions.

Except for those babies born with a hypospadias, prematurely, or very small, circumcisions are generally done within a week or two of birth. This procedure may be done in the hospital or your doctor's office and is typically performed by either your baby's doctor or your obstetrician. Insurance companies may or may not pay for this procedure. Outside of the newborn period, a urologist may perform medically necessary circumcisions. These may require general anesthesia in the hospital because older babies are thought to have more pain sensors and are apt to bleed more.

Following a circumcision, the head of the penis may appear purple-red and/or swollen for about a week. You can also expect a moist or even goopy-looking scab to remain on the head of the penis while it heals. A little Vaseline, Bacitracin, or KY Jelly often helps keep the scab from sticking to the diaper, and is therefore most useful while the circumcised area is still raw. In general, parents should avoid giving their newborns full baths until the penis has healed completely (see "Prelude to a Bath" on page 135). Contact your pediatrician if you think you see pus or notice any bleeding that leaves a spot of blood bigger than a quarter on your baby's diaper.

When to Call a Foul Ball

There are a few commonly mentioned conditions involving a baby boy's scrotum and testicles that you may want to familiarize yourself with. If your baby's testicular area doesn't look quite right, he may have

- **A hernia.** Hernias tend to be more common in premature babies and are 10 times more likely to occur in boys than in girls. This is a condition where there is a small opening in the belly wall that allows part of the intestine to creep down into the scrotum, or testicular sac (or the groin area in girls). When a baby has a hernia, his scrotum and/or groin area may appear full and larger than normal. The bulge of a hernia tends to appear or enlarge when babies cry because crying puts more pressure on the belly. If you suspect that your baby has a hernia, contact your pediatrician. Surgery will usually be required to make sure the intestine doesn't become stuck, twisted, or swollen.

- **A hydrocele.** Excess fluid surrounds the testicle(s) and will make the scrotum look large. This fluid will transilluminate, meaning if you hold a flashlight against the scrotum, it will "glow" and appear fairly translucent (reminiscent of ET's glowing index finger). Hydroceles usually disappear by 1 year of age without any intervention. They occur in about 10% of baby boys.

- **Undescended testes.** Over the course of fetal development, a baby boy's testicles move down from the abdomen and ultimately settle themselves in the scrotum. Sometimes the testicles (one or both) are slow to descend— taking their own sweet time to move down into the scrotum during the first few months. Other times the testicle does not descend and therefore does not develop as it should and won't function properly if left to fend for itself in the abdomen. If and when surgery is indicated, it is usually recommended when your baby is between 6 to 18 months of age.

On the Surface—Your Newborn's Skin

Visualize what happens to skin that has been soaked for a long time in a tub full of warm water. It gets shriveled and soft and has a tendency to become a bit dried out afterward. Now if you consider the fact that your newborn has been soaking in an amniotic fluid bath for 9 months, you'll better understand why her skin looks like it does—most likely dry, cracked, and/or peeling. If you think about it, it's actually amazing that a newborn's skin doesn't look worse than it does after delivery. While we find that almost all new parents come to us in search of a way to remedy the dry skin situation, there's really not much to be done except exercise patience. Moisturizers only serve to temporarily slick down the dead, flaky skin that is destined to be sloughed off anyway, and given that many young babies have sensitive skin to begin with, we suggest avoiding the use of lotions in the first month unless otherwise directed by your doctor.

Rashes

Newborns frequently develop rashes on the skin, most of which are common and harmless. In an effort to familiarize you with what you may be faced with (because many newborn rashes tend to show up on the face), we have put together the following list. Whether due to maternal hormones or tiny pores that are easily clogged, these common newborn rashes rarely require anything more on your part than patience and a hands-off approach, with the exception of an occasional wipe with a wet washcloth.

- **Baby acne.** Although baby acne doesn't tend to show up until a month or so of age, we're listing this first because it tends to be the most concerning for parents. Just as in puberty, these pimples appear due to the effect of hormones on the oil glands, only this time it's mom's hormones from pregnancy that are the culprit. Baby acne tends to last for a few months before going away and may get worse before finally getting better.
- **White bumps (milia).** These tiny bumps are usually found on newborn noses and usually disappear within a few weeks without requiring anything on your part.
- **Erythema toxicum.** This red, splotchy, bumpy rash with little blister-like lesions in the center can make newborns look as if they've been attacked by fleas. E tox, as it is often called, often appears shortly after birth—within hours or days—and can be expected to go away within about a week. Individual spots can actually come and go within hours (similar to hives) and should not be poked, prodded, or popped. Because any blister-like rash needs a doctor's evaluation, be sure to get confirmation that it's erythema toxicum you're dealing with.
- **Heat rash.** Warm clothes or sweat can cause fine pink pimples on your baby's skin—most commonly on the face and in and around skin folds. Try to keep him cool and dry to avoid heat rash or get rid of it once it appears.

Birth Marks by Color
- **Pink or red.** Splotchy, flat red or pink spots on the eyelids, forehead, or back of the neck and scalp are called angel kisses, salmon patches, or stork bites (the technical term is nevus simplex). These often fade over the first few years and they tend to get brighter when your baby cries. Darker red areas on the skin are called port-wine stains (think Gorbachev's forehead), or nevus flammeus. Hemangiomas are bumpy strawberry-like collections of blood vessels that may be found anywhere on the body and can be of any size. They often grow a little in the first year before gradually shrinking over the next several years. Some disappear on their own, while others may require laser treatment or even surgery (if found in areas like the eyes or near the neck or throat).

- **Blue.** Mongolian spots are bluish-green flat birthmarks often seen in babies with darker skin. They are frequently located on the lower back or buttocks but can be found on other body parts as well. They tend to fade with time, but until they do, it's a good idea to make sure their presence is documented in your baby's medical record to decrease the likelihood that they will be mistaken for unexplained bruising.
- **Brown.** Flat, light brown birthmarks are called café au lait spots. These usually require no intervention, but on occasion (usually when someone has 6 or more of them) can be associated with other symptoms or rarely be associated with neurologic conditions. Spots called moles or nevi may also be brown but tend to be darker and in some cases raised.

Blue or Mottled

Because babies don't have great circulation, you may well see your fair share of mottled or even bluish skin, especially of your newborn's hands and feet. If you notice this, simply make sure your baby is warm enough by covering up cool extremities and repositioning her to get the blood flowing. Should your newborn's lips or skin around the mouth appear blue, on the other hand, contact your pediatrician without delay because this more centrally located blueness may mean your baby is not getting enough oxygen.

Fingers and Toes

Not a whole lot to say—it's usually a matter of counting 10 of each and you're done. Well, almost. Every now and then a baby is born with an extra finger or a toe that curls a bit—neither of which are likely to be a big deal in the grand scheme of things. If either situation applies to you, just discuss it with your pediatrician. We've found that the real story from a practical standpoint is not your newborn's fingers and toes, but what lies in store for you on the tips of them. What really throws some parents for a loop is the recurrent challenge of nail management.

Nails, Nails Everywhere

Did you know that fingernails grow 0.00012 inches per hour? Neither did we, until we looked it up. While that may not seem like much, let us assure you that it will keep you busy. Keeping up with your newborn's fingernails as they continuously grow as much as 1/2 inch per month is a very demanding task. As far as we're concerned, the real purpose baby nails serve is to break you into parenthood. They will likely require trimming or filing at least once a week because long nails on the hands of newborns with little to no control of them predictably result in stray scratches. If you happen to fall behind on your nail clipping, your baby will inevitably remind you (and make you feel guilty) by scratching his face when his nails get too long (or if you leave sharp corners or points when clipping).

THE BABY MANICURE-PEDICURE

A handful of parents are intimidated by the prospect of having to cut their baby's nails and would probably opt for a professional manicure-pedicure if only they were generally available. No such luck. If you're lucky, your hospital nurse will be able to help demonstrate the correct technique, but some hospitals actually discourage their personnel from doing so, because any unintentional injury may be a liability problem. And while we aren't exactly recommending it (or admitting to doing it ourselves), we're well aware of the fact that some parents opt to bite or peel off their newborn's nails rather than fiddle with clippers or scissors. Because clippers and scissors can trim nails in a more controlled fashion, you'll be better off using one or the other (or both), or simply using a nail file to keep things under control.

For best results, trim or file your baby's nails when she's asleep and her hands are less of a moving target.

Push down on the fingertip skin so you can get the clipper or scissors around both sides of the nail and avoid cutting your baby's finger (or toe).

Then, just as a professional manicurist would, finish off any sharp or rough edges with an emery board and...

Voila! Not so bad after all once you get the hang of it.

Hand Exploration

Many parents cover their newborn's hands with baby mittens or socks to prevent wayward nails from scratching their faces. As your baby develops over the next several weeks (and you become more skilled at nail clipping), it's a good idea to allow your baby plenty of time during which he can freely explore with his hands. If scratches continue to be a problem, we suggest limiting covered time to when your baby is sleeping.

Curved Legs and Feet

After being curled up in her mother's body for 9 months, it's not surprising to find that a baby's legs and feet come out a bit footloose and fancy-free—appearing to be curved. These positional effects will gradually improve over the first months and years of life. A few babies will have problems with the bones of the feet, which may require casting or surgery. Make sure your pediatrician checks your baby's feet, especially if they seem rigid and can't be moved from the curved position.

Reflexes

Reflexes are actions that happen automatically. Newborns are born with several of them, many of which they will grow out of as their nervous systems develop and take control over the next several months. We've listed some common normal reflexes that you'll probably come across.

- **Grasp.** We consider the newborn grasp reflex to be one of the most endearing. It causes your baby to grasp tightly to your finger if you place one into the palm of his hand. Pressing on the bottom of his feet will also cause his toes to curl up.
- **Sucking.** The sucking reflex is present even before birth, as witnessed in many a prenatal ultrasound. You'll find the reflex is so strong that your baby may want to suck even if he's not hungry. Rather than overfeed him, consider offering a pacifier or clean finger to satisfy his urge (see "Sucking Sense and Sensibility" on page 56).

- **Moro or startle reflex.** When newborns are startled by loud noises or sudden changes in position, they may well throw their arms and legs out and even start to cry. You can chalk up this entire sequence to what is known as a startle reflex.

- **Fencing pose.** We included this reflex only as a point of general interest. Watch your newborn as he lies on his back. Whichever side his head is turned to is likely to be the side he reflexively extends his arm, while the opposite arm will bend at his side (resembling the pose of a fencer).

CHAPTER 19

fever: trial by fire

As you're probably well aware, fever is a hot topic that applies to everyone—young and old. We all get plenty of firsthand experience with it long before we reach parenthood, yet there's nothing quite like a baby's first fever to make even the most well-prepared parents feel a bit hot and bothered themselves. Whether it happens at 1-1/2 weeks, months, or years, fever can admittedly be quite unnerving. While as pediatricians we are committed to making sure that you develop a healthy respect for fever—especially in the first few months after your baby is born—as parents we're convinced that having a good understanding of what causes fever, its implications, and what may (or may not) need to be done about it will help prepare you to manage your baby's first and future fevers safely and confidently.

Fending Off Fever

Before you read up on what to do in the event that your newborn gets a fever, let us first offer you some simple strategies for putting off your first run-in with fever for as long as possible.

- **Limiting exposure.** You may find that you have many well-wishers waiting in the wings even before you get home from the hospital. While you should be sure to express your gratitude for their support, be selective about whom you allow to share their best wishes in person. By coming over to see and/or hold your baby, they may share their viruses as well.
- **Hand washing.** Now is not the time to be shy about requiring that anyone and everyone who wants to lay hands on your susceptible bundle of joy has to wash them (their hands, that is) first. All rules of in-law etiquette aside, don't hesitate to postpone all hugs and pinches as long as possible, but at least long enough to ask for a show of clean hands first.

- **Don't go looking for trouble.** There's nothing inherently risky about taking an appropriately dressed newborn out of the house, but it's wise to be a bit choosy about where you go. Crowded areas and small closed-in spaces are perfect places to come into contact with unwanted germs. Taking a walk outdoors or sticking to wide open spaces will decrease the likelihood that your baby will be coughed on, sneezed at, or touched by people who are sick.

- **Help is only a wipe away.** Despite all your best fever-fighting efforts, you may find at some point in the not too distant future that someone somehow has managed to break through all lines of defense and touch your baby with the same hand recently used to hold a snot-filled tissue or cover a cough. Given that this can and has happened to the best of us, we suggest keeping a handy supply of baby wipes nearby to wash off the "contaminated" area at your earliest convenience. Even though we don't have hard-core evidence proving that this works, the basic principles of infection control strongly support such a simple effort and we therefore consider it well worth a shot.

Fever in Newborns

Instead of venturing into great detail about what causes fever and whether it truly warrants your fear and respect, we first want to point out what we consider to be our most important take-home message: Discussing what needs to be done about a newborn with a fever is *very* different from fever considerations in older infants and children. The reason is straightforward: The younger the infant, the less prepared their immune system is to fight infection. Therefore, the best way to sum up a new parent's healthy approach to fever is that it's *always* better to be safe than sorry. You should never wonder about whether to bother your newborn's doctor about a fever: Just make the call. Sure, most fevers during the first few months are likely to be caused by the same common cold viruses that plague the rest of us, but a newborn's risk of having a serious underlying infection, while relatively small, is nevertheless real. It is for this reason that *any infant with a fever during the first few months of life should be brought to the immediate attention of a doctor.* What happens from there depends on the age of the baby and the circumstances. In some cases, babies simply need close observation. In others (especially in the first month of life) you should be prepared for your baby's doctor to check blood, urine, and even spinal fluid for signs of infection. In general, the younger a baby is and the sicker she seems, the more likely she is to require hospitalization and treatment with antibiotics in addition to the tests listed above.

 ## IN THE ABSENCE OF FEVER

While new parents are routinely warned to take fevers very seriously, we know that some serious types of infections have the potential to cause little or no fever in newborns. In the absence of fever, babies who seem to be less responsive than normal—anywhere from a bit listless to downright lethargic—or are having problems eating need to be taken just as seriously as those with fevers and evaluated to determine the cause. If you ever find yourself concerned about your baby's health, don't waste any time sitting around waiting for a fever before consulting with your baby's doctor.

Overcoming the Fever Fear Factor

Now that we've done our duty in delivering the "take all fevers seriously in your newborn" warning, we also feel obliged to give you a bigger picture perspective and point out that there's a fine line between taking fevers seriously and living in constant fear of a rise in your baby's temperature. We hope that the additional information that follows will help eliminate the fever fear factor and better prepare you to rise to the occasion.

The Body's Built-in Thermostat

You've probably heard it on the news or read it in print—fever serves a purpose. While we won't belabor this point and make you suffer through all we learned on the subject in our own medical training, it's worth reminding yourself every now and then. Fever not only acts as a warning sign for infections, but it is actually thought to help the body in its effort to fight them. A part of the brain called the hypothalamus is responsible for regulating body temperature—similar to the way a thermostat controls the temperature in your house. In general, infants and young children have much more sensitive "thermostats" than adults. When viruses, bacteria, or other fever-causing agents trigger the hypothalamus to raise the body's set point, body temperatures rise. You can therefore think of fever as the body's equivalent of having its thermostat setting turned up.

Fever Defined

The natural question that begins most discussions involving fever is: Exactly what temperature is considered a fever? You'd think you could get a straight answer to such a seemingly straightforward and commonly asked question, but chances are good that if you asked around you'd get a wide range of answers starting anywhere from 99°F on up to 100.4°F or more. That's because several factors go into defining fever.

 IT'S A MATTER OF DEGREE

Normal body temperature is generally defined as 98.6°F. A rectal temperature of 100.4°F or higher is typically used to define a fever in newborns. How the numbers that fall in between are interpreted tends to vary considerably. In part, that's because body temperature fluctuates normally over the course of any given day—generally rising a bit in the afternoon and evening. The degree of variation is thought to increase with age; while a child's or adult's temperature can vary as much as 2°F (1.1°C) over the course of the day, you should expect your newborn's range of normal to be much smaller.

Using Thermometers for Good Measure

Back in the days when we were kids, pretty much everyone used a glass mercury-containing thermometer. While we'll spare you a long-winded discussion of the potential dangers of broken glass and the risks associated with exposure to spilled mercury, suffice it to say, these thermometers are not just out of style, they are no longer recommended. From a practical standpoint, it's also a good thing; we have yet to talk to anyone who found mercury thermometers easy to read. In contrast, the readily available digital thermometers currently in vogue are (almost) foolproof—put them in the right place and the numbers just appear.

Hot Spots—Fever by Location

The easiest way to categorize thermometers is according to the part of the body where the temperature is taken (axillary = underarm, tympanic = ear, oral/pacifier = mouth, temperature strips = forehead, and rectal =

self-explanatory). Temperature strips, albeit temptingly easy, are generally frowned on as being notoriously inaccurate. Even when taken using some of the more accepted temperature-taking routes, such as placing a thermometer in a child's mouth or armpit, the resulting temperatures can vary quite a bit. That is why the definition of fever usually includes some reference to the location.

 FEVER ON LOCATION

The following represent the temperatures typically used to define fever:

99°F (37.2°C) axillary
100°F (37.8°C) oral
100.4°F (38°C) rectal

When reporting a temperature to your pediatrician, there's really no need for you to add, subtract, or otherwise mathematically manipulate the results based on where you took the temperature. Instead, just be sure to mention how/where you measured it.

You should be aware that almost all doctors recommend only using rectal thermometers for newborns because the resulting readings are considered the most accurate measure of a newborn's core body temperature.

 EAR THERMOMETERS

Ear thermometers are marketed to parents as quick and easy alternatives to rectal thermometers and have been shown to be a relatively accurate method of measuring temperature. If you happen to have one already, you don't need to get rid of it. Just be aware that it's a good idea to steer clear of this type of thermometer until your baby reaches at least 3 months of age because they require a good fit in the ear (all newborns' ear canals are pretty darn small) and it's hard to get a reliable measurement.

Bottoms Up: Taking a Rectal Temperature

While you're certain to find plenty written about the ins and outs of using each type of thermometer, we decided that your time and ours would be best spent focusing on the rectal approach. There's no way around it: Rectal temperatures are considered the gold standard of temperature taking, especially in infants younger than about 3 months. When it comes to figuring out whether your newborn has a fever, you should settle for nothing less. If you are now squirming at the thought (which we're pretty sure some of you are), take a minute to get used to the idea and then we'll walk you through the process. Despite the dread many new parents seem to experience, you just have to believe us that taking an infant's rectal temperature is not all that difficult or uncomfortable—for the baby or the parent. In fact, many parents sweat their way through taking their first temperature only to be pleasantly surprised when their babies don't seem to mind. Some even sleep right through the whole "ordeal"!

The easiest way to get set up is to lay your baby on a comfortable but firm, flat surface. Place him across your lap if you like, or consider using a changing table, sofa, or the floor—whatever you find easiest and most convenient. You can either put him on his belly or lay him on his back. If you opt for the back, then hold up your baby's legs just as you would if you were changing his diaper. Be forewarned that regardless of how you approach it, taking a rectal temperature has the potential to trigger pooping—especially in young infants—so you might want to place a towel or changing pad underneath your baby in advance. Disposable probe covers are optional but can make cleanup that much easier. You may also want to dab a little lubricating jelly (such as Vaseline or KY Jelly) onto the short, round metal tip of the thermometer. Then carefully insert the tip into the rectal (anal) opening just until the metal tip is no longer showing (between 1/2 and 1 inch). Then all you need to do is keep the thermometer in place by gently squeezing your baby's butt cheeks closed around it until a reading has been made. Once you're done using the thermometer, remember to give it a quick rinse with some hot soapy water (especially if you didn't use a probe cover) and be sure to put it away somewhere handy along with a mental note that this is now designated "for rectal use only"—not that it couldn't technically be used for any other type of temperature taking, but the thought of mistakenly doing so really causes people to cringe!

Over-Bundled = Overheated?

It is a commonly held belief that over-bundled infants can end up with an elevation in their temperature. There is a certain degree of truth to this belief because babies' skin temperatures have been shown to rise noticeably with bundling and cool down again once they are unbundled and their temperature rechecked. Rectal temperature, on the other hand, is thought to be relatively unaffected by bundling, especially if you get a reading of 100.4°F or above. Bottom line: Never write off an elevated rectal temperature as simply the result of too many layers of clothing or blankets—especially if it doesn't come down.

 CLIMATE CONTROL

In general, there seems to be consensus amongst parenting experts that a comfortable room temperature for babies is anywhere between 68°F and 72°F. There seems, however, to be a bit of a difference of opinion when it comes to what is appropriate indoor attire for the youngest members of the household. Some feel that babies are adequately dressed wearing the same number of layers as everyone else, while others recommend one more layer of clothing than an adult would wear in the same room. We really don't think it makes that much difference and suggest you start out either way. Then if your baby seems to be uncomfortably warm or cool, just adjust her clothing and/or your thermostat accordingly.

Getting a Feel for Fever

Forgoing a thermometer in favor of feeling your baby's forehead is never considered an acceptable measure of fever in a newborn. Even for older children, for whom this thermometer-less method of temperature taking has been shown to be a decent way to tell if they are hot or not, you still cannot rely on your hand alone to determine just how hot. In other words, parents may well be accurate in saying that their older children have fevers simply because they feel hot, but estimating just how hot—101°F versus 103.5°F—is always best left to a thermometer.

TOO MUCH OF A GOOD THING

Having done our best to inform you about the gravity of fever, let us now do our best to spare you and your newborn a lot of unnecessary probing. Given that most newborns actually make it all the way through the first several months of life without ever needing to have their temperature taken, there is definitely such a thing as taking a baby's temperature too often. Quite a few new parents have come to our offices having paid heed to all of the abundant cautionary advice about fever in the newborn period, and consequently are under the impression that they need to take and record their babies' temperatures on a daily basis (or even more frequently). We can think of very few (if any) reasons that would warrant such routine measurements in the absence of any suspicious symptoms. Big picture perspective: Some of you may benefit by giving your new thermometer a break (figuratively speaking, anyway)—whipping it out only for good reason (ie, make sure you didn't skip the beginning part of this chapter).

Understanding Febrile Seizures

Febrile seizures are seizures caused by fever. While approximately 95% of all children *never* have a febrile seizure, we've nevertheless found that the very idea causes most parents a certain degree of anxiety—much of it unnecessary—now and throughout parenthood. And that's why we thought we'd give you a bit of perspective on the subject to carry with you in the months and years to come. For purposes of easing your current state of mind we want to start by pointing out that the statistics are quite reassuring: Newborns are unlikely to experience this type of seizure because they typically occur between the ages of 6 months and 5 years. Furthermore, and contrary to popular opinion, the likelihood of having a febrile seizure is not based on how high a fever gets but rather on how fast it rises. If a child is destined to have a febrile seizure, it will most likely occur early on in the course of the fever(s), not days into an illness. And finally, to set the record straight, febrile seizures by themselves don't cause permanent damage and are rarely predictive of a long-lasting seizure disorder.

Treating a Fever

It is short and easy to tell you how to treat a newborn's fever: If you suspect your newborn has a fever, your immediate course of action is to seek medical advice and/or attention. Everything you may know or have heard about fever medications, lukewarm baths, or the potential benefits of fever all take a back seat at this age. End of discussion.

OK, so we aren't really going to leave it at that, but we definitely do mean it when we say that you don't have to bother yourself with the information below right now if you don't want to. In fact, we seriously considered not including it at all because we didn't want to give any of you the impression that there is any room for interpretation of fever in newborns without involving your pediatrician. Then we gave it a second thought and decided that when it comes to parenthood and fevers, there are a lot of inquiring minds out there who undoubtedly want to know more—if only for future reference.

Fever Medications

We don't intend to tell you when and how much fever medication you should use for your newborn because a) this book is not about our practicing medicine; b) we've already told you the golden rule—that you should first and foremost be talking to your baby's doctor; and c) your baby's doctor, in turn, will tell you which medicine to use and how much, if any (all of which will depend on your baby's age and weight). Instead, we've listed below some of the basics of fever medications that we think every parent should know.

- Just about all medications commonly used to treat fevers in infants contain either acetaminophen (eg, Tylenol, Tempra, Feverall) or ibuprofen (eg, Advil, Motrin).
- Fever medication meant for use in infants comes in either liquid form (concentrated drops or suspensions) or as rectal suppositories.

- Fever medications are always dosed according to a baby's weight.
- There are 2 typical sizes of droppers used to measure liquid infant fever medication. "One dropperful" can mean either 0.8 mL (milliliters) or 1.25 mL depending on which type and brand of infant drops you're using, so always pay close attention to the markings and use the dropper that came with the bottle.
- Infant drops are much more concentrated than the children's suspension form. Always make yourself double-check that the dose you are using is correct for the type of medication you're using.
- Be sure to read the fine print on the label about how often the medicine can be given and take it very seriously! Acetaminophen is not to be given more often than every 4 to 6 hours. Ibuprofen should only be repeated every 6 to 8 hours.

 SETTING ASPIRIN ASIDE

Aspirin should never be given to newborns, infants, or children (except in rare and specific instances when it is prescribed by a doctor) because it has the potential to cause a serious illness called Reye syndrome that can result in brain and liver damage.

Feed a Fever?

You may have heard the expression "feed a fever, starve a cold." While we've never been clear on the benefits of starving a cold, "feeding" a fever actually does have its merits. Fever is one of the factors that can cause dehydration, so encouraging your baby to continue drinking or nursing as much as possible is a good idea whenever possible.

CHAPTER 20

seeing yellow: jaundice

In our humble but medical opinion, all new parents should add the color yellow to their list of newborn traits to be familiar with, watch for, and be poised and ready to bring to medical attention if and when it shows up. That's because more than half of all full-term healthy newborns stand a good chance of turning at least a light shade of yellow—in other words, developing some degree of jaundice—during the first weeks of life. In most cases, jaundice is harmless; in some cases, it requires treatment. In any case, you'll want to be prepared to recognize jaundice and discuss its appearance with your pediatrician without delay.

Behind the Scenes

We thought it would be quite useful to first provide you with a basic understanding of what lies just below the surface of yellow-tinged skin. To do that, it helps to understand what bilirubin is because it is the culprit behind jaundice. From birth and throughout our lives, our bodies are responsible for continually breaking down and getting rid of old red blood cells while all the while replacing them with new ones. Bilirubin is simply a normal breakdown product of red blood cells. Our livers are given the ongoing task of processing bilirubin, which is ultimately disposed of by the intestines in the form of poop. Jaundice results when, for whatever reason, too much bilirubin accumulates in the body.

Who Gets Jaundice?

There are several straightforward reasons why some healthy, full-term newborns develop higher than normal levels of bilirubin and end up looking yellow. Not only do newborns have a proportionately larger number of red blood cells than adults—inevitably requiring more in the way of breakdown and processing—but it may take a baby's liver several days before it is able to rise to the occasion and function at full speed. This in turn tends to be determined by how many red blood cells are being broken down, how effectively they are being processed, and how efficiently they are being disposed of—all factors that can vary from baby to baby.

It's in the blood

- **More blood.** As we mentioned, babies are born with a higher concentration of red blood cells than adults and older children, increasing the demands placed on the liver.
- **Bruising.** Many newborns sustain bruising or even hematomas (usually egg-like swellings of blood in the scalp) from the pressure of childbirth. The collections of blood cells in these areas as they are broken down and cleared away may be enough to lead to jaundice.
- **Blood type differences.** Jaundice is sometimes caused when mom and baby have different blood types. For the most part, a mother's blood remains separate from her fetus's throughout pregnancy. During delivery, however, some of it manages to pass through the placenta and umbilical cord and make its way into her baby's bloodstream. Recognizing these stray red blood cells as foreign, the baby's body reacts against them by breaking them down—posing the potential for a more rapid accumulation of bilirubin.

Slow to Go

- Babies tend to have slow liver function at first and may have some evidence of jaundice as their livers quickly mature over the first several days.
- Newborns who are slow to figure out how to eat may in turn be slow to poop. There may be other medical reasons a baby may have problems with pooping. The end result is bilirubin staying in the body rather than being pooped out.
- Much less commonly, a baby may have a problem with the liver. Certain disorders can cause the liver not to function properly, resulting in a buildup of bilirubin and sometimes pale-colored (almost white) poop.

Taking It From the Top

As higher levels of bilirubin are found in the bloodstream, regardless of cause, the more bilirubin will make its way into the skin and cause a baby to appear yellow. Interestingly, the yellow tends to show up in a fairly predictable fashion—first on the face and then gradually spreading down toward the toes. How far down on a newborn's body the yellow goes is thought to be roughly indicative of how high the bilirubin levels are in the blood. The lower down on the body the yellow extends, the higher the bilirubin level is likely to be. On a side note, the actual shade and intensity of the yellow, which can sometimes approach pumpkin colored, is not thought to offer much of a clue as to just how high the bilirubin level is.

Time Course

Most term babies reach their peak levels of jaundice at 3 to 5 days before improving completely; premature babies peak a few days later. After peaking, the jaundice should resolve within a few weeks. Newborns who appear jaundiced earlier or stay jaundiced much longer than typically expected may have an underlying medical problem that should be evaluated by a pediatrician.

- **Early jaundice.** Any jaundice that appears within the first 24 hours after birth needs medical evaluation. Sometimes it can indicate a problem with the liver or a baby's blood cells that needs to be addressed, but in all instances it suggests that the bilirubin level needs to be watched closely and treated appropriately.
- **Typical jaundice.** Regular newborn jaundice (also called physiologic jaundice) appears gradually after the first couple days. The bilirubin level generally peaks by about 5 days for term babies and about 1 week for those born prematurely.
- **Late jaundice.** Babies with what is referred to as breastfeeding jaundice may not start to turn yellow until about 2 weeks of age. Sometimes this is treated by briefly stopping breastfeeding, but you'll certainly want to talk to your pediatrician before coming to any conclusions, regardless of whether you think your baby might have this type of jaundice.

- **Persistent jaundice.** Regardless of when jaundice sets in, babies whose livers can't keep up, for whatever reason, get progressively more yellow. In some liver conditions a baby's poop can also lose its color and become pale in color. This is one of the many reasons why pediatricians routinely express sincere interest in the color of baby poop (see "The Many Colors of Poop" on page 66). Another symptom to be on the lookout for in conjunction with jaundice is poor growth because just about any underlying medical problem can cause newborns to gain weight more slowly than expected. On occasion, red blood cell abnormalities are also known to cause jaundice that lasts longer than a few weeks. Before you assume the worst, read on because good old-fashioned, run-of-the-mill jaundice can certainly take a while to fade away.

 EASY COME, SLOW TO GO

Although jaundice appears fairly predictably from head to toe while bilirubin levels are rising, the yellow color does not always disappear in reverse as they subsequently fall, and it can take weeks to fade away completely. In general, the whites of the eyes are usually the last things to return to normal.

Spot-Checking for Jaundice

Just as with fever in the newborn period, trust us when we say that your doctor will want to know if you're seeing yellow. While some babies become unmistakably yellow, easily alerting parents and pediatricians alike that they need to be evaluated, we have found that others pose more of a challenge. That's because the color changes of some newborns' skin can be more subtle—whether due to varying underlying skin tones, ruddy complexions, dim room lights, sleep deprivation, or simply because jaundice has a way of gradually creeping up on new parents unnoticed. To be more effectively on the lookout for jaundice, we suggest you

- Move to a well-lit area, preferably one that offers you natural light.
- Gently press on your baby's skin and then remove your finger.
- Before blood flow returns and makes it appear pink again, take a look to see if the underlying area appears yellow. If you're not sure, compare it to a spot much farther down on the body using the same technique.

- If the first area you check appears to be yellow, make your way down your baby's body—the upper chest, at the nipple line, then the belly—continuing to spot-check until you find a level at which the jaundice stops.
- You can then keep a watchful eye to see if the jaundice increases.

Measuring Bilirubin Levels

Skin color changes offer parents and/or pediatricians the first hint that bilirubin is on the rise. Subsequently, the rate at which the yellow color spreads from head to toe can give us a vague idea of how fast the bilirubin level is increasing. Whenever the degree of jaundice is in question, a simple blood test currently is considered the most accurate way of determining where things stand. If your baby becomes jaundiced, don't be surprised if he is subjected to one or more heel pokes or blood draws to collect the necessary sample(s). How many bilirubin levels your doctor decides to check will depend not only on what's causing your baby's jaundice and how many days old your baby is when it appears, but also how high the first level is, how fast it seems to be rising, and how likely it is to be effectively cleared. On the horizon—the hope that already available technology (that determines bilirubin levels using a special form of light applied to the skin's surface and referred to as transcutaneous bilirubin monitoring) will prove itself equally effective, more widely accepted, and readily available as an accurate way to follow bilirubin levels noninvasively (ie, no bloodletting involved).

Taking Care of Business—Treating Jaundice

Getting Pooped Out

Because we know that bilirubin is primarily cleared out of the body in poop—something that some newborns produce in much more abundant supply than others in the first few days of life—it only stands to reason that those newborns who get off to a slower start pooping may, in turn, become a bit more yellow than those who fill their diapers early and often. When it comes to jaundice, the more you can do to encourage feeding (and, therefore, pooping) the better. You may have been advised to feed your baby at least every 3 to 4 hours, but if your baby is interested in eating even sooner, go ahead and feed her, because this will help clear out the bilirubin. If possible, feed your baby slightly more milk at each sitting (a few more minutes per side, for example, if breastfeeding, or by offering an extra ounce or so if bottle-feeding) to help increase the poop output. Just be sure not to overdo it in the name of getting rid of the bilirubin; you may end up with a spitting up problem.

 LET THE SUNSHINE IN

Rumor has it that in the 1950s an observant nurse noticed that babies placed near the window in the newborn nursery were less likely to become jaundiced than their (relatively) in-the-dark colleagues on the other side of the room. Whether this story is actually true, we're not sure, because we didn't devote any time to checking it out. What we do know is that sunlight plays a useful role in changing bilirubin into a form that the body can dispose of more easily. In fact, "sunbathing" your baby with few clothes on in the indirect sunlight that streams through the windows of your home for as little as 15 minutes a few times a day can help keep jaundice in check.

Let the Lights Begin

On further study of the "let the sunshine in" principle of treating jaundice, a particular wavelength of blue light was found to speed up the bilirubin breakdown and elimination process. Phototherapy simply makes use of this blue wavelength in the form of a bili blanket and/or special lights to treat babies with high bilirubin levels easily and effectively. This lighting is often done in the hospital, but sometimes the equipment can be sent to your house for the few days your baby might need it.

A Positive Perspective on Rising Bilirubin

While we have done our best to prepare you for the possibility of jaundice in your newborn, we are well aware of the fact that facing a yellow newborn with rising bilirubin levels requiring repeated trips to the pediatrician's office (or blood work in the hospital) all in the first week or so of parenthood is not only challenging, but often enough to make concerned new parents feel that their babies are unhealthy and themselves ill-equipped for the demands of parenthood. We wanted to make sure to give you a more positive big-picture perspective. It is certainly true that high levels of bilirubin can have serious effects on babies. Fortunately, modern-day medicine allows us to recognize and treat rising bilirubin levels before they reach dangerous levels, and severe jaundice is rare and tends to occur in premature or critically ill newborns. Any poking, prodding, repeated doctor's visits, phototherapy, or hospitalization prescribed to treat bilirubin levels that are on the rise is done to keep them from ever getting to the point where your baby is at risk.

PART VI

thanks for the memories

Time Flies—So Catch It!

Time certainly may not seem to fly by when you're buried knee-deep in diapers and facing your umpteenth night of interrupted sleep or anxiously awaiting the birth of your child, but one of the almost universal insights parents gain with time is just how fast the days, weeks, months, and years go by. A cliché? Yes, but definitely worth taking note of at the start of your parenting career.

Reality Check

Before we jump right into our advice about how you can creatively archive your parenting memories, we feel the need to add a short disclaimer: Neither of us comes close to qualifying as Martha Stewart disciples when it comes to craftiness (although Laura on occasion has to curb her urges). Nonetheless, we've found that our own relatively simple creations and those suggestions we've collected and shared over the years about preserving childhood memories rank high on the list of our most popular advice—especially because they don't require a lot of artistic talent, immense creativity or, for that matter, time. The most important ingredient, in fact, is foresight. Some of the following suggestions may not strike your fancy, while others may help you to think up your own ideas that may be even better than ours. In either case, the point is that you won't be joining the ranks of the countless numbers of parents who have found themselves regretfully saying, "What a great idea—If only I'd thought to do it myself! …Sooner!…With my first child!…When I had time!"

CHAPTER 21

birth memories

Whether the birth of your child has yet to become a reality or is an event so recently ingrained in your memory that the possibility of forgetting any of the details seems quite unlikely, we want to forewarn you that even birth memories fade and blur over time. That's fine for those of you content with simply remembering the date and time of the big event along with a few random details interjected into the picture. If you aim to remember more—for your own sake and to share with your child some day—you will want to continue reading this section. The ideas we've included are simple and straightforward, yet while you're swimming in all the novelties of parenthood, you might not otherwise think of them.

Keys to Photographic Success in the Delivery Room

The birth of your child will undoubtedly be a momentous occasion—one worthy of capturing for posterity—however, it's one thing to envision the perfect shot of your baby in the delivery room and another to get it. Short of signing up to be the next featured delivery on The Learning Channel's "A Baby Story," it is going to be up to you to figure out exactly how much of "the moment" you want to capture and how you're going to go about doing it.

- **Plan ahead.** If and when you fall into delivery preparedness mode and pack your suitcase in anticipation of your trip to labor and delivery, don't forget to include your camera and whatever accessories it may require. Even beyond showing up with your camera equipment, we suggest you take a few minutes between breathing exercises and OB appointments to discuss a simple photographic game plan. First and foremost, be sure to find out if your hospital has any photographic restrictions. If there are any, you'll want to be sure to factor them in as you think about your photographic goals. If you've got your heart set on capturing a particular shot, the odds of getting it will be better if you make your wishes known ahead of time. Don't forget to figure out a place to keep your camera that's out of the way but easily accessible. While all of this advanced planning may seem a little extreme to some of you (especially those of you less "into" photography than we are), trust us when we say that the resulting photos will speak for themselves.

- **Decide if you're going digital.** There's no question that as a society, we've entered the digital age. Whether you choose to use a digital camera or a good old-fashioned print one is up to you, but for those of you who have not yet made the switch to digital, let us just point out that the ability to actually see each picture as you take it and know instantly whether it turned out to your satisfaction is a priceless feature— especially when the event you're photographing is as completely irreproducible as the birth of your child. And the thought of entrusting an irreplaceable, not to mention potentially revealing, roll(s) of film to local film developers is often enough to convince some parents to use a digital camera. If you've ever found a scratch on a prized negative, you'll know what we mean.

- **Delegate.** If you don't consider yourself much of a photographer, have no desire to rise to the occasion and focus your efforts on capturing the moment, or just plain anticipate having too many other things on your mind when you deliver—don't hesitate to delegate. If you plan on having any family or friends in the delivery room, pick the one you consider to be the best photographer (and the one least likely to be overcome with emotion when it's time to click the shutter), and make it clear what pictures you hope to have when it's all over. Whichever type of camera you choose, make sure you or your designated photographer is comfortable using it, as well as prepared to load new rolls of film, swap out memory cards, and/or replace batteries. In short, the delivery room isn't a great place to sit down with a new camera and the instruction book.

- **Use discretion.** You don't have to have gone through labor and delivery or witnessed one before to realize that there's not a whole lot of privacy involved in the process. That does not, however, mean that you can't control the degree of exposure evident in the commemorative photo-graphs. I'm sure you all know what we're talking about because you inevitably have to give at least some thought to how to take pictures of a baby being born *without* getting the infamous crotch shot. Fathers-to-be (or other family members or friends) who might otherwise find themselves caught up in the moment often do quite well in their role as photographer if you've not only delegated the job ahead of time, but made it very clear what you would and would not like to see revealed in the family photo album for years to come.

- **Consider composition.** Now you may be thinking to yourself "who has the time to consider composition? I'm just focused on maintaining some degree of composure," but that's why it's worth mentioning the concept to you now and not in the delivery room. After all, many a new parent has regretted not discussing photographic discretion in advance of the big event, much less having the designated photographer give some quick thought to such photographic challenges as an open window for a backdrop on a bright sunny day. How much forethought you choose to devote to this subject will depend purely on how important the photographic end result is to you.

 THE PERFECT POSE

Before you deliver, you may want to set your sights on our favorite delivery room picture. While not all deliveries are conducive to being captured on film, the cutting of the cord is definitely a pose well worth a shot. Now, before you laugh this photographic feat off as an impossibility, let us assure you that it can be done—if not by you, then at least by someone else in the delivery room. Long before I (Laura) went into labor, someone suggested that I try to take a photo of my baby on the delivery room scale so I could use it as my birth announcement photo. Having made that my personal goal, I instructed my husband to keep track of our camera and give it to me as soon as I delivered. Little did I know I'd find myself armed with a camera well before my son made his way to the scale—in time to snap photos of my squawking baby in the obstetrician's arms as his father did the honors on the cord. Thrilled with what I considered to be the ultimate once in a lifetime photo, I decided to try again with my next child. Two years later I ended up with an even better photo of my husband cutting the cord—this time complete with a clock in the immediate background bearing witness to the event.

Video

It seems that video recorders have made their way up to the top of the expectant parents' purchase list. Whether you decide to have the tape rolling in your delivery room or ban all live coverage of the event is purely a matter of personal preference (unless there is some related hospital policy, of course). Just remember that the photographic considerations we discussed for photographs in the delivery room apply to video as well—only more so. Unless you plan on doing a whole lot of editing, whoever is in charge of the video camera should be well versed in discretionary limits, not to mention the use of common sense when deciding when to put the camera down and get out of the way.

CHAPTER 22

commemorative creations

Saving Time in a Bottle

Even if you've never dried and preserved flowers before, here's your chance to create a great keepsake that is inexpensive to make and priceless. If you happen to receive roses or other flowers in recognition of your baby's birth, remember to take them home with you and hang them upside down (or put someone else in charge of doing so) until they are *completely* dry. Especially if you have no prior experience with flower drying, please pay particular attention to our emphasis on the word "completely." Trust us when we tell you from personal experience that anything short of fully dried flowers has a very high likelihood of turning into a progressively moldy bunch of old flowers sealed in a jar. Fortunately, most flowers can be left drying for as long it takes you to come up with a few spare minutes (which, from personal experience, can easily be a couple of months). Then simply get a glass jar that has a tight-sealing lid, cut the stems off the flowers, and carefully place them in the jar along with any additional small mementos you might have saved or purchased (such as pink or blue confetti or ribbon), and then seal the jar so it's airtight. A pink or blue ribbon and bows around the outside of the jar can make a nice finishing touch. While quick and easy to make, this keepsake is likely to become far more valuable than the effort you put into it. We hope you'll be thanking us for years to come.

Tipping the Scales

We haven't met a parent yet who hasn't appreciated the suggestion of taking a picture of their newborn on the delivery room scale—capturing baby and his official birth weight in one shot. This is a relatively easy to get and likely to be treasured picture that makes a great stand-alone keepsake, but better yet makes the perfect choice if you're considering a photo birth announcement.

On the Day You Were Born

It may seem hard to imagine as you settle into a routine of caring for a newborn that one day, in the not too distant future, this same child will ask you as many questions as she can come up with about more subjects than you can presently imagine—including the day she was born. As we mentioned at the beginning of this chapter, your memories of childbirth and the events surrounding it may seem so vivid now that you figure you can afford to wait a while before taking the time to write them down. Well, we suggest you learn from our mistakes and spend a few minutes writing down for your child what will certainly become a cherished gift—your account of the day she was born. Include as many details as you can, no matter how trivial they may seem now. You'll be surprised to find out which details your 4- or 5-year-old considers to be the most entertaining, whether it's the pre-labor dinner that didn't sit so well during delivery or the fact that she peed on her daddy when he first held her. We do suggest, however, that you censor out any inappropriate language that may have found its way into your delivery room and simply stick to what was wonderful about the day.

Putting the Day on Display

The beauty of creating a shadow box frame that displays all of the para-
phernalia you collect from the day your child is born is that just about
anyone can do it quite easily with only a little forethought, at very little
expense, and in a relatively sleep-deprived state.

- **Collecting memorabilia.** This is where the forethought part comes in,
  because you'll want to remember to gather together as many small items
  as you can think of that relate to the day your baby was born. Some
  suggested items include

  - Baby hat from the hospital
  - Hospital clothing or outfit your baby wears home from the hospital
  - Cord clamp
  - Hospital name card (usually attached to baby's crib throughout
    hospital stay)
  - Wrist ID bracelets
  - Birth announcement
  - Dried flowers
  - Recent ultrasound picture
  - Headlines and date cut out from the local newspaper
  - An issue of your favorite magazine from that week to remind you
    of news and current pop culture
  - Any souvenirs of the day, such as movie ticket stubs and a take-
    out menu or matchbook from a restaurant (with matches removed,
    of course)

- **Supplies.** You can either decide to wait and purchase the necessary supplies after your baby is born, or plan ahead and purchase them when
  your hands aren't yet so full. We've found that the latter option certainly
  increases the likelihood that you'll have your project hanging on the
  wall before your baby's first birthday. Either way, as long as you man
  age to gather together the memorabilia, it's not important *when* you
  actually get inspired to actually sit down and work on putting together
  your shadow box display. When you do, useful supplies to have on
  hand include

- *A shadow box frame.* While there's no reason you can't get this whole project done professionally, it's really quite easy (and less expensive) to buy a shadow box from a craft store or frame shop. Choose your frame size based on how many mementos you intend to include.
- *Decorative paper.* Many of the craft store shadow boxes simply come with an inset made of white cardboard. If you're partial to a plain white background, you can skip decorative paper. Otherwise, look for some craft paper—pink or blue checkered paper seems to be quite popular—or even gather up some fabric or new baby wrapping paper to line the inside of the shadow box.
- *Scissors*
- *Tape, glue, and/or staples.* Check with your local craft store regarding which types of tape and glue are best suited for this type of project.
- *Additional decorations.* Using additional items such as ribbon, tiny decorative pink or blue flowers, or even new-baby confetti (which comes in the shape of tiny little rattles and baby bottles) can definitely help spruce up your shadow box.

The rest is really quite easy. After figuring out what you want to use as a backdrop—whether it's plain white, the day's newspaper headlines, your baby's birth announcement, or decorative paper—and preparing the inside of your shadow box accordingly, play with the layout of your trinkets until they look good to you. You may want to consider using photocopies of newspaper headlines or ultrasound photos because the originals will run the risk of yellowing over time. Then simply secure your memorabilia, along with some decorative ribbon, confetti, and/or flowers, and voila! Without requiring much in the way of artistic skills, you'll have a commemorative creation worth displaying in your home for years to come.

CHAPTER 23

capturing the moments
along the way

Before going any further, we feel obliged to tell those of you who aren't already aware that there are entire craft books dedicated to the subject of preserving childhood memories, and many who profess to be expert in this field. While expert we are not, we have more than enough experience dealing with the regrets and missed opportunities of other parents (and, at times, of our own) that we decided to offer you a sampling of suggested ways you can continue to preserve in time some of the moments.

Photo Clubs

The point of mentioning photo clubs to you now is to make sure you are aware that they exist. While there are many variations on the theme, the basic idea behind photo clubs is that you pay a membership fee (often in the $25–$35 range) that buys you a full year or two of no sitting fees. Having this type of membership is great if you're not particularly handy with a camera, but in our opinion well worth considering even for those of you who take your own shots. We've found that new parents with photo club memberships (ourselves included) find themselves getting pictures taken not only more economically, but also more regularly and frequently— whether at the local JCPenneys, Sears, or any of the other local photographic studios that offer them.

A WORD ABOUT BABY BOOKS

Perhaps one of the easiest ways to start out is with a baby book. Those of you who didn't already get one (or 2 or 3) as baby gifts should have no difficulty finding one that suits your tastes—anything from a calendar-style book (where you can fill in the blanks for everything from the birth weight and head circumference to the first visitor, first smile, first tooth, and first birthday) to a book with blank pages that you can fill in as you please. Our advice to you is to document some of the early details of your child's life for posterity, and then continue the habit later in life. Those of you who are more technologically inclined may wish to keep an electronic journal instead. Some parenting Web sites even offer this feature. Explore your many options (ideally ahead of time) and go with what best suits you.

Big Before You Know It

The only reason we thought to include the suggestion of preserving your child's footprints and handprints is because we can't tell you the number of times parents have thought the idea of doing so was great, marveled at another parent's footprint creation, but never got around to doing it themselves. After all, who hasn't looked at a little pair of shoes, a birth certificate with imprints from a newborn's tiny feet, or a toddler's handprints on a piece of construction paper and wistfully remembered the days when they were that small. It's quick, it's easy, and there are more than a few retail products out there that eliminate any need for creative talent. Some suggestions include

- Simply frame a piece of paper with your baby's handprints or footprints on it. Adding your baby's name and birth information or putting the prints onto decorative paper is an easy way to embellish your work of art.
- Place your baby's first pair of shoes in a shadow box alongside a footprint made when the shoes were worn.
- Make an imprint or 3-dimensional plaster mold of your baby's hand or foot. Mold kits, some of which will allow you to adorn, paint, or otherwise enhance your creation, are readily available at most craft shops or stores that sell baby products.

- Go to a pottery painting store and use baby-safe paint to preserve your baby's handprint or footprint on a dish, serving plate, tile, or any of the large number of other pottery pieces generally available.
- Create a handprint (or footprint) photo frame.

 HELPFUL HANDPRINT HINTS

It's easiest to get a good handprint if you wait until your baby is asleep before attempting it. You may also find the activity less challenging if you wait a few weeks or months before choosing hand over foot, because newborns are notorious for keeping their hands in a tight fist—when awake and asleep— much to the dismay of their handprint-seeking parents.

CHAPTER 24

sharing the memories

Although you're undoubtedly familiar with the abundance of jokes made about having to watch someone else's home videos or look through old photo albums, as a new parent you're not likely to find a shortage of interested parties when it comes to sharing in your child's progress. Of course this may be truer with some friends and family members than with others. We've found that grandparents and other relatives generally rank at the top of the "marvel at the new baby" list. Finding a few simple ways to share captured moments with them—especially when close family and friends aren't able to share them directly—is generally much appreciated. When it comes to showing off your child in style, some recent gadgets as well as some time-tested ideas may serve you well as a new parent. They include

(Almost) Instant Access

- **Internet viewing.** The use of e-mail and Web pages for showing off your baby has become quite popular among our generation. If you're already adept at setting up a Web page, or at least uploading pictures to your computer and e-mailing them, then you're already ahead of the game. If not, having a new baby in the family may be what it takes to finally convince you to learn. The beauty of it is that the actual process is really not all that hard to master; it's fast and inexpensive, and it doesn't take much advanced planning. And for those of you with parents or grandparents who are easily flustered by such modern-day conveniences as e-mail and the Internet, accessing Web pages or e-mailed photos requires little more than the basic hardware and a 2-minute tutorial. Many free Web-based companies also allow you to store your photos in a password-protected album. You can allow access to your family and friends by giving them the site and password information. Printed photos can be ordered and then sent to friends and family as well.

- **Digital photo frames.** Although definitely more pricey than a simple Web page, this relatively new gadget wins hands down—at least when it comes to the Jana family. After investing in the actual frame, signing up, and paying a fee for monthly service, interested friends and family simply need to register their frame and plug it into a phone line and a power source. Then they can sit back as you upload photos onto your computer and select which ones to have displayed as a slide show on their frame.

     MEANINGFUL THANK YOUS

Once you've had a child, you'll find that the gifts just keep on coming with the passing of each holiday and birthday. While your baby can't exactly be counted on to deliver the proper thank you, as his parent you can help to provide his gift givers more meaningful thanks by photographing him lying on, wearing, reading, or using each gift and then sending the photo to whichever friend or relative was kind enough to give it. As your child gets older and is able to play a more active role in expressing his appreciation, you'll be able to continue in the tradition of capturing special moments, events, trips, or gifts from others on film and giving a copy to the person as a meaningful way of saying thank you.

PART VII

parting insights

You have now reached the end of this book, but you are only just starting your lifelong adventure. We thought long and hard about what parting insights we wanted to leave with you because in the end—all diapers and joking aside—we love being parents and we want you to enjoy this noblest of professions as much as we do. When we tried to think of how to finish things off in a meaningful way, everything that came to mind seemed to have been said before—mostly in the form of clichés. The one we feel is nevertheless worth repeating is that you will soon become the person who knows your baby best—what she wants, needs, likes, and dislikes. This expertise will come naturally over time, so it is worth reminding yourself every so often that parenthood is not a race. As for the rest of the clichés, you're certain to hear from others that your baby will grow big before you know it and how they're only young once. Instead of elaborating, we thought we'd lighten things up a bit by leaving you with a few thoughts that occurred to us while writing this book—all of which relate to a concept that has become quite apparent to us: Becoming a parent is really quite a lot like writing a book on parenting.

- It starts to seem like everyone's doing it.
- It's a guaranteed adventure.
- If you're lucky you fall right into your new role, but for the rest of us it takes a good bit of time, effort, and patience.
- It has a way of taking over your life, but you find that you wouldn't want it any other way.
- It serves as a reminder that everything is always easier said than done.
- You are bound to run into obstacles along the way, and you will be the exception to the rule if you don't have days when you doubt yourself.
- Having faith and sticking with it always pay off in the end.
- People are going to judge you. Regardless of what they think, if you do your best you'll always have something to be proud of.
- Striving for perfection is great, but expecting to achieve it is a setup for failure.
- And finally…

this end is really only the beginning!

index